MW00682948

Rose Murray's
A–Z VEGETABLE
COOKBOOK

from asparagus to zucchini
and everything in between,
250+ delicious and simple recipes

Rose Murray.

ROSE MURRAY
Illustrations by Eila Hopper Ross

For Bernie,

Enjoy your vegetables.

check out page 163.

Do you remember?

June 14, 2015.

Formac Publishing Company Limited
Halifax

Formac Publishing Company Limited recognizes the support of the Province of Nova Scotia through the Department of Communities, Culture and Heritage. We are pleased to work in partnership with the province to develop and promote our culture resources for all Nova Scotians. We acknowledge the financial support of the Government of Canada through the Canada Book Fund for our publishing activities. We acknowledge the support of the Canada Council for the Arts which last year invested $157 million to bring the arts to Canadians throughout the country.

This book is a companion to Rose Murray's 1983 book *Rose Murray's Vegetable Cookbook*. This book contains 100 entirely new recipes in edition to over 150 updated recipes from the 1983 book.

Cover image: Shutterstock

Library and Archives Canada Cataloguing in Publication
Murray,   Rose,   1941-,   author
        Rose Murray's A–Z Vegetable Cookbook : from asparagus to zucchini and everything in between, 250+ delicious and simple recipes / Rose Murray. -- Second edition.

Includes   index.
ISBN 978-1-4595-0371-7 (bound)

        1. Cooking (Vegetables). 2. Cookbooks. I. Title.

TX801.M87 2015   641.6'5   C2014-907491-3

Formac Publishing Company Limited
5502 Atlantic Street
Halifax, Nova Scotia, Canada
B3H 1G4
www.formac.ca

Printed and bound in China

To the memory of my mother, Josephine Varty, with whom I spent happy hours in our farm garden and kitchen.

CONTENTS

INTRODUCTION

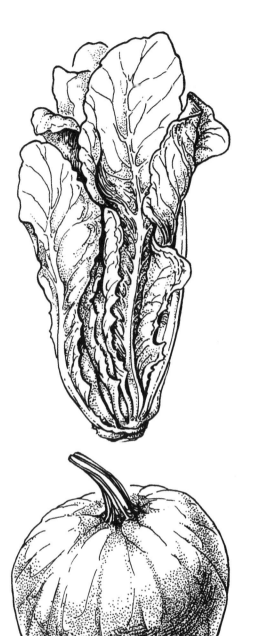

The Peerless Cook Book, published in Montreal around 1890, gave the following boiling times for vegetables: green peas, ½ hour; string beans, 3 hours; asparagus, 20 minutes; cabbage, 2 hours; turnip, 1 ½ hours; carrots, 2 hours; beets, 4 hours; shelled beans, 1 hour; and spinach, 1 ½ hours. Granted, these were old varieties of vegetables that did require longer cooking, but imagine the grey, mushy results of such long boiling! The notion of vegetables being good for you was very vague indeed and no one had any idea that such long cooking destroyed their natural vitamins and minerals.

No wonder early settlers used vegetables as a kind of fuel. The nineteenth-century Canadian author Catharine Parr Traill writes about a whole peck of potatoes being consumed at a log-house building bee.

Overcooking aside, there are some great vegetable dishes to be found in early Canadian cooking. Baked beans with pork and homemade pea soup are just two of the ways early settlers used limited ingredients to their best advantage. But, especially in rural areas, settlers lacked the time and means to fuss with fresh vegetables so they were relegated to a secondary role.

All that's changed and nowadays we give fresh vegetables the respect they deserve. We have quick-cooking strains of familiar vegetables as well as many unfamiliar varieties imported from around the world. New Canadians from regions like Asia and the Middle East, where fresh vegetables abound and are dealt with superbly, have brought interesting techniques and ideas. Today we stir-fry, add herbs and spices to bring out natural flavours and colours, and have a greater appreciation for the texture, appearance and flavour of our produce. Recipes from other countries have been adapted for vegetables that grow well in Canada. As we have become more interested in using fresh produce to its best advantage, we have learned to appreciate the succulence and bright colour of vegetables, like fresh beans or sugar snap peas, cooked simply and perfectly.

Today we prepare vegetables so they stimulate the eye as well as the taste buds, and the harvest of vegetables we have in Canada is finally assuming its rightful central place in our cuisine.

HOW TO COOK VEGETABLES

When preparing vegetables, rule number one is don't overcook them. This does not mean serving them "raw" if, in fact, they are supposed to be cooked. Most cooked vegetables are at their best when they're tender but still slightly crisp, with a bright colour and all their natural nutrients intact. Cooking times for any vegetable will vary tremendously with the age, size and variety of the vegetable, as well as the cooking method used. So use cooking times in recipes as a guide because much depends on careful watching and your own valuable experience.

Freshly harvested vegetables taste best and are most nutritious but even if you have to "gather" your vegetables from a supermarket, buy the freshest you can find, don't store them for too long and prepare them just before cooking.

Whenever possible, leave vegetables whole with their skins on to help hold in vitamins and minerals. When you do chop or slice them, cut just before cooking. Since nutrient loss (especially vitamin C) from a cut vegetable increases with exposure to oxygen and water, avoid soaking prepared vegetables, except in special cases such as potatoes for deep-frying (see Potatoes, page 113). Cook in the smallest amount of water possible (see exceptions to this below) and for as short a time as possible.

TO BAKE

Vegetables that are high in moisture and contain enough cellulose to hold their shape, like most root vegetables, are good cooked this way. Always prick their skins to allow steam to escape so the vegetables do not explode and, with the exception of potatoes (see Potatoes, page 113), bake them in a preheated 350°F (180°C) oven. If you're already roasting meat or poultry, baking or roasting the vegetables alongside also helps conserve energy.

TO BLANCH OR PARBOIL

These terms refer to a brief boiling period or immersion in boiling water to set colour, soften food or control the enzymes that cause undesirable changes in flavour, colour and texture of vegetables during freezing.

Before freezing vegetables, blanch them in a large pot of boiling water for 2 to 5 minutes, depending on the toughness of the vegetable. Drain well, then plunge into ice water to stop the cooking process. Drain again, then dry well by whirling the vegetables in a salad spinner. Pack in freezer bags, drawing out any air with a straw. Remember frozen vegetables cook more quickly than fresh because they are blanched. To minimize the loss of vitamin C, do not thaw frozen vegetables before cooking.

Blanching also makes certain vegetables, like tomatoes, easier to peel (see Tomatoes, page 142).

Some vegetables are parboiled before roasting (potatoes) or before being stuffed and baked (Corn-Stuffed Peppers, page 113).

TO BOIL

For most vegetables, place them in a small amount of boiling, salted water. As soon as the water returns to a boil, cover and cook until tender but still slightly crisp. Drain, season and serve at once. The cooking water can be added to soups, stews or used as part of the liquid for an accompaniment, like a cream sauce.

The exceptions are green vegetables which should be cooked, uncovered, in a large amount of boiling, salted water. During cooking, green vegetables release natural acids that dull their colour but cooking them in an uncovered saucepan in a large amount of water allows these acids to disperse. Don't add baking soda to the water (as people once did to neutralize the acid) since it makes the vegetables mushy and destroys vitamins.

For members of the cabbage family, turnips and other strong-tasting vegetables, cooking them in a large amount of water also helps rid these vegetables of their strong (sometimes bitter) taste and unpleasant odour. Of course, vegetables boiled in a large amount of water also release more nutrients. You might compromise in some cases by partially covering the saucepan.

TO BRAISE

Cook vegetables in a saucepan in hot butter or oil until starting to soften, then add a small amount of liquid (such as broth or water), cover and cook over low heat until tender.

TO DEEP-FRY

When cooking vegetables in a large amount of hot fat or oil, the temperature of the fat or oil is important—so it's worth investing in a candy thermometer if you're planning to deep-fry.

Cooking at too low a temperature causes the food to soak up too much fat, while a temperature that is too high will burn the food. Starchy vegetables like potatoes can simply be sliced before deep-frying, but other vegetables require a coating of batter or bread crumbs first.

TO GLAZE

Root vegetables are a great choice for glazing. Simply cook until tender but still slightly crisp, drain well, then sauté in butter and a sweetener like honey, maple syrup, sugar, jelly or liqueur. (Check the index for glazed recipes in this book.)

TO MICROWAVE

Cooking vegetables in a microwave oven is an excellent method of preserving texture, nutrients and colour. It's best to follow the manufacturer's instructions, but check if the vegetables are done before the time given in the manual since microwave cooking times are often too long. Be sure to prick unpeeled vegetables so the steam will escape and they won't burst. If you use a liquid, add salt to it. Otherwise, do not salt the vegetables since it will dehydrate them and interfere with the microwave pattern, leaving dark spots where the salt has been sprinkled.

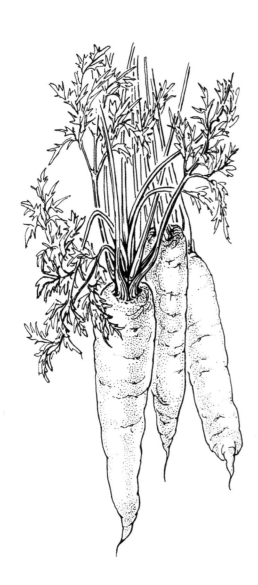

TO PRESSURE-COOK

As a time-saving device, the pressure cooker is the forerunner of the microwave oven, allowing vegetables to cook in a fraction of the time needed for boiling and, in the process, preserving nutrients and flavour. Timing is crucial when pressure-cooking since even a few extra seconds will overcook the food. (If you have a pressure cooker, refer to the manual for vegetable cooking times and techniques.)

TO SAUTÉ

Sautéing means cooking food in a small amount of hot fat over fairly high heat while frequently stirring the food or shaking the skillet. While this is usually done as a first step before cooking the food by another method, there are some recipes included in this book where the vegetables are sautéed until done. The oil seals in their flavour and juices and preserves their vitamin content.

TO STEAM

Vegetables lose fewer nutrients during steaming since they do not come in contact with the liquid, or with oxygen since the air in the saucepan is replaced by steam. Suspend vegetables in an expandable steamer basket above a small amount of rapidly boiling water. Cover the saucepan and cook until tender but still slightly crisp.

TO STIR-FRY

This method of cooking food over high heat in a small amount of oil is a popular way to retain the texture and colour of vegetables. As with sautéing, it is also a good way to retain nutrients. Firmer vegetables (like carrots, broccoli stems, celery, cauliflower) should be cut into small pieces so they'll stir-fry quickly.

Heat a large skillet or wok and add oil (about 1 tablespoon for every 1 lb/500 g vegetables). When hot, add the vegetables (and garlic and/or fresh ginger, if you wish) and stir and toss until tender but still a little crisp. Stir-fried vegetables (especially firmer ones) are sometimes finished by a short steaming period. To do this, add a few drops of water and cover the wok or skillet for a few minutes.

PRESERVING

Before making any of the pickles or relishes in this book, take a look at these hints and tips:

- Due to the high acid content in pickles, use glass or stainless steel bowls and stainless steel saucepans for preparing and cooking ingredients.

- Use jars specifically designed for preserving.

- Check that any jars you're reusing are free of chips and cracks.

- Use new discs (lids) for every jar. Jar rings or bands, if they are not bent or rusted, last a few trips through the canner. Before sealing the jars, warm the discs in a bowl of barely hot water.

HOW TO USE A BOILING-WATER CANNER

- Heat the jars before filling them with pickles or relishes. Fill a boiling-water canner two-thirds full with hot water. Place the clean, empty jars upside-down on the rack in the canner. Cover and bring to a simmer (10 minutes to sterilize), timing this process so the jars are hot and ready to fill when the pickles or relishes are ready. With canning tongs, remove the jars, drain well, then set them upright on a tray.

- When you are filling the jars with pickles or relish, use a funnel and small metal cup or ladle, and fill up to the headspace level recommended in each recipe. For chunky pickles, run a plastic knife down the inside of the jars to press out any air bubbles. Adjust the headspace level, if necessary.

- Wipe the jar rim, if necessary. Centre a disc on top of the jar and screw on a jar ring or band until you meet resistance, tightening without forcing so it's fingertip tight.

- Place the jars upright on the rack in the canner. Lower the rack and add more boiling water, if necessary, to come 1 inch (2 ½ cm) above the top of the jars. Cover the canner. Bring to a boil and start timing the processing time from this point.

- Once the jars have been processed for the time stated in the recipe, turn off the heat, uncover the canner and let the boiling subside, about 5 minutes.

- Using canning tongs, transfer the jars to a rack or folded towel to cool, about 1 day.

- Check that the discs have snapped down and are well sealed. The lids should be slightly curved down. If, by chance, one of the jar discs did not seal (the disc will be curved up, not down), refrigerate the jar and use the contents within three weeks.

- Wipe and label the jars. Remove the jar rings if desired. Store in a cool, dry, dark place.

ASPARAGUS

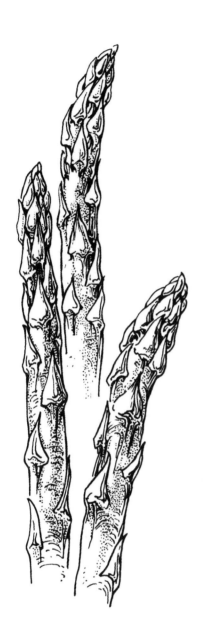

Asparagus was cultivated in ancient Greek and Roman gardens, and derived its name from the Greek word *asparag*, meaning sprout. In the seventeenth century, Italians grew fields of asparagus as a profitable crop, but it wasn't until late in the nineteenth century that asparagus was established as a garden crop in Canada. Ontario now produces two-thirds of Canada's asparagus.

I like serving it all by itself as an appetizer, either hot and drizzled with melted butter and lemon, or cold with a vinaigrette (page 170).

Canadian asparagus is in season from early May until late June. Asparagus is a good source of vitamins A and C and is low in calories.

CHOOSING

Look for straight, crisp, round stalks about 5 inches (12 cm) long. Each stalk should be bright green for most of its length and have a tightly closed green or purple tip. The secret of good asparagus lies in its freshness, not the thickness of its stalks, although thicker stalks tend to have more flavour. Use straight, even stalks when serving them whole and reserve crooked ones for soups.

One pound (500 g) yields 2 to 4 servings, depending on the recipe.

STORING

Texture, flavour and colour are all at their best when asparagus is cooked the day it's harvested. When this is not possible, wrap the bottoms of the stalks in damp paper towels, place in a plastic bag and store in the crisper. Or place unwrapped stalks upright in a container of water (like a bouquet of flowers) and refrigerate until ready to use.

To freeze asparagus, blanch small stalks for 2 minutes, medium stalks for 3 minutes and large stalks for 4 minutes. Cook straight from the freezer.

PREPARING

To prepare asparagus, snap off and discard the tough, white woody ends; they'll snap easily where the tender part begins. Wash thoroughly to remove any sand and cut an X in the bottom of each stalk to speed the cooking of this thicker part. For older, less tender asparagus, use a vegetable peeler to peel off the outer skin from the base of the stalk to within 2 to 3 inches (5 to 8 cm) from the tip.

COOKING

Because the tips cook more quickly than the stalks, stand asparagus upright in 2 inches (5 cm) boiling water in a tall coffee pot or the bottom of a double boiler. Cover the pot or invert the top of the double boiler over the asparagus. Cook until tender but still slightly crisp, 5 to 7 minutes. Alternatively, use a large skillet with a tight-fitting lid to boil or steam the stalks. Asparagus loses colour, texture, flavour and nutrients if overcooked.

CREAM OF ASPARAGUS SOUP

5 cups chicken broth
1 lb (500 g) asparagus, trimmed and cut into
   1-inch (2 ½ cm) pieces
¼ cup chopped onion
¼ cup chopped celery
2 tbsp chopped chives
¼ cup unsalted butter
3 tbsp all-purpose flour
1 cup milk
1 cup half-and-half cream (10% MF) or table
   cream (18% MF)
2 tbsp dry sherry
1 tbsp fresh lemon juice
Salt and freshly ground white pepper to taste

This full-flavoured soup is equally good served hot or cold, and makes an elegant starter for a spring dinner.

In a large pot, bring the broth to a boil over high heat. Add the asparagus, onion, celery and chives. Cover and bring back to a boil. Reduce the heat to medium-low and simmer, covered, for 5 minutes.

With a slotted spoon, remove 12 asparagus tips and set aside. Continue cooking the asparagus mixture until the vegetables are tender, about 2 minutes. Let cool slightly.

Use an immersion blender in the pot to blend the soup until smooth, or purée the soup in batches in a countertop blender (a blender, rather than a food processor, makes a smoother soup). Set aside.

In a heavy saucepan, melt the butter over medium heat. Add the flour and cook, stirring, for 2 minutes.

Remove the saucepan from the heat and gradually whisk in the milk. Return the saucepan to medium heat and cook, stirring constantly, until sauce comes to a boil and thickens.

Add the cream, sherry and asparagus purée. Heat gently until very hot, but do not boil. Add the lemon juice and season to taste with salt and pepper. Serve hot or cold, garnished with reserved asparagus tips.

Makes 5 to 6 servings

ASPARAGUS ON TOAST

1 cup Low-Fat Hollandaise (page 172) or Cream
   Sauce (page 172)
1 lb (500 g) asparagus, trimmed and cut into
   2-inch (5 cm) pieces
4 slices buttered white toast
5 hard-cooked eggs, shelled and sliced

This simple dish was a favourite lunch my mother made for us when I was a child.

Prepare the hollandaise or cream sauce and set aside. Cook the asparagus (see page 11) until just tender, about 5 minutes.

Meanwhile, cut the toast into 1-inch (2 ½ cm) strips and arrange on individual warm plates.

When the asparagus is tender, drain it well and arrange on top of the toast. Top the asparagus with sliced hard-cooked eggs and sauce.

Makes 4 servings

2 lb (1 kg) asparagus, trimmed

LEMON-MUSTARD SAUCE

1 hard-cooked egg, shelled and halved
1 raw egg yolk*
1 ½ tsp Dijon mustard
½ cup olive oil
¼ tsp finely grated lemon zest
1 ½ tbsp fresh lemon juice
2 tsp well-drained capers
Salt and freshly ground white pepper to taste
1 tbsp finely chopped pimento or sweet red
   pepper
1 tbsp finely chopped parsley

ASPARAGUS IN LEMON-MUSTARD SAUCE

A zesty mayonnaise-style sauce dresses this pretty salad that's a perfect accompaniment to roast lamb or ham.

Cook the asparagus (see page 11) until just tender, about 5 minutes. Drain and refresh immediately under cold water to stop further cooking and to retain its colour. Place the asparagus on a serving dish and let cool but don't refrigerate.

For the lemon-mustard sauce, finely chop the hard-cooked white and set aside. In a food processor or blender, process the hard-cooked yolk, raw egg yolk and mustard until smooth.

With the motor running, slowly add the oil. Process until thick and creamy. Add the lemon zest and juice and pulse until well combined. Scrape the sauce into a small bowl. Add the capers and season to taste with salt and pepper.

Spoon the sauce over the asparagus, leaving the tips exposed. Sprinkle with the reserved finely chopped egg white, pimento and parsley.

Makes 6 servings

* When using raw eggs in a recipe, choose Canada Grade-A eggs within their best-before date; these eggs have been properly handled and graded by a registered farmer.

MAKE-AHEAD

Wrap the cooled asparagus in a tea towel and refrigerate. Refrigerate the sauce. Thirty minutes before serving, remove the asparagus from refrigerator. Just before serving, stir the sauce and spoon it over the asparagus.

STIR-FRIED ASPARAGUS

Just a handful of ingredients in this quick stir-fry brings out the flavour of fresh asparagus.

2 tbsp peanut or canola oil
1 clove garlic, minced
1 tsp minced fresh ginger
1 lb (500 g) asparagus, trimmed and cut into
   2-inch (5 cm) pieces
½ tsp granulated sugar
Salt to taste
1 tbsp water
1 tbsp sesame seeds

In a large skillet or wok, heat the oil over medium-high heat. Add the garlic and ginger and stir-fry for a few seconds.

Add the asparagus and stir-fry to coat with oil. Sprinkle with sugar, and salt to taste. Add the water, then cover and cook over low heat for 5 minutes.

Remove the lid and increase the heat to medium-high. Cook until the moisture evaporates and the asparagus is tender but still slightly crisp, 1 to 3 minutes. Sprinkle with sesame seeds.

Makes 4 servings

STIR-FRIED BROCCOLI

Substitute 1 lb (500 g) broccoli, cut into small florets, for the asparagus.

OVEN-ROASTED ASPARAGUS

1 lb (500 g) fat asparagus, trimmed
1 tbsp canola or olive oil
Salt and freshly ground black pepper to taste

One year, when I was doing a lot of work with asparagus, I discovered that oven-roasting it at a high temperature was not only fast but also easy and provided a new dimension to the vegetable: it becomes nuttier, with a more substantial texture. I cook asparagus this way often, and it never fails to impress. Sometimes I add a drizzle of balsamic vinegar just before serving. The recipe can be doubled easily.

Preheat the oven to 500°F (260°C). Spread the asparagus out in a single layer in a large shallow baking pan or on a rimmed baking sheet. Drizzle with oil, and sprinkle with salt and pepper to taste.

Roast, uncovered and stirring once, until tender but still slightly firm, about 8 minutes.

Makes 4 servings

OVEN-ROASTED ASPARAGUS WITH HAZELNUT VINAIGRETTE

2 tbsp finely chopped shallots
2 tbsp finely chopped toasted hazelnuts (see sidebar)
1 tbsp hazelnut or olive oil
1 tbsp red wine vinegar
½ tsp Dijon mustard
1 lb (500 g) asparagus, freshly roasted (see above)

Here is a delicious variation on simple roasted asparagus that I developed for a national magazine. My editor there said, "It's so delicious two people could happily share a portion this size." With less greedy people at the table, it could easily serve four.

In a small bowl, whisk together the shallots, hazelnuts, hazelnut oil, vinegar and mustard.

Transfer the hot, freshly roasted asparagus to a warm platter and spoon the dressing over the top. Toss gently to coat the asparagus with the dressing.

Makes 2 to 4 servings

HOW TO TOAST NUTS

Spread the nuts out on a baking sheet and bake in a 350°F (180°C) oven for about 5 minutes, watching carefully. (In the summer, I use my toaster oven to toast nuts to avoid heating up the kitchen.) When toasting hazelnuts, wrap the warm nuts in a clean tea towel and rub vigorously to remove their loose, brown skins before using.

BEANS (DRIED AND FRESH)

DRIED BEANS

Without dried beans and peas in their larders, many of our early settlers would have starved during the long Canadian winters. Native Canadians first introduced beans to French settlers, who quickly made them a staple part of their diet. For decades these low-cost vegetables were a crucial source of nutrition before refrigeration and year-round fresh produce were readily available. In various parts of the country, especially the Maritimes, baked beans served with brown bread became a Saturday night tradition.

Cooked dried beans contain very little fat and no cholesterol, and are a good source of iron, calcium, phosphorous, magnesium, potassium and three of the B vitamins. Bean-based dishes are an excellent source of complete protein if combined with meat, fish, grains or dairy products.

Of the twenty-five varieties of dried beans and lentils grown and used in Canada, the white pea bean or navy bean is the most popular. Ontario's second-largest crop is the yellow-eye bean, a Maritime favourite with molasses. Soy beans are now under wide cultivation in Ontario, and Saskatchewan grows more lentils than any other province.

CHOOSING

Look for bright beans of uniform colour and size with less than 10 per cent volume of broken, wrinkled or blistered beans.

One pound (500 g) of dried beans (2 cups) yields about 6 cups cooked beans (6 to 8 servings).

PREPARING

Pick over and rinse beans in a sieve under cold, running water.

SOAKING

Although dried beans can be cooked without soaking them first, the soaking process reduces their cooking time by up to 2 hours. Do not add baking soda to the water because it destroys the vitamins in the beans. There are two ways you can soak beans:

- In a large pot, cover the beans with three times their volume of cold water and soak overnight. Drain the beans before using.

- Or cover the beans with three times their volume of cold water in a large pot, then bring to a boil. Boil for 2 minutes. Cover the pot, remove from the heat and let sit for 1 hour. Drain the beans before using.

FRESH BEANS

Fresh garden beans are native to North America and were cultivated for centuries by Canada's First Nations. Almost all beans stocked by seed houses during the nineteenth century were varieties native to Canada.

Snap beans are the most familiar to Canadians. They are available year round and are easily grown by home gardeners. They're so-called because the young, crisp beans will "snap" when broken. There are two types: pole beans whose plants require some support, and green or yellow (wax) bush beans that appear on low-growing plants. Wax beans, which get their name from their shiny, yellow colour, were not common until the latter part of the nineteenth century.

The purple Royal Burgundy bean, sometimes available in markets, is a variety that turns green when cooked.

The term string bean comes from the tough string that had to be removed from old varieties.

CHOOSING

Choose lean, firm pods without any brown marks (known as rust). To avoid rust when harvesting your beans, pick them on a dry day.

One to 1 ½ pounds (500 to 750 g) of fresh beans yield 4 servings.

STORING

Don't wash the beans, but refrigerate in a plastic bag and use as soon as possible.

PREPARING

Wash the beans, then snap off the ends. Leave whole or cut as desired.

COOKING

When fresh from the garden or market, whole green beans can simply be steamed for 3 to 5 minutes or boiled, uncovered and in plenty of water, for 5 to 7 minutes. (Wax beans should be cooked, covered, in a minimum amount of water.) In either case, don't overcook them or the beans will be pale and limp.

Season cooked beans with butter, lemon juice, and salt and pepper to taste and serve as a side dish.

TARRAGON-DRESSED CORN AND BEAN SALAD

3 ears corn, shucked

12 oz (375 g) green beans, trimmed and sliced (about 3 cups)

1 stalk celery, thinly sliced diagonally

½ cup light mayonnaise

1 small clove garlic, minced

2 tsp finely chopped fresh tarragon leaves

½ tsp Worcestershire sauce

Salt and freshly ground black pepper to taste

1 tbsp well-drained capers (optional)

¼ cup toasted pine nuts or sliced almonds (see page 14)

Tarragon is a licorice-flavoured herb that's delicious in the dressing for this salad, but if it doesn't grow in your garden or isn't easy to find, try fresh sage or substitute ½ tsp dried tarragon leaves. Capers are the pickled buds of a Mediterranean shrub. You can find them in the condiments section of your supermarket or, if you prefer, simply omit them from the recipe.

In a large pot of boiling, salted water, cook the corn and beans until just tender, 3 to 4 minutes. Drain and cool under running water. Put the beans in a large bowl.

Cut the kernels from the corn and add to the beans, along with the celery.

In a small bowl, whisk together the mayonnaise, garlic, tarragon, Worcestershire sauce and salt and pepper to taste. Stir in the capers, if using.

Pour the dressing over the vegetables and toss to coat well. Refrigerate, covered, for at least 30 minutes. Stir in the pine nuts just before serving.

Makes 6 servings

YELLOW BEANS WITH QUICK TOMATO SAUCE

1 lb (500 g) yellow beans, cut into 1-inch (2 ½ cm) pieces (about 4 cups)

QUICK TOMATO SAUCE

2 slices bacon, chopped

¼ cup finely diced onion

¼ cup seeded and finely diced sweet green pepper

¼ cup finely diced celery

1 clove garlic, minced

3 or 4 medium tomatoes, peeled, seeded and chopped

1 tsp finely chopped fresh basil or ¼ tsp dried basil leaves

¼ tsp granulated sugar

Salt and freshly ground black pepper

2 tbsp finely chopped parsley

Use regular side bacon or pancetta for this colourful side dish.

In a large pot of boiling, salted water, cook the beans until almost tender, about 4 minutes. Drain.

For the quick tomato sauce, cook the bacon in a medium saucepan over medium heat until it is almost crisp. Add the onion, green pepper, celery and garlic. Sauté until tender.

Stir in the tomatoes, basil, sugar, and salt and pepper to taste. Reduce the heat to low and cook, uncovered, for 10 minutes. Add the beans and parsley and cook just until beans are heated through.

Makes 6 servings

GREEN BEANS IN SOUR-CREAM SAUCE

1 lb (500 g) green beans, sliced (about 4 cups)

SOUR-CREAM SAUCE

4 slices side bacon, diced
½ cup finely chopped onion
2 tbsp all-purpose flour
1 tsp granulated sugar
Salt and freshly ground black pepper to taste
1 cup sour cream
2 tbsp white vinegar

A German influence on Canada's vegetable cuisine is evident in this kind of sauce.

In a large pot of boiling, salted water, cook the beans until tender but still slightly crisp, about 4 minutes. Drain.

For the sour-cream sauce, cook the bacon in a large skillet over medium heat until crisp. Remove with a slotted spoon and set aside.

In the fat remaining in the skillet, sauté the onion over medium heat until soft. Blend in the flour, sugar and salt and pepper to taste. Reduce the heat to low and cook, stirring, for 2 minutes.

Remove the skillet from the heat and stir in the sour cream, vinegar and cooked beans. Return the skillet to low heat and cook, stirring gently, until the beans are heated through. Serve topped with the bacon.

Makes 4 servings

BRUSSELS SPROUTS IN SOUR-CREAM SAUCE

Substitute 1 lb (500 g) Brussels sprouts for the green beans.

SAVOURY GREEN BEANS

2 lb (1 kg) green beans, trimmed (about 8 cups)
¼ cup olive oil
2 large cloves garlic, halved
Salt and freshly ground black pepper to taste
2 tsp fresh lemon juice
1 tbsp finely chopped fresh summer savory or 1 tsp dried savory leaves

This is my favourite way of preparing green beans for company since they just need a quick sauté to finish them off.

Bring a large saucepan of salted water to a boil. Gradually add the beans and cook, uncovered, over medium-high heat, until just tender, about 5 minutes. Drain the beans in a colander and refresh under cold running water. (Beans can be prepared ahead to this point.)

In a large skillet, heat the oil over medium heat. Brown the garlic halves in the oil. Discard the garlic. Add the beans and shake the skillet to coat them with oil. Season to taste with salt and pepper.

Cover the skillet and cook over low heat until the beans are heated through, about 2 minutes. Stir in the lemon juice. Arrange on a shallow serving dish and sprinkle with savory.

Makes 6 to 8 servings

BEANS

2 cups dry white navy beans*

1 medium onion, peeled and halved

1 large clove garlic, halved

1 tbsp salt

Freshly ground black pepper to taste

¼ cup seeded and diced sweet red pepper

¼ cup finely chopped parsley

¼ cup chopped chives or green onion tops

DRESSING

¼ cup fresh lemon juice

2 large cloves garlic, minced

1 tsp dry mustard

1 tsp ground cumin

Salt and freshly ground black pepper to taste

½ cup olive oil

Boston or leaf lettuce

12 black olives

2 tbsp chopped parsley

1 3-quart (3 L) basket yellow or green beans, trimmed

3 cups water

1 ½ cups granulated sugar

1 ½ cups white vinegar

WINTER BEAN SALAD

A tangy dressing adds lots of flavour to this easy salad. Enjoy it for lunch with whole wheat rolls. You can cheat by using canned beans if you wish. I always keep cans of beans of all types in my pantry to add to soups or to make salads like this.

For the beans, clean and soak them according to one of the methods on page 15. Drain the beans and place in a saucepan with enough cold water to cover them by 1 inch (2 ½ cm).

Add the onion, garlic, salt and pepper to taste. Bring to a boil, then reduce the heat and simmer, covered, until tender, about 45 minutes (do not overcook or the beans will be mushy).

Drain well, discarding the onion and garlic. Gently stir in the sweet pepper, parsley and chives. (The beans don't have to be cooled.)

For the dressing, whisk together the lemon juice, garlic, mustard, cumin and salt and pepper to taste in a small bowl. Slowly whisk in the olive oil.

Pour the dressing over the bean mixture and gently stir again to mix everything well. Taste and add more salt if needed. Cool, then cover and refrigerate.

To serve, line a large salad bowl with lettuce leaves. Spoon in the salad and arrange the olives on top. Sprinkle with parsley.

Makes 8 to 10 servings

* Or substitute 2 cans (each 19 oz/540 mL) navy beans, drained and rinsed, and skip the soaking and cooking instructions. Add the sweet pepper, parsley and chives to the beans and continue with the recipe.

DIANE SLIMMON'S PRESERVED BEANS

For more detailed instructions on how to preserve vegetables, see Preserving on page 9.

Cut the beans as for Edna Staebler's Schnippled Bean Salad, below.

In a small saucepan, stir together the water, sugar and vinegar. Bring to a boil and boil for 3 minutes.

Meanwhile, bring a large pot of salted water to a boil. Add the beans, bring back to the boil and blanch until almost tender, about 2 minutes.

Drain the beans well and pack into 3 hot, 2-cup (500 mL) preserving jars.

Pour the hot syrup into the jars to cover the beans, leaving a ½-inch (1 cm) headspace. Seal with prepared discs and rings. Boil in a boiling-water canner for 10 minutes. Remove the jars and let cool on a rack.

Makes three 2-cup (500 mL) jars

EDNA STAEBLER'S SCHNIPPLED BEAN SALAD

1 lb (500 g) fresh yellow or green beans
  (about 4 cups)
1 small onion, sliced
Salt to taste
¾ cup sour cream
1 tbsp granulated sugar
1 tbsp white vinegar
Freshly ground black pepper to taste

Edna Staebler (1906–2006) was one of the first Canadian writers to celebrate local, regional food in her bestselling *Schmecks* cookbooks. Her sour cream bean salad, which the author Pierre Berton requested each time he visited Edna, became one the area's long-lasting specialties. My Kitchener friend, Diane Slimmon, makes this bean salad in the summer with market-fresh wax or green beans, but she also preserves beans in a vinegar-sugar syrup (see page 19) so that she can enjoy the salad all year round. She drains a pint of her preserved beans and uses Edna's sour cream dressing. Edna refers to her mother making a similar syrup to pickle beans in her book, *More Food that Really Schmecks*. She explains, "To make bean salad, Mother drained the beans and stirred into them a blend of salt and pepper to taste, a teaspoon of sugar and enough sour cream to give the beans a thin coating."

Cut the beans diagonally in very thin slices, about 3 or 4 slices per bean. (In Ontario's Waterloo County, beans cut this way are called schnippled beans.)

In a large saucepan of boiling, salted water, cook the beans until tender-crisp, 3 to 4 minutes for garden- or market-fresh beans. Drain and let cool.

Meanwhile, in a small bowl, sprinkle the onion liberally with salt. Stir it around and let stand for at least 15 minutes, giving it a stir occasionally.

In a bowl large enough to hold the beans, stir together the sour cream, sugar, vinegar and salt and pepper to taste. Squeeze the juice from the onion and add the onion to the sour cream mixture.

Add the drained beans to the bowl and stir with the dressing until the beans are well coated.

Makes 4 to 6 servings

2 cups dry white navy beans

5 cups water

1 bay leaf

1 small onion, stuck with 6 whole cloves

2 large cloves garlic, cut in half lengthwise

1 medium onion, chopped

4 oz (125 g) salt pork, rinsed and diced

2 tbsp Worcestershire sauce

2 tsp white vinegar

1 ½ tsp dry mustard

Salt and freshly ground black pepper to taste

¼ cup maple syrup

¼ cup molasses

BAKED BEANS WITH PORK

A specialty of New Brunswick and Quebec, baked beans are a favourite winter meal everywhere in Canada.

Clean and soak beans according to one of the methods on page 15.

In a large pot, combine the drained beans with the water, bay leaf, clove-studded onion and garlic. Bring to a boil over high heat. Reduce the heat to medium-low and simmer, covered, for 30 minutes. Discard the onion and bay leaf. Drain the beans in a colander, reserving the liquid.

Preheat the oven to 325°F (160°C). Put the beans in a large bean pot or 10-cup (2 ½ L) baking dish. Add the chopped onion, salt pork, Worcestershire sauce, vinegar, mustard and salt and pepper to taste. Add enough of the reserved liquid to cover the mixture.

Cover and bake until the beans are tender, about 5 hours. Stir often and add more reserved liquid or water, if needed, to keep beans covered with liquid during cooking.

One hour before serving, remove the lid to let the beans brown. Thirty minutes before serving, stir in the maple syrup and molasses.

Makes about 10 side-dish or 6 main-course servings

SEE ALSO:

Black Bean Chili 162

Hearty Chili Soup 164

Hodge Podge 168

Squash and Bean Stew with Chipotle Cream 167

Tuscan Kale and White Bean Soup 138

BEETS

Beet roots were developed by gardeners in the Middle Ages in northern Europe where they became a common vegetable. Imported into Canada by early settlers, they thrived here because of our cold climate.

Flat-bottomed and round varieties are relatively recent; until as late as 1800, beets had pointed roots like a turnip. The golden beet, a new variety, has tasty, tender tops and doesn't bleed its colour during cooking. You might encounter an Italian variety called Chioggia with red-and-white-striped flesh.

Beets contain calcium, phosphorous, sodium, potassium, and vitamins A and C. Cooked beet tops are a good source of iron, sodium and vitamin A, while raw tops contain many more nutrients.

CHOOSING

Choose small, smooth, firm beets that do not look shrivelled. Soft spots indicate decay, and any roughness means the beet will be tough. As beets grow larger, they may become coarse and woody.

Twelve small (1 inch/2 ½ cm) beets yield 3 to 4 servings.

STORING

Beets store well in the crisper for up to two weeks. Remove the tops, leaving an inch or two (2 ½ to 5 cm) of stem and root to preserve nutrients, tenderness and colour.

Beets can be pickled, canned or frozen for long-term storage. Cook them and remove their peel before freezing.

PREPARING

Scrub beets thoroughly and leave the root and stem end attached to prevent too much bleeding. For most recipes, do not peel beets until after cooking.

COOKING

Drop beets into enough boiling, salted water to cover them. Cover the pot and cook for 10 to 20 minutes, until pressure applied to the skin causes it to move. The cooking time varies greatly according to size and freshness of the beets and the time of year. You can also test for tenderness with the point of a sharp knife or a fork, although every time you do this, there is a certain amount of bleeding. Drain and cool under cold, running water. When cool enough to handle, slip off the skins.

Baking beets helps retain flavour and juices. For 1 ½-inch (4 cm) beets, bake, covered, in a 300°F (150°C) oven for about 1 hour or until tender.

Steaming is also an excellent method of cooking beets. Whole beets will take about 40 minutes.

Grated raw beets are a good addition to salads.

The tops of young, early beets are tasty if steamed and served with butter, salt, pepper and lemon juice.

CHILLED BEET AND CUCUMBER SOUP

1 lb (500 g) beets, cooked and sliced (about 6 medium)

3 cups chicken broth

2 tbsp finely chopped onion

1 large clove garlic, minced

1 tsp finely chopped fresh dill

1 tbsp fresh lemon or lime juice

1 cup plain yogurt

Salt and freshly ground black pepper to taste

1 medium cucumber

Additional yogurt for garnish

1 lime, thinly sliced

This refreshing and colourful soup makes a good starter for dinner on a hot day.

In a food processor or blender, purée the beets until smooth.

In a large saucepan, bring the broth to a boil over high heat. Add the puréed beets, onion, garlic and dill. Reduce heat to medium-low and simmer, uncovered, for 3 minutes. Let cool.

Add the lemon juice or lime juice, yogurt and salt and pepper to taste. Beat with a whisk until thoroughly blended. Chill for several hours or overnight.

Just before serving, peel, seed and dice the cucumber. Stir it into the soup.

Pour the soup into chilled soup bowls. Place a small dollop of yogurt in the centre of each portion and top with two thin slices of lime.

Makes 6 servings

TARRAGON-BUTTERED BEETS

36 tiny beets (approx.)

⅓ cup butter

1 tsp finely chopped fresh tarragon or ½ tsp dried tarragon leaves

½ tsp finely grated lemon zest

2 tsp fresh lemon juice

Salt and freshly ground black pepper to taste

1 tbsp chopped parsley

Here's a make-ahead side dish that combines beets with the licorice flavour of tarragon.

Wash the beets. Remove all but 1 inch (2 ½ cm) of the stems but leave the roots on. In a large pot of boiling, salted water, cook the beets until they're tender when pierced with a fork, 15 to 18 minutes.

Drain the beets and, when cool enough to handle, peel the beets, removing stems and roots. (The beets can be prepared ahead up to this point.)

In a large, heavy skillet, heat the butter over medium heat. When the foam subsides, add the beets, tarragon, lemon zest and juice and salt and pepper to taste. Shake the pan well or stir gently until the beets are heated through, about 5 minutes. Serve on a heated platter with a sprinkling of parsley.

Makes 8 servings

BEET AND STILTON SALAD

6 medium beets
1 tbsp red wine vinegar
Salt and freshly ground black pepper to taste
1 cup light mayonnaise
1 tbsp each, Dijon mustard and olive oil
4 oz (125 g) Stilton cheese, coarsely crumbled
2 stalks celery, sliced
½ cup toasted walnut pieces (see page 14)
Lettuce leaves, arugula or watercress

Stilton cheese gives a tangy creaminess to this colourful salad, but if you have another blue cheese on hand, give it a try. Remember that fresher beets cook faster and are easier to peel than those stored for a while, although both have good flavour.

Wash the beets. Remove all but 1 inch (2 ½ cm) of the stems but leave the roots on. In a large pot of boiling, salted water, cook the beets until they're tender when pierced with a fork, 15 to 18 minutes.

Drain the beets and, when cool enough to handle, peel the beets, removing stems and roots. Cut the beets into bite-sized cubes. Toss with the vinegar and salt and pepper to taste. (The beets can be prepared up to 24 hours ahead to this point, cooled, covered and refrigerated.)

In a small bowl, whisk together the mayonnaise, mustard, olive oil and salt and pepper to taste. Pour over the beet mixture and toss gently to coat. Gently stir in the cheese and celery. (The salad can be covered and refrigerated for up to 4 hours.)

Just before serving, toss in the walnuts and arrange the salad on a lettuce-lined platter.

Makes 8 servings

BORSCHT

2 tbsp canola oil or lard
1 lb (500 g) lean stew beef, diced
8 cups beef broth or water
Salt to taste
2 tbsp butter
1 ½ cups grated raw beets
1 medium onion, chopped
¾ cup grated carrots
¾ cup grated turnip
2 tbsp tomato paste or purée
2 tbsp red wine vinegar
2 large cloves garlic, minced
1 tsp granulated sugar
½ small head cabbage, shredded
2 bay leaves
Freshly ground black pepper to taste
3 tbsp finely chopped parsley
1 cup sour cream

Ukrainian settlers have contributed many recipes to our national cuisine. One of the best is this delicious and hearty fall soup.

In a large, heavy saucepan, heat the oil or lard over medium-high heat. Add the beef and brown on all sides. Add the broth and salt to taste. Bring to a boil over high heat. Reduce the heat to medium-low and simmer, covered, until the meat is tender, about 1 ½ hours.

Meanwhile, in another large saucepan, melt the butter over medium heat. Add the beets, onion, carrots, turnip, tomato paste, vinegar, garlic and sugar. Reduce the heat to medium-low and cook, covered and stirring often, for 15 minutes. Add the cabbage and cook, covered, until vegetables are almost tender, about 10 minutes.

Stir vegetable mixture and bay leaves into meat mixture. Season to taste with salt and pepper. Cook, covered, until vegetables are very tender and flavours have blended, about 20 minutes. Remove and discard the bay leaves. Taste the soup and add more sugar and vinegar, if desired.

Ladle into soup bowls and sprinkle with chopped parsley. Serve with a bowl of sour cream or put a dollop of sour cream on each serving.

Makes about 8 servings

BEET AND APPLE SALAD

3 cups cooked beets, cut into julienne strips
   (about 6 medium)
2 cups peeled and diced apples (about 3
   medium)
1 small onion, finely chopped
1 tbsp fresh lemon juice
¾ cup sour cream
¾ cup mayonnaise
2 tbsp liquid honey
¼ tsp ground cloves
Salt to taste
Lettuce leaves or watercress

Add some hard-cooked egg wedges to this easy salad and it becomes a light first course. If you wish, add ½ cup thinly sliced fennel to the beet mixture.

In a medium bowl, combine the beets, apples, onion and lemon juice.

In a small bowl, stir together the sour cream, mayonnaise, honey, cloves and salt to taste. Pour the dressing over the beet mixture and stir gently. Refrigerate, covered, for at least 3 hours before serving. (The salad will keep well for several days in the fridge.)

Serve on a bed of lettuce or watercress.

Makes 6 to 8 servings

MUSTARD BEET SALAD

10 small beets (1 ½ inches/4 cm)
2 tbsp red wine vinegar
1 large clove garlic, minced
1 tsp finely chopped fresh dill or ¼ tsp dried dill
   weed
1 tsp Dijon mustard
½ tsp mustard seeds
¼ tsp granulated sugar
Salt and freshly ground black pepper to taste
⅓ cup olive oil
Boston lettuce leaves to serve

Serve this pretty salad on a bed of lettuce for a colourful first course or as part of a buffet menu.

Wash the beets. Remove all but 1 inch (2 ½ cm) of the stems but leave the roots on. In a large pot of boiling, salted water, cook the beets until they're tender when pierced with a fork, 15 to 18 minutes.

Drain the beets and, when cool enough to handle, peel the beets, removing stems and roots. Cut the beets into 1 ½- x ¼-inch (4 cm x 6 mm) julienne strips. Place in a glass bowl and set aside.

For the dressing, stir together vinegar, garlic, dill, mustard, mustard seeds, sugar and salt and pepper to taste in a small bowl. Slowly whisk in the oil. Pour the dressing over the cooked beets and stir gently to coat. Refrigerate for several hours or overnight before serving.

Drain the beets. Line a serving platter with lettuce leaves. Arrange the beets on top of the lettuce.

Makes 8 servings

STUFFED BEETS

Instead of cutting the cooked beets into julienne strips, scoop out the centre of each beet with a knife and a spoon or an apple corer. Use the insides in the stuffing or in another recipe. Slice off a thin section from the bottom of the beets, if necessary, so they'll stand up.

Prepare the dressing as for Mustard Beet Salad. Marinate the hollowed-out beets in the dressing for 30 minutes to 1 hour, basting occasionally. Just before serving, drain the beets and fill their cavities with Beet and Apple Salad (above) or ham, shrimp, egg or herring salad, or another favourite salad.

BRAISED GRATED BEETS

6 large beets (about 1 lb/500 g)
2 medium onions, grated
1 large potato, peeled and grated
⅓ cup butter
⅛ tsp granulated sugar
Salt and freshly ground black pepper to taste
2 tbsp finely chopped parsley
2 tbsp fresh lemon juice or lime juice

This French Canadian recipe is appealing in both appearance and taste, especially if you serve it in a white bowl.

Wash and peel the beets, then grate them coarsely.

In a large, heavy skillet, combine the beets, onions, potato, butter, sugar and salt and pepper to taste. Cover and cook over very low heat, stirring often, until the vegetables are just tender, about 35 minutes.

Just before serving, sprinkle with parsley and lemon juice.

Makes 6 to 8 servings

BAKED GRATED BEETS
Combine grated beets, onions, potato, butter, salt, pepper and sugar in a baking dish and add 1 tbsp water. Cover and bake in a 350°F (180°C) oven for 30 minutes, stirring occasionally.

BEET GREENS WITH SOUR CREAM AND HORSERADISH

2 lb (1 kg) beet greens
¼ cup sour cream
2 tbsp prepared horseradish
1 tsp packed brown sugar
1 tsp lemon juice
Salt and freshly ground black pepper to taste

I always look for beets with fresh, healthy tops when I buy them at our market. Beet tops are particularly good steamed and tossed with butter, salt, pepper and lemon juice, but sometimes I dress them up with the addition of sour cream and horseradish.

Wash the greens well and trim off any coarse stems. Place the greens in a large, heavy saucepan with just the water that clings to the leaves. Cover tightly and cook over medium heat until tender, about 15 minutes. Drain the greens. Chop them and return to the saucepan.

Stir in the sour cream, horseradish, sugar, lemon juice and salt and pepper to taste. Heat just until hot but do not boil.

Makes 6 servings

BEETS WITH SOUR CREAM AND HORSERADISH
Substitute 4 cups cooked, sliced beets for the beet greens and increase the sour cream in the dressing to ½ cup.

PICKLED BEETS

5 lb (2 ⅕ kg) small red beets (about sixty 1- to 1 ½-inch/2 ½ to 4 cm beets)

3 cups white vinegar

1 ½ cups lightly packed brown sugar

1 ½ cups water

1 ½ tbsp coarse pickling salt

¾ tsp each, ground cinnamon and ground allspice

¼ tsp ground cloves

¼ tsp freshly ground black pepper

Having pickled beets in the pantry provided early settlers with an extra vegetable for winter meals when fresh produce was not so available, and it's still comforting to see a shelf of homemade pickles. For more detailed instructions on how to preserve vegetables, see Preserving on page 9.

Wash the beets. Remove all but 1 inch (2 ½ cm) of the stems but leave the roots on. In a large pot of boiling, salted water, cook the beets until they're tender when pierced with a fork, 15 to 18 minutes.

Drain the beets and, when cool enough to handle, peel the beets, removing stems and roots.

Meanwhile, combine the vinegar, sugar, water, salt, cinnamon, allspice, cloves and pepper in a stainless steel saucepan. Bring to a boil over high heat. Boil for 2 to 3 minutes, then remove from the heat.

Pack the beets in hot 2-cup (500 mL) preserving jars to within ¾ inch (2 cm) from the rim. Pour the hot syrup over them leaving a ½-inch (1 cm) headspace. Using a plastic knife, press out any air bubbles and add more syrup, if necessary, to adjust the headspace. Be sure the syrup covers the beets. Seal with prepared discs and rings. Boil in a boiling-water canner for 30 minutes. Remove the jars and let cool on a rack.

Let stand for three to four weeks before using.

Makes about six 2-cup (500 mL) jars

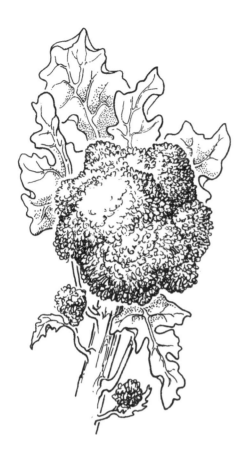

BROCCOLI

A member of the cabbage family, broccoli with its small green heads and condensed flowers, is a close relative of cauliflower. Although broccoli has been a favourite in Italian cooking since early Roman times and popular in the British Isles since the 1700s, it has been cultivated only since 1920 in the United States and more recently in Canada. Broccoli is one of the few imported vegetables that's worth buying fresh during winter months because it's a sturdy vegetable that travels well.

Broccoli contains large amounts of calcium, iron, B vitamins and vitamins A and C.

CHOOSING

Look for firm, compact, fresh, dark green or purplish green heads. Avoid any with yellow blossoms since this indicates tough, stringy stems.

About 2 pounds (1 kg) of broccoli yield 4 servings.

STORING

Refrigerate broccoli immediately so that it retains its crispness. Store in a perforated plastic bag up to a week.

To freeze, cut according to the instructions below, and blanch for 3 to 4 minutes depending on floret size.

PREPARING

Trim off leaves and tough stem ends. If you think there might be any insects present, soak in salted water for 15 minutes. Cut off florets, peel any thick stalks and slice stalks lengthwise into thin spears. Lay stalks on the bottom of a saucepan, placing florets on top, and cook, uncovered, in a large amount of salted boiling water about 5 minutes.

Or steam, arranging the vegetable in a steamer basket in the same way, until tender but still slightly crisp, 8 to 12 minutes. The florets should still be bright green when done.

Broccoli is also a favourite served raw on a crudité platter.

RAPINI

A relative of broccoli and a member of the cabbage family, rapini has the same health benefits of both. Low in calories, rapini is high in iron, calcium, potassium, magnesium and vitamins A, C and E.

When cooking, keep the lid off to prevent darkening and don't add any acidic ingredients until just before serving.

BROCCOLI-BRIE SOUP

1 large bunch broccoli

2 tbsp butter

1 onion, chopped

1 stalk celery, chopped

1 potato, peeled and chopped

1 tsp dried thyme leaves

5 cups chicken broth

4 oz (125 g) brie cheese (rind removed), diced

Salt and freshly ground black pepper to taste

Any cheese complements broccoli, but brie makes this simple soup interesting enough to serve to company as well as for a family lunch. My good friend Kathryn Wardropper often makes the soup for guests, sometimes substituting Stilton for the brie.

Separate the broccoli into florets and stems. Reserving ¾ cup tiny florets to garnish the soup, chop the remaining florets. Peel and coarsely chop the stems.

In a large saucepan, melt the butter over medium heat. Add the onion, celery, potato and thyme. Cook for 5 minutes, stirring occasionally.

Add the broth and bring to a boil over high heat. Reduce the heat to medium-low and simmer, covered, until the potato is tender, about 5 minutes.

Add the chopped broccoli florets and stems and bring back to a boil. Simmer, uncovered, until the broccoli is just tender, about 3 minutes.

Use an immersion blender in the pot to blend the soup until smooth. Or purée the soup in batches in a countertop blender (a blender, rather than a food processor, makes a smoother soup). If necessary, pour the soup back into the rinsed-out saucepan. (The soup can be prepared ahead, cooled, covered and refrigerated for up to 1 day.)

When ready to serve, bring the soup to a simmer over medium-high heat. Add the cheese, and salt and pepper to taste, stirring until the cheese melts (do not let the soup boil after adding the cheese). Ladle into warm soup bowls and garnish with reserved broccoli florets.

Makes 4 to 6 servings

BROCCOLI SLAW

1 bunch broccoli

½ cup each, slivered red onion and thinly sliced celery

Half sweet red pepper, seeded and slivered

⅓ cup each, white vinegar and vegetable oil

3 tbsp granulated sugar

1 tsp paprika

Salt and freshly ground black pepper to taste

½ cup roasted unsalted sunflower seeds

This make-ahead salad adds crunch and colour to your menu. To save time, buy a bag of broccoli that's already been chopped for a slaw.

Separate the broccoli into florets and stems. Cut the florets into small pieces. Peel the stems and chop coarsely. In a large salad bowl, stir together the broccoli, onion, celery and red pepper.

In a 2-cup (500 mL) liquid measure, whisk together vinegar, oil, sugar, paprika and salt and pepper to taste. Continue to whisk until the sugar melts and the dressing thickens slightly. Pour the dressing over the broccoli mixture and toss well. Refrigerate the salad, covered, for at least 4 hours or up to 24 hours.

Just before serving, add sunflower seeds to the salad and toss well.

Makes 8 servings

HOT BROCCOLI AND RED PEPPER SALAD

2 tbsp fresh lemon juice

¼ cup finely chopped shallots

½ tsp dry mustard

¼ tsp hot pepper sauce

Salt and freshly ground black pepper to taste

¼ cup olive oil

2 bunches broccoli (1 ½ lb/750 g total)

1 sweet red pepper, seeded and slivered

If you're serving a menu that includes a smooth vegetable purée, this crunchy, colourful salad is a nice contrast. If the broccoli is all ready to steam and the dressing made ahead, the salad takes only minutes to finish.

In a small bowl, whisk together the lemon juice, shallots, mustard, hot pepper sauce and salt and pepper to taste. Gradually whisk in the oil. Let stand at room temperature for at least 1 hour or up to 6 hours.

Separate the broccoli into florets and stems. Cut the florets into small pieces. Peel the stems and cut them into ¼-inch (6 mm) slices. Steam the florets and stems until just tender but still bright green, 4 to 5 minutes (do not overcook).

Whisk the dressing to recombine it. In a salad bowl, toss the hot broccoli with the dressing and red pepper. Serve at once.

Makes 8 servings

GAI LAN STIR-FRIED WITH OYSTER SAUCE

8 oz (250 g) gai lan

2 tbsp canola oil

1 tbsp minced fresh ginger

2 cloves garlic, minced

2 green onions, sliced

2 tbsp oyster sauce

½ tsp hot pepper flakes

Sometimes called Chinese broccoli, gai lan doesn't flower out as much as its cousin, regular broccoli. My good friend, Anne Noronha, brought me a huge bag of gai lan last time she visited and showed me her favourite way of cooking it. Anne brings a large pot of water to the boil, adds a couple of drops of vegetable oil, then the chopped gai lan. As soon as the water comes to a boil again, she drains it and perhaps adds a bit of oyster sauce…or not. I couldn't resist transforming it into a quick stir-fry with ginger and garlic after the blanching.

Cut gai lan stems into 1-inch (2 ½ cm) diagonal pieces and shred the leaves into 1-inch (2 ½ cm) strips. Blanch as described above, then drain and refresh under cold running water.

In a large skillet or wok, heat the oil over medium-high heat. Add ginger and garlic and stir-fry for 30 seconds.

Add the gai lan and green onions and stir-fry until tender, 3 to 4 minutes. Stir in the oyster sauce and hot pepper flakes. Serve at once.

Makes 2 servings

SAUTÉED BROCCOLI WITH CHEESE

1 large bunch broccoli
¼ cup butter
2 large cloves garlic, minced
½ cup freshly grated Parmesan cheese
Freshly ground black pepper to taste

Parmesan cheese is always good teamed with broccoli. Instead of grating it, you might prefer to thinly slice the cheese with a vegetable peeler.

Separate the broccoli into florets and stems. Cut the florets into small pieces and the stems into small spears. In a saucepan of boiling, salted water, blanch the florets and stems until almost tender, about 2 minutes. Drain well.

In a large skillet, melt the butter over medium heat. Add the garlic and sauté until softened nut not browned, 2 or 3 minutes.

Add the broccoli and sauté for 2 minutes. Stir in the cheese and sprinkle with lots of pepper.

Makes 4 to 6 servings

RAPINI SAUTÉED WITH WALNUTS AND ANCHOVIES

1 bunch rapini (1 lb/500 g)
¼ cup olive oil
2 shallots, finely chopped (about ½ cup)
¼ tsp hot pepper flakes
½ cup chopped walnuts
Salt and freshly ground black pepper to taste
3 anchovies, drained and chopped
2 tbsp fresh lemon juice

Also called broccoli rabe, this skinny cousin of our more familiar broccoli is, like its relative, loaded with nutrients but is not as popular because of its slightly bitter taste. Lately, however, more and more people are taking to its pungent, earthy flavour, especially when combined with interesting ingredients like nuts and anchovies.

Trim off 1 inch (2 ½ cm) from the bottoms of the stems and wash the rapini well. Cook, uncovered, in a large pot of boiling, salted water until just tender, about 2 to 3 minutes. Drain and refresh under cold running water to cool. Squeeze out any excess liquid and pat dry. Coarsely chop. (The blanched rapini can be refrigerated in a plastic bag for up to 24 hours.)

In a large skillet, heat the oil over medium-high heat. Sauté the shallots and hot pepper flakes until the shallots are soft, about 2 minutes. Add the walnuts and sauté for 2 minutes.

Add the rapini and cook, stirring often, until heated through, about 3 minutes. Season to taste with salt and pepper. Stir in the anchovies and lemon juice.

Makes 4 to 6 servings

¼ cup olive oil

8 anchovies, drained (optional)

6 large cloves garlic, minced

¼ tsp hot pepper flakes

1 bunch rapini (about 1 lb/500 g)

4 cups short pasta, such as orecchiette, penne or gemelli (about 1 lb/500 g)

Freshly grated Parmesan cheese to serve

RAPINI AND PASTA

Rapini—think broccoli or kale with a deliciously bitter edge—is here tempered with garlic, anchovies, olive oil and the merest sprinkle of hot pepper flakes in a wonderful pasta dish from my very good friend and sometime co-author, Elizabeth Baird. Elizabeth advises that, although the anchovies are optional, they're recommended. If you prefer, omit the pasta and cheese and serve the rapini as a side dish.

In a large, heavy saucepan, heat the olive oil over low heat. Mash the anchovies (if using) into the oil. Add the garlic and pepper flakes. Cook, stirring often, until the garlic is tender, but not golden. Set aside.

Rinse the rapini and trim bottoms of the stems. Cut the stems from the leafy tops. In a large pot of boiling water, cook the stems until just tender, about 2 minutes. Add the leaves and cook until wilted, about 1 minute.

Leaving the rapini cooking water in the pot, scoop the stems and leaves into a bowl of ice water to chill them. Drain well, pressing gently to reduce any clinging moisture. Cut the leaves and stems crosswise into ½-inch (1 cm) pieces.

Bring the rapini cooking water back to the boil. Add the pasta and boil until just tender to the bite, about 8 minutes.

Meanwhile, add the rapini to the garlic mixture and heat through over medium heat, tossing well.

Drain the pasta and return to the pot. Add the rapini mixture and toss well. Serve in warmed bowls, topped with freshly grated Parmesan cheese.

Makes 4 to 6 servings

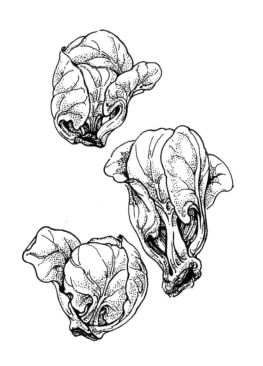

BRUSSELS SPROUTS

These tiny, elegant members of the cabbage family originated around Brussels during the Middle Ages but were not widely used in Europe until the nineteenth century. They were introduced to North America in the early 1800s and have become increasingly popular.

Resembling miniature cabbages on a stalk, Brussels sprouts develop as large buds on tall stems.

Brussels sprouts are ready late in the season and can be gathered even after very light frosts. They are rich in vitamin C and contain good amounts of vitamin A and iron.

CHOOSING

The buds mature from the bottom of the stalk to the top and can be harvested when they're one to two inches (2 ½ to 5 cm) across. Look for compact, firm, bright green sprouts with no blemishes. Select Brussels sprouts of similar size for more even cooking.

One pound (500 g) of Brussels sprouts yields about 4 servings.

STORING

Because Brussels sprouts get stronger in flavour with storage, they are best eaten soon after harvest. They will, however, keep for 1 to 2 days if you discard any loose or discoloured leaves and store them, unwashed, in a perforated plastic bag in the crisper.

To freeze Brussels sprouts, blanch small sprouts for 3 minutes, medium for 4 minutes and large for 5 minutes.

PREPARING

Wash Brussels sprouts, remove any damaged leaves, trim their bases and cut an X in the core of each so they'll cook faster and more evenly. If you suspect there might be insects present, soak the Brussels sprouts in warm, salted water for 15 minutes.

COOKING

Steam for 6 to 12 minutes, depending on size, until just tender when pierced with a knife, or boil, uncovered, in a large saucepan of salted water for 4 to 10 minutes, depending on size. Serve immediately so they won't lose their colour or flavour.

For marinated salads, refresh the Brussels sprouts after cooking by rinsing them under cold running water.

Season hot sprouts with salt, pepper, butter and lemon juice, or slice in half after cooking, sauté in butter and season with lemon juice.

Serve with a cheese sauce, or bake around a pork or beef roast for the last 20 to 25 minutes, basting often with the drippings.

A B C D E F G H I J K L M N O P Q R S T U V W X Y Z

BRUSSELS SPROUTS IN LEMON BUTTER

4 cups Brussels sprouts (about 1 ¼ lb/625 g)

2 cups chicken broth

¼ cup fresh lemon juice

⅓ cup cold butter, cut into small pieces

2 tsp finely grated lemon zest

Salt and freshly ground black pepper to taste

This tasty sauce will turn anyone into a Brussels sprouts fan.

Cut the end from each sprout and remove any damaged outer leaves. Cut an X in the bottom of each.

In a large saucepan, bring the chicken broth to a boil over high heat. Add the sprouts and cook, partially covered, until just tender, but still bright green, 12 to 20 minutes. Drain and discard the broth. Put the Brussels sprouts in a serving dish and keep warm.

Meanwhile, in a small saucepan, boil the lemon juice until it is reduced to 1 tbsp. Reduce the heat to low and gradually whisk in the butter, one piece at a time, blending each in thoroughly before adding the next. Stir in lemon zest and season to taste with salt and pepper. Pour the sauce over the warm sprouts and serve at once.

Makes 6 servings

BROCCOLI IN LEMON BUTTER

Substitute 1 ¼ lb (625 g) broccoli for the Brussels sprouts, but cook broccoli for only about 5 minutes.

SHREDDED SPROUTS SAUTÉED WITH PANCETTA

1 lb (500 g) Brussels sprouts

1 tbsp olive oil

2 oz (50 g) pancetta, diced (about ½ cup)

½ tsp hot pepper flakes

2 tbsp fresh lemon juice

Many people avoid Brussels sprouts because they've only ever eaten overcooked, grey versions of these little cabbage cousins. In this new fast way of cooking them, there is lots of lively colour and flavour, which is sure to appeal to everyone.

Cut the end from each sprout and remove any damaged outer leaves. Cut each sprout in half lengthwise, then thinly slice each half crosswise. (The sprouts can be shredded hours ahead of time and refrigerated.)

In a large skillet, heat the oil over medium heat. Add the pancetta and cook, stirring often, until crisp, about 4 minutes. With a slotted spoon, remove to drain on paper towels. Discard all but 2 tbsp drippings from the pan.

Add the shredded sprouts and hot pepper flakes and sauté for 3 minutes. Cover the skillet and cook until sprouts are tender-crisp, 2 to 3 minutes. Stir in the lemon juice, sprinkle with pancetta and serve at once.

Makes 4 servings

1 lb (500 g) small Brussels sprouts (about 3 cups)

0 oz (250 g) small baby carrots

8 oz (250 g) small cauliflower florets (about 1 cup)

½ cup dry white wine

½ cup fresh lemon juice

¼ cup water

¼ cup olive oil

2 large cloves garlic, quartered

2 tsp granulated sugar

1 tsp finely chopped fresh oregano or ¼ tsp dried oregano leaves

1 tsp finely chopped fresh basil or ¼ tsp dried basil leaves

1 tsp finely chopped fresh thyme or ¼ tsp dried thyme leaves

Salt and freshly ground black pepper to taste

MARINATED BRUSSELS SPROUT SALAD

This colourful salad can be prepared ahead and looks lovely on a buffet table.

In separate saucepans, steam Brussels sprouts for 10 to 12 minutes, carrots for 4 to 5 minutes and cauliflower for 2 to 3 minutes, or until each vegetable is barely tender.

Refresh each vegetables under cold running water, drain well and gently combine all the vegetables in a large glass bowl.

In a medium saucepan, combine the wine, lemon juice, water, olive oil, garlic, sugar, oregano, basil, thyme and salt and pepper to taste. Bring to a boil over high heat. Pour over the vegetables and stir gently.

Let cool, then cover and refrigerate at least 3 hours, stirring occasionally. Remove from the refrigerator 20 minutes before serving.

Makes 6 to 8 servings

SEE ALSO:

Brussels Sprouts in Sour-Cream Sauce   18

CABBAGE

Jacques Cartier brought the first cabbage seeds to Canada on his third voyage in 1541. Other varieties were introduced by colonists from eastern Europe, and most types of cabbage now grown in North America have come from Germany, Denmark, the Netherlands and Belgium.

Because it is a late vegetable that grows well in our climate, cabbage has always been an important part of our diet. Many early settlers preserved it as sauerkraut to use for hearty, nourishing winter meals.

Most familiar to us are the round, tightly packed green and red cabbages and the curly leafed Savoy. Recently Chinese cabbage, a leafy member of the mustard family, has been available in our markets.

Cabbage is an economical vegetable we can buy year-round and is rich in minerals, calcium and vitamins A and C, but low in calories.

CHOOSING

Select firm heads, heavy for their size, with crisp-looking outer leaves. Allowing cabbages to grow beyond their prime causes them to have a stronger flavour and odour.

About 1 ½ pounds (750 g) of cabbage yields 4 servings.

STORING

There are many references to early settlers storing cabbages in a hole in the ground. Besides providing them with a cool place, this method would keep the strong odour of cabbages out of the house. and also deal with the concern among early Canadians that green vegetables kept below living quarters in the house would cause sickness, "agues, intermittent, remittent and lake-fevers." (*The Backwoods of Canada*, Catharine Parr Traill, 1836.)

However, outside storage is not ideal since repeated thawing and freezing will affect the keeping qualities of the cabbage. It needs a cool, moist area for storage. Cut a thin slice off the end of the stalk and place the cabbage in a plastic bag in the refrigerator for up to 2 weeks. If storing a large number of cabbages for a longer time, a cold root cellar is ideal.

To freeze cabbage, blanch wedges for 2 minutes and shredded cabbage for 1 minute.

PREPARING

Just before cooking, discard any wilted outer leaves and wash the cabbage well. Chop or shred, depending on the recipe, cutting out the core as you go.

COOKING

Be careful not to overcook cabbage or it will have a strong flavour and mushy texture. Steam sliced cabbage for about 5 minutes and wedges for 6 to 9 minutes.

Boil wedges gently, uncovered, in a large pot of salted water for 6 to 9 minutes.

Since flavour and nutrients are retained if a vegetable is eaten raw, cabbage is popular for salads and coleslaws.

To ensure red cabbage retains its colour, add an acid like lemon juice or vinegar to the cooking water. Vinegar also makes a good seasoning for cooked green cabbage.

COLESLAW

I make a large jar of this tangy salad to have on hand over the holidays when I know I'll be cooking for family and friends. It keeps very well for days in the refrigerator.

1 medium green cabbage
2 large carrots, grated
1 small sweet green pepper, seeded and chopped
1 small sweet red pepper, seeded and chopped
1 medium onion, chopped
1 tbsp salt
Ice cubes
¾ cup granulated sugar
¾ cup white vinegar
½ cup canola oil
¼ cup water
1 tsp celery seeds
1 tsp dry mustard

Shred the cabbage finely by hand or in a food processor fitted with a slicing disk. In a large bowl, combine the cabbage, carrots, peppers, onion and salt. Cover with ice cubes and let the mixture sit to crisp for at least 1 hour. Remove the ice cubes and drain cabbage mixture well.

For the dressing, combine the sugar, vinegar, oil, water, celery seeds and mustard in a small saucepan over medium-high heat. Bring to a boil, stirring constantly. Pour the hot dressing over the cabbage mixture and let cool. (The coleslaw will keep in a lidded container in the fridge for up to 2 weeks.)

Makes 12 to 14 servings

CREAMY COLESLAW

Combine 6 cups finely shredded green cabbage and ½ cup each, diced red onion and diced unpeeled English cucumber. Whisk together ⅔ cup light mayonnaise, 2 tbsp cider vinegar, 4 tsp brown sugar, ½ tsp salt and ⅛ tsp of paprika. Pour over the cabbage mixture and toss to coat; cover and refrigerate for at least 1 hour or up to 4 hours. Makes 6 servings

BRAISED CABBAGE WITH APPLES

This easy dish tastes even better if made ahead and reheated. Try teaming it with Baked Beans with Pork (page 21).

6 slices side bacon, chopped
1 small green cabbage, shredded (about 8 cups)
2 large tart apples, peeled, cored and coarsely chopped
½ cup finely chopped onion
1 tsp seasoned salt
½ tsp freshly grated nutmeg
¼ cup cider vinegar
1 tbsp granulated sugar
⅛ tsp cayenne

In a large skillet over medium heat, cook the bacon, stirring often, until crisp. Remove with a slotted spoon and drain well on paper towels. Discard all but 2 tbsp of the fat remaining in the skillet.

Add the cabbage, apples, onion, seasoned salt and nutmeg to the bacon drippings. Stir well to mix. Cover tightly and cook over low heat for 20 minutes, stirring often.

In a 1-cup liquid measure, stir together the vinegar, sugar and cayenne until the sugar has dissolved. Add vinegar mixture to the skillet. Cook, uncovered, until cabbage is tender, about 5 minutes. Serve sprinkled with bacon.

Makes 4 to 6 servings

½ cup parboiled rice

1 lb (500 g) lean ground beef

8 oz (250 g) mushrooms, sliced (2 ½ cups)

1 onion, chopped

2 cloves garlic, minced

1 tsp Worcestershire sauce

Freshly ground black pepper to taste

1 can (7 ½ oz/213 mL) tomato sauce

½ cup sour cream

2 cups sauerkraut, drained and rinsed

1 cup fresh bread crumbs

1 tbsp butter, melted

QUICK SAUERKRAUT "CABBAGE ROLL" CASSEROLE

In the markets around the Waterloo region of Ontario, soured heads of cabbage are often available for making cabbage rolls. Here, I've incorporated the flavour of these delicious rolls into a quick and easy casserole. Serve with pickled beets (page 27) and whole wheat bread or rolls.

Cook the rice in 2 cups of boiling, salted water for 5 minutes. Drain well.

Meanwhile, in a large skillet over medium heat, cook the beef, mushrooms, onion and garlic, breaking up the meat and stirring often, until the beef is no longer pink and the vegetables are softened, about 8 minutes. Drain off any fat.

Stir in the Worcestershire sauce, and season to taste with pepper. Stir in the rice, tomato sauce and sour cream.

In a deep, 6-cup (1.5 L) baking dish, alternately layer three layers of sauerkraut and two of beef mixture.

In a small bowl, stir together the crumbs and butter. Sprinkle evenly over the top. (The casserole can be prepared to this point, covered and refrigerated for up to 8 hours. Let stand at room temperature for 30 minutes before baking.)

When ready to bake, preheat the oven to 350°F (180°C). Cover the baking dish with a lid or foil and bake until the rice is tender and the topping golden brown, about 45 minutes.

Makes 4 servings

QUICK FRESH CABBAGE "CABBAGE ROLL" CASSEROLE
Substitute 3 cups chopped fresh cabbage for the sauerkraut. Before adding the cabbage to the casserole, cook it in 1 tbsp butter just until wilted, about 5 minutes.

RED CABBAGE WITH MUSTARD SAUCE

1 medium head red cabbage

1 tbsp fresh lemon juice

MUSTARD SAUCE

¼ cup butter

½ cup finely chopped onion

1 egg, beaten

¼ cup red wine vinegar

2 tbsp packed brown sugar

2 tbsp dry red wine

2 tsp German-style prepared mustard

Salt and freshly ground black pepper to taste

Braised red cabbage is always a welcome side dish during the colder months. It goes particularly well with roast beef or goose.

Remove the outer leaves of the cabbage and set aside. Chop the rest of the cabbage coarsely. Cook in a large saucepan in a small amount of boiling, salted water and the lemon juice until barely tender, about 8 minutes. Drain well and keep warm.

For the mustard sauce, melt the butter in the same saucepan over medium heat. Add the onion and sauté for 5 minutes.

In a small bowl, stir together the egg, vinegar, sugar, wine, mustard and salt and pepper to taste. Add the egg mixture to the onion, along with the cooked cabbage. Cook, stirring, until the cabbage is coated with the sauce, about 2 minutes.

Line a warm serving bowl with the reserved cabbage leaves and pour cooked cabbage into it. Serve at once.

Makes 8 servings

BRAISED RED CABBAGE WITH CRANBERRIES

1 red cabbage (1 ½ lb/750 g)

¼ cup red wine vinegar

2 tbsp canola oil

2 small onions

2 apples, peeled and chopped

1 ¼ cups granulated sugar

¼ cup fresh orange juice

4 whole cloves

3-inch (8 cm) cinnamon stick, broken

4 cups cranberries

Strips orange zest (outer rind) for garnish

The wonderful people who worked at the well-loved Cookbook Store in Toronto (now sadly out of business) always told me what they liked cooking out of my books, and this was one of their favourites. It's a delicious side dish that goes well with roast goose or duck.

Core the cabbage and thinly shred it. In a large glass bowl, toss the cabbage with the vinegar. Set aside.

In a large stainless steel saucepan, heat the oil over medium heat. Chop one of the onions, add to the skillet and cook until softened. Stir in the apples, sugar and orange juice. Push the cloves into the remaining onion. Add the onion to the saucepan, along with the cinnamon stick.

Stir in the cabbage mixture and bring to a boil over high heat. Reduce heat to low and simmer, partially covered and stirring occasionally, until the cabbage is tender, about 15 minutes.

Increase the heat to medium-high and add the cranberries. Cook, uncovered and stirring often, until the cranberries begin to pop, about 5 minutes. Discard the whole onion and cinnamon stick. (The cabbage can be spooned into a serving bowl, cooled, covered and refrigerated for up to 1 day. Bring to room temperature to serve.)

Garnish with orange zest and serve warm or at room temperature.

Makes 8 servings

CLASSIC CABBAGE ROLLS

1 large cabbage or 2 small cabbages, cored*

FILLING

1 cup long grain rice

1 ½ cups boiling water

2 lb (1 kg) lean ground beef

1 can (10 oz/284 mL) condensed beef
  consommé, divided

1 onion, finely chopped

1 egg, beaten

2 cloves garlic, minced

1 tsp Worcestershire sauce

Salt and freshly ground black pepper to taste

SAUCE

¼ cup butter, divided

½ cup packed brown sugar, divided

2 tbsp all-purpose flour

2 onions, sliced

1 can (28 oz/796 mL) whole tomatoes with their
  juice

1 can (14 oz/398 mL) tomato sauce

¾ cup cider vinegar

2 tsp Worcestershire sauce

Salt and freshly ground black pepper to taste

A number of years ago, Ontario's Ministry of Culture sponsored a food show at the Ontario Science Centre in Toronto. Part of the show was a series of ongoing food demonstrations by the province's authors and cooks. This was the recipe I demonstrated at the show.

The recipe makes a large batch of cabbage rolls, so you can freeze some for future flavourful meals. It's also a good, big-batch recipe to cook with a friend so you can divide the result between you.

In a large pot of boiling water, blanch the cabbage for 2 minutes. Remove the cabbage from the pot, reserving the water.

Remove the outer leaves from the cabbage. Place any torn leaves in the bottoms of two 13- x 9-inch (3 L) shallow baking dishes and set the unblemished leaves aside. When it becomes too difficult to remove the leaves from the cabbage, blanch it again.

Without cutting through the leaves, trim the thick rib from the outside of each unblemished leaf for easier rolling.

For the filling, add the rice to the boiling water in a medium saucepan. Cook for 1 minute. Cover, turn off the heat and let stand until the water is absorbed, about 10 minutes.

Meanwhile, stir together the beef, ½ cup undiluted consommé, onion, egg, garlic, Worcestershire sauce, and salt and pepper to taste in a large bowl. Stir in the prepared rice.

Place about ⅓ cup filling in the centre of each cabbage leaf. Fold the sides over the filling and roll up from the stem end. Secure with toothpicks.

For the sauce, melt half of the butter in a large skillet over medium heat. Stir in 2 tbsp of the brown sugar.

Working in batches and adding the remaining butter and sugar as needed, add the cabbage rolls and cook until glazed on all sides, about 5 minutes. Remove the toothpicks and arrange the rolls close together and seam side down over the cabbage leaves in the baking dishes.

Preheat the oven to 325°F (160°). In a small bowl, whisk together the flour and remaining consommé until smooth. Stir into the skillet. Add the onions, tomatoes, tomato sauce, vinegar, Worcestershire sauce and salt and pepper to taste. Bring to a boil over medium-high heat. Reduce the heat to medium-low and cook, stirring, until slightly thickened, 3 to 5 minutes.

Pour the sauce over the cabbage rolls. Bake, covered, until the cabbage is tender, about 2 ½ hours.

Makes about 30 rolls

* Where I live in the Waterloo region of Ontario, soured heads of cabbage for making cabbage rolls are often available at the farmers' markets. These soured heads need no blanching.

½ small head red cabbage

¼ cup red wine vinegar, divided

8 oz (250 g) side bacon, diced

2 tbsp well-drained capers

¼ cup canola oil

2 cloves garlic, minced

Freshly ground black pepper to taste

1 cup crumbled soft goat cheese (6 oz/175 g)

WARM RED CABBAGE AND GOAT CHEESE SALAD

Serve this colourful, interesting salad as a first course or, with crusty rolls, as a lunch. You can substitute blue cheese or feta for the goat cheese.

Remove the core and shred the cabbage. Put cabbage in a large glass bowl and sprinkle with 2 tbsp of the vinegar. Set aside.

In a large skillet over medium heat, cook the bacon until crisp. Remove with a slotted spoon to drain on paper towels. Sprinkle the bacon and capers over the cabbage.

Pour off all but ½ cup fat from the skillet. Add the oil, garlic, remaining vinegar and pepper to taste. (The recipe can be prepared to this point and set aside at room temperature for up to 3 hours.)

Heat the dressing in the skillet until hot. Pour over the cabbage and toss well. Sprinkle with goat cheese. Serve at once.

Makes 4 generous appetizer servings

SEE ALSO:
Corn Relish   60

CARROTS

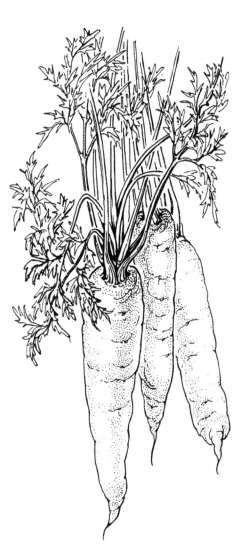

For years the carrot was valued more for its decorative foliage than its edible root: the feathery plumes adorned hats and mantelpieces alike. Related to parsnip, fennel and Queen Anne's lace, carrots were originally white; the bright orange varieties we have today were developed by the Dutch in the Middle Ages.

As well as orange carrots, we can now choose from a selection of coloured (primarily purple and red) heritage carrots, but be careful when you cook these heritage varieties together with a light-coloured vegetable, like fennel, since the colour will leach out of them and tint the other vegetable. (Orange carrots don't leach their colour.)

Their bright colour and crisp texture make carrots a success in salads, stews, soups and many other dishes. Because of their natural sugar content, they have often been used in desserts. There are many nineteenth-century references to sweet carrot pie. Carrot pudding became a popular and economic substitute for fruit pudding at Christmas, and carrot cake is a modern favourite.

Nowadays carrots are one of our most popular vegetables. They're easy to grow, available fresh all winter, low in calories and high in vitamin A. Carrots also contain B vitamins and minerals.

CHOOSING

Select firm, smooth, well-shaped carrots with bright colour.

About 1 to 1 ¼ pounds (500 to 625 g) of carrots yield 4 servings.

STORING

Remove the carrots' tops and stems immediately because they drain the moisture from the root. Brush and wash clean, dry well and store in a perforated plastic bag in the crisper for up to two weeks. If storing longer, change the plastic bag because moisture will build up inside and rot the carrots. Don't store with apples since the fruit emits a gas that gives carrots a bitter taste.

For longer storage of large quantities of carrots, layer in moist sand in a well-ventilated cold cellar.

To freeze carrots, blanch whole carrots for 5 minutes and pieces for 3 minutes.

PREPARING

Just scrub them if the carrots are young, and peel thinly if older. Slicing them lengthwise rather than crosswise, retains more nutrients during cooking.

COOKING

Steam whole small carrots about 10 minutes and pieces about 4 minutes.

Boil, covered, in a small amount of salted water for about 8 minutes for whole carrots or 3 to 4 minutes for pieces. Cooking time varies with the age of the vegetable.

Bake a casserole of shredded carrots with butter, salt, pepper and a little water or broth for about 40 minutes in a 350°F (180°C) oven. Or coat whole carrots or chunky pieces with melted butter or oil and bake around a roast of pork, beef or lamb.

Carrots are also delicious braised with butter in a tightly covered skillet.

CHILLED CARROT AND ORANGE SOUP

2 tbsp butter

1 ½ lb (750 g) carrots, coarsely chopped (about 6 medium)

2 medium onions, coarsely chopped

¼ cup water

1 cup fresh orange juice

1 cup plain yogurt

2 tsp finely grated orange zest

¼ tsp ground cinnamon

¼ tsp freshly grated nutmeg

Salt and freshly ground white pepper to taste

Finely chopped parsley or chives for garnish

A hint of orange and some zesty spices give extra interest to this cold carrot soup, which makes a refreshing starter to a summer supper.

In a large, heavy saucepan, melt the butter over medium heat. Add the carrots, onions and water. Cover tightly and steam until the vegetables are tender, about 20 minutes. Let cool slightly.

Use an immersion blender in the pot to blend the carrot mixture until smooth. Or purée the soup in batches in a countertop blender (a blender, rather than a food processor, makes a smoother soup). Add the orange juice, yogurt, zest, cinnamon, nutmeg and salt and pepper to taste. Blend until smooth. Chill, covered, for 4 hours or overnight.

Serve in chilled soup bowls and garnish each portion with parsley.

Makes about 6 servings

CARROTS IN GINGER CREAM

1 lb (500 g) carrots

2 tbsp butter

1 tsp ground ginger

Salt and freshly ground black pepper to taste

¼ cup reserved cooking liquid

¼ cup table cream (18% MF)

1 egg yolk

1 tbsp finely chopped parsley

Ginger is always good with carrots, while a bit of cream adds a touch of luxury.

If the carrots are small, young ones, just scrub them and leave whole. Otherwise, scrape them and cut into matchstick pieces. Cook in a saucepan of boiling, salted water to cover until almost tender, about 5 minutes. Drain the carrots, reserving ¼ cup of the cooking liquid.

In a large skillet, melt the butter over medium heat. Add the carrots, tossing to coat well with butter. Sprinkle with ginger and salt and pepper to taste. Pour in the reserved cooking liquid. Cover and simmer until tender, 10 minutes for whole carrots, less for cut ones.

In a small bowl, beat together the cream and egg yolk. Stir the cream mixture into the carrots. Heat for a few seconds, uncovered and stirring gently, until the sauce thickens (do not let it boil). Serve sprinkled with chopped parsley.

Makes 4 servings

CARROT AND RED LENTIL SOUP WITH PARSLEY CREAM

2 tbsp olive oil

1 lb (500 g) carrots (about 6 small), sliced

1 onion, chopped

1 small sweet red pepper, seeded and chopped

2 cloves garlic, minced

2 tsp ground ginger

6 cups chicken broth

1 cup red lentils, picked over and rinsed

2 tsp fresh lemon juice (approx.)

Salt to taste

PARSLEY CREAM

¼ cup parsley leaves

1 green onion, sliced

⅓ cup sour cream

⅛ tsp cayenne

Simple to make but comforting and delicious, this soup is just right for company or family. To save time, skip the parsley cream garnish and just top the soup with croutons.

In a large saucepan, heat the oil over medium heat. Add the carrots, onion, red pepper, garlic and ginger and cook, stirring often, for 5 minutes.

Add the broth and lentils and bring to a boil over high heat. Reduce the heat to medium-low and simmer, covered, until the carrots are very tender, 15 to 20 minutes. Let cool slightly.

Use an immersion blender in the pot to blend the soup until smooth. Or purée the soup in batches in a countertop blender (a blender, rather than a food processor, makes a smoother soup). If necessary, pour the soup back into the rinsed-out saucepan and bring to a simmer. Add 2 tsp lemon juice and season to taste with salt and more lemon juice if desired.

For the parsley cream, finely chop the parsley and green onion in a mini chopper. Add the sour cream and cayenne and process until well combined. Or finely chop the parsley and onion by hand and combine with the sour cream and cayenne in a small bowl.

Serve the soup in warm bowls and spoon a dollop of parsley cream onto each portion.

Makes 4 servings

MARINATED CARROTS

1 lb (500 g) carrots (about 5)

¼ cup dry white wine

¼ cup white wine vinegar

¼ cup water

¼ cup olive oil

1 clove garlic, minced

1 tsp granulated sugar

3 large sprigs fresh thyme or ½ tsp dried thyme leaves

1 bay leaf

Salt to taste

This easy salad needs no refrigeration so is perfect for a buffet table.

Cut the carrots in half crosswise, then in half lengthwise.

In a large saucepan, combine the wine, vinegar, water, oil, garlic, sugar, thyme, bay leaf, and salt to taste. Bring to a boil over high heat. Add the carrots. Reduce the heat to medium and cook, uncovered, in the marinade until just tender, about 7 minutes.

With a slotted spoon, remove the carrots to a shallow serving dish. Strain the liquid over the carrots and let them cool in it. (Salad can be prepared to this point and refrigerated, covered, for 1 day.)

If carrots have been refrigerated, let them come to room temperature before serving. Drain the carrots and place in a serving bowl.

Makes 4 to 6 servings

MAPLE-GLAZED CARROTS

1 ½ lb (750 g) whole baby carrots, or larger carrots cut into matchstick pieces

3 tbsp butter

¼ cup maple syrup

Salt to taste

2 tbsp finely chopped parsley or fresh mint

These sweet roots make a lovely accompaniment to a pork roast.

In a large skillet, cook the carrots in boiling, salted water until almost tender, about 5 minutes. Drain the carrots, reserving ¼ cup of the cooking liquid.

In the same skillet, melt the butter over medium heat and roll the carrots in it. Add the reserved liquid, maple syrup and salt to taste.

Cook, uncovered, until the liquid is thickened and carrots are tender, about 10 minutes for whole baby carrots, less time for cut carrots. Serve sprinkled with parsley or mint.

Makes 6 servings

HONEY-GLAZED PARSNIPS
Substitute diced parsnips for the carrots, and ¼ cup honey for the maple syrup.

HONEY-GLAZED RUTABAGA
Substitute diced rutabaga for the carrots, and ¼ cup honey for the maple syrup.

CARROT-HERB STUFFING FOR FISH

8 small carrots or one large carrot, grated

4 oz (125 g) button mushrooms, chopped

1 small onion, finely chopped

¼ cup finely chopped parsley

1 tbsp finely chopped fresh summer savory or 1 tsp dried savory leaves

1 large clove garlic, minced

1 ½ tbsp fresh lemon juice

½ cup fine, dry bread crumbs

¼ cup canola oil (approx.)

Salt and freshly ground black pepper to taste

1 egg

3 to 4 lb (1 ½ to 1 ⅘ kg) cleaned fish, such as salmon

This flavourful stuffing recipe comes from my sister Muriel Barbour who lived in Vancouver. It was a favourite of hers for filling a whole fresh salmon. Try it, too, with whole whitefish or rainbow trout.

Preheat the oven to 450°F (230°C).

In a large bowl, stir together the carrots, mushrooms, onion, parsley, savory and garlic. Sprinkle over the lemon juice. Stir in the bread crumbs, ¼ cup oil and salt and pepper to taste. Add the egg and stir until well combined.

Sprinkle more salt on the inside of the fish and stuff it loosely with the carrot mixture. Fasten the opening with small skewers or toothpicks and loop string around them. Or sew the opening with a large needle and coarse thread.

Place the stuffed fish in a greased shallow roasting pan and brush with a little more oil. Measure the depth of the stuffed fish at its thickest part. Bake, uncovered, for 10 minutes per inch (2 ½ cm) of thickness. When done, the flesh will be opaque and will flake easily with a fork (do not overcook).

Makes enough stuffing for a 3 to 4 lb (1 ½ to 1 ⅘ kg) cleaned fish

CARROT AND PARSNIP PURÉE

8 oz (250 g) carrots (about 3 medium)

8 oz (250 g) parsnips (about 3 medium)

¼ cup butter

¼ cup whipping cream (35% MF)

2 tsp finely grated lemon zest

1 tbsp fresh lemon juice

¼ tsp ground ginger

Salt and freshly ground black pepper to taste

1 tbsp finely chopped parsley

This easy side dish can be prepared ahead, then cooled, covered and refrigerated for up to one day. Bring out to room temperature, then reheat, covered, in a 350°F (180°) oven until heated through, about 30 minutes.

Peel the carrots and parsnips. Cut roughly into 2-inch (5 cm) matchstick pieces, removing the cores from the parsnips if they're hard or woody.

In a medium saucepan, bring a small quantity of salted water to a boil. Add the carrots and cook, covered, for 5 minutes. Add the parsnips and cook until tender, about 5 to 10 minutes. Drain the vegetables, reserving the cooking liquid.

Return the vegetables to the saucepan and add the butter, cream, lemon zest and juice. Mash together well. Use an immersion blender in the saucepan to blend the vegetables to a smooth purée. Or purée the vegetables in batches in a countertop blender or food processor. If the purée is too stiff, add a little of the reserved cooking liquid.

Return the purée to the saucepan if necessary. Stir in the ginger and season to taste with salt and pepper. Heat through until piping hot. Spoon into a warm serving dish and sprinkle with chopped parsley.

Makes 3 to 4 servings

CARROT AND RUTABAGA PURÉE
Substitute cubed rutabaga for the parsnips and add them along with the carrots. Omit lemon juice and zest, if desired.

SPICY CARROT COOKIES

2 cups peeled and thinly sliced carrots (about 4 medium)

⅓ cup seedless raisins

⅓ cup orange juice

1 cup butter, softened

¾ cup firmly packed brown sugar

1 egg

2 tbsp finely grated orange zest

1 tsp vanilla

1 ¼ cups whole wheat flour

2 tsp baking powder

1 tsp cinnamon

¼ tsp freshly grated nutmeg

¼ tsp salt

⅓ cup chopped walnuts or pecans

These easy cookies are moist and chewy. If you prefer a crisper cookie, increase the baking time slightly. Either way, they'll keep well in an airtight container for up to 1 week in the refrigerator or for up to 1 month in the freezer.

In a small saucepan, cook the carrots, uncovered, in a small amount of simmering water until quite soft, about 12 minutes. Drain well and mash. Don't worry if the mixture is not absolutely smooth.

Preheat the oven to 350°F (180°C).

In a small bowl, combine the raisins and orange juice and set aside.

In a large bowl, cream the butter, add the brown sugar and beat until light and fluffy. Beat in the egg. Stir in the orange zest, vanilla and mashed carrots.

In a separate bowl, sift together the flour, baking powder, cinnamon, nutmeg and salt. Stir into the butter mixture.

Drain the raisins well, discarding the orange juice. Add the raisins to the batter and stir in the nuts. Mix until well blended.

Drop by rounded teaspoonfuls onto lightly greased or parchment-paper-lined cookie sheets. Bake in the centre of the oven until light brown and set, about 15 minutes. Cool on wire racks.

Makes 4 to 5 dozen cookies

CARROT CAKE

This classic cake stays moist for more than a week in the refrigerator and it also freezes well. If you prefer, the same batter will fill two 9- x 5-inch (2 L) loaf pans and take just 1 hour to bake.

2 ½ cups all-purpose flour

2 tsp baking powder

2 tsp cinnamon

1 tsp baking soda

1 tsp salt

½ tsp freshly grated nutmeg

4 eggs

1 ½ cups firmly packed brown sugar

¾ cup canola oil

1 cup undrained crushed pineapple

2 ½ cups lightly packed grated carrots
   (about 5 medium)

1 cup raisins

½ cup chopped walnuts or pecans

ICING

1 pkg (250 g) brick cream cheese, softened

¼ cup softened butter

3 ½ cups icing sugar

2 tsp vanilla

1 tsp fresh lemon juice

Orange slices and pecan or walnut halves for
   garnish

Preheat the oven to 325°F (160°C). Grease and flour a 10-inch (3 L) tube pan.

In a medium bowl, sift together the flour, baking powder, cinnamon, baking soda, salt and nutmeg. Set aside.

In a large bowl, beat the eggs well until thick and lemon-coloured. Add the sugar gradually and continue to beat until light and fluffy. Add the oil and beat well. Stir in the pineapple, then the carrots, raisins and nuts. Mix well.

Stir the dry ingredients into the creamed mixture until just combined. Pour the batter into the prepared pan. Bake in the centre of the oven until a skewer inserted in the centre of the cake comes out clean, about 1 hour and 15 minutes.

Let cool in the pan for 30 minutes, then turn out onto a wire rack and let cool completely.

For the icing, blend together the cream cheese and butter in a medium bowl, then beat until fluffy. Beat in the sugar ½ cup at a time. Beat in the vanilla and lemon juice.

When the cake is cool, slice it horizontally into three layers. Spread the icing between the layers and on top. Ice the sides of the cake, if desired. Garnish with orange slices and pecan or walnut halves.

Makes 12 servings

CAULIFLOWER

Another member of the cabbage family, cauliflower was developed in the Middle East and by the sixteenth century was being grown in Europe.

Because cauliflower can be tricky to grow, it was not a staple of Canada's early settlers, as cabbage was. Today, however, the familiar creamy white variety, and the new purple and orange cauliflowers, are popular raw and cooked.

Cauliflower is high in calcium, potassium and vitamins A and C.

CHOOSING

Select compact, solid and blemish-free heads with heavy, green outer leaves.

One medium head of cauliflower yields about 4 servings.

STORING

Cut a thin slice from the stalk, but leave the outer leaves attached and store in a perforated plastic bag in the crisper. Use within 4 days.

To freeze cauliflower, blanch the florets for 3 minutes.

PREPARING

Remove the outer leaves, wash the cauliflower well and cut off the stem at the base of the head. Cut out the core. Leave the head whole or separate it into florets. Unblemished outer leaves can be used in the bottom of the cooking pot, as part of the presentation of a whole, cooked head, or chopped and added to soup.

COOKING

Raw cauliflower adds a delicious accent to green salads and is a favourite on a tray of crudités.

When cooking, cauliflower passes quickly from being underdone to being overcooked; watch carefully so it doesn't end up mushy.

Boil cauliflower in a large amount of salted water, uncovered, for 12 to 20 minutes for a whole head or 4 to 6 minutes for florets. For really white cooked cauliflower, add 1 tablespoonful milk or 1 teaspoonful fresh lemon juice to the cooking water. Steaming takes slightly longer.

Cauliflower is also excellent in stir-fries or braises. A rich cheese sauce (see page 172) is a popular and delicious final touch to cooked cauliflower.

CAULIFLOWER CHEESE SOUP

1 medium cauliflower

¼ cup butter

2 medium potatoes, peeled and finely diced

2 medium carrots, finely diced

1 cup finely chopped onion

1 cup diced celery

2 medium cloves garlic, minced

5 cups chicken or vegetable broth

1 tsp finely chopped fresh thyme or ¼ tsp dried thyme leaves

1 tsp finely chopped fresh marjoram or ¼ tsp dried marjoram leaves

1 ½ cups shredded old cheddar cheese

1 ½ cups milk, half-and-half cream (10% MF) or table cream (18% MF)

¼ tsp dry mustard

Salt and freshly ground black pepper to taste

Chopped green onion or celery leaves for garnish

The classic combination of cauliflower and cheese, plus the addition of fresh herbs, makes a delicious fall soup.

Trim the cauliflower and separate into small florets.

In a large, heavy saucepan, melt the butter over medium heat. Add 2 cups of the cauliflower florets and sauté for about 2 minutes. Reduce the heat to low and cook, covered, until tender-crisp, about 2 minutes. Remove cauliflower florets with a slotted spoon and set aside.

In the butter remaining in the saucepan, sauté the remaining cauliflower, potatoes, carrots, onion, celery and garlic over medium heat for about 5 minutes.

Stir in the broth, thyme and marjoram. Bring to a boil. Reduce the heat to medium-low and simmer, partially covered, until the vegetables are tender but not mushy, about 20 minutes. Let cool slightly.

Use an immersion blender in the saucepan to blend the soup until smooth. Or purée the soup in batches in a countertop blender (a blender, rather than a food processor, makes a smoother soup). If necessary, pour the soup back into the rinsed-out saucepan.

Stir in the cheese, milk or cream, dry mustard and reserved cooked cauliflower florets. Season to taste with salt and pepper. Heat slowly until hot but do not boil. Serve garnished with chopped green onion or celery leaves.

Makes about 10 servings

WHOLE CAULIFLOWER WITH HERBS

1 large cauliflower

Milk, as required (see method)

¼ cup butter, melted

1 tbsp finely chopped chives

1 tbsp finely chopped fresh summer savory or 1 tsp dried savory leaves

1 tbsp seeded and chopped sweet red pepper

1 tbsp fresh lemon juice

This recipe turns cauliflower into a spectacular presentation for a dinner party.

Remove most of the outer green leaves of the cauliflower, but leave two or three of the nicest ones next to the head.

Pour enough milk into a large saucepan to give a depth of 1 inch (2 ½ cm). Bring to a boil over medium-high heat.

Place the whole cauliflower, stem end down in the saucepan. Bring back to a boil. Reduce the heat to medium-low and simmer, covered, until the stalk is tender-crisp, 15 to 20 minutes. Drain well and transfer to a warm shallow serving dish.

In a small bowl, combine the melted butter, chives, savory, red pepper and lemon juice. Spoon the butter mixture over the cauliflower and serve at once. Use a sharp knife and a large serving spoon to the serve the cauliflower.

Makes 6 servings

BREADED SAUTÉED CAULIFLOWER

A quick and easy finish perks up cooked cauliflower.

1 large cauliflower
1 tbsp fresh lemon juice
¼ cup unsalted butter
1 cup fresh bread crumbs

Trim the cauliflower and cut into small florets. Cook, uncovered, in a small amount of boiling, salted water to which the lemon juice has been added, until barely tender, about 6 minutes. Drain well.

In a large, heavy skillet, cook the butter over medium heat until it starts to brown, but do not let it burn. Add the bread crumbs and cook, stirring, until bread crumbs are golden brown.

Add the cauliflower to the skillet and stir until heated through and coated with browned crumbs, about 5 minutes.

Makes 6 servings

CURRIED CAULIFLOWER

Curry spices add interest to a side dish that would be excellent with something full-flavoured like grilled lamb chops.

1 large cauliflower
2 tbsp canola oil
2 tsp mustard seeds
2 tbsp minced fresh ginger
½ tsp turmeric
2 tsp ground cumin
1 tbsp water
Salt and freshly ground black pepper to taste
¼ each, sweet green and red pepper, seeded and slivered

Trim the cauliflower and cut into small florets about inch ¾ (2 cm) across.

In a large skillet or wok, heat the oil over high heat. Add the mustard seeds and immediately cover the skillet. When the seeds start to pop, add the ginger and cook, stirring, until lightly browned. Remove the skillet from the heat, add the turmeric and stir for 30 seconds.

Add the cauliflower and return the skillet to medium heat. Cook, stirring, until the florets are golden.

Stir in the cumin and cook, stirring, for 1 minute. Add the water, and salt and pepper to taste. Increase the heat to high. Cook, covered, for 1 minute.

Reduce the heat to very low and steam until the florets are tender-crisp, 10 to 15 minutes.

During the last 5 minutes, add the sweet pepper slivers. Just before serving, cook, uncovered and stirring well, to evaporate any moisture. Serve at once.

Makes 6 servings

SEE ALSO:
Curried Harvest Vegetables with Lentils   157

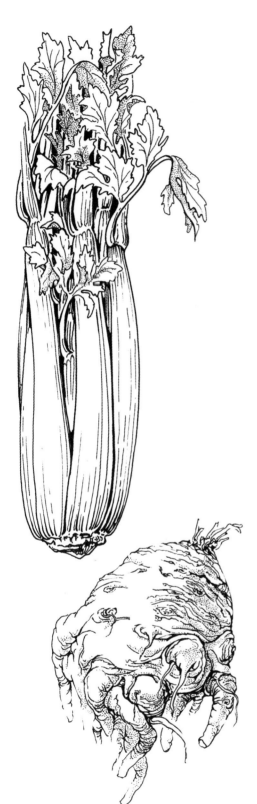

CELERY AND CELERIAC

CELERY

Celery and celeriac are both members of the carrot family. Celery was cultivated by French and Italian gardeners in the seventeenth century and eventually made its way to North America. Although not a staple in early Canadian households, celery can be found in almost every kitchen now. This low-calorie vegetable adds crispness and colour in salads, and flavour to stews, soups and casseroles. Don't waste celery leaves; they make a great addition to your stockpot and can also be used as a garnish.

CHOOSING

Select firm, crisp, compact stalks. I prefer the flavour of lighter rather than dark green celery.

One bunch of celery yields about 6 servings.

STORING

Celery keeps well for up to 2 weeks enclosed in a plastic bag in the crisper. As soon as you bring it home, trim off the root end and any damaged leaves, and separate the celery into individual stalks. Wash and dry well, then wrap. Do not freeze celery.

COOKING

Celery is used most often raw, but is also good braised in butter for about 5 minutes, or stir-fried.

CELERIAC

Also called celery root, celery knob or turnip-rooted celery, this rather shaggy-looking vegetable has been more popular in Europe than here. Recently, however, I have noticed it more often in our markets. It has a delicate celery flavour and is excellent used raw in salads, which is especially welcome since it's available primarily during the fall and winter. It can also be substituted in most recipes calling for cooked celery.

CHOOSING

Look for medium, round roots that are neither soft nor withered. It is difficult to detect hollow or pithy centres without cutting into the celeriac; it may be necessary to cut out this soft part.

About 1 ½ pounds (750 g) of celeriac yield 4 servings.

STORING

Store unwashed celeriac for up to 1 week in the refrigerator. For longer storage, bury it in sand in a cold cellar.

PREPARING

Have ready a container filled with 4 cups of cold water and 1 tablespoonful fresh lemon juice. Peel the celeriac and plunge immediately into the acidulated water since the flesh will darken quickly when exposed to air.

COOKING

Cook as you would potatoes. Peeled celeriac darkens if steamed.

SMOKED FISH AND CELERIAC CHOWDER

2 tbsp butter

1 onion, chopped

2 stalks celery, thinly sliced

2 cloves garlic, minced

1 medium celeriac, peeled and cut into ½-inch (1 cm) cubes

¾ tsp dried thyme leaves

2 bottles (each 240 mL) clam juice

1 cup water

1 cup dry white wine

2 red-skinned potatoes, unpeeled and cut into ½-inch (1 cm) cubes

12 oz (375 g) smoked rainbow trout fillets, skinned and flaked

1 cup fresh or frozen and thawed corn kernels

1 cup whipping cream (35% MF)

Salt and freshly ground black pepper to taste

¼ cup finely chopped parsley

2 tbsp fresh lemon juice

Celery leaves and paprika for garnish

This hearty chowder gets its rich flavour from smoked fish. If smoked rainbow trout is unavailable, substitute other smoked fish fillets, such as mackerel.

In a large, heavy saucepan over medium heat, melt the butter. Add the onion, celery and garlic. Cook, stirring often, until the onion is soft but not brown, about 5 minutes. Add the celeriac and thyme. Cook, stirring, for 1 minute.

Stir in the clam juice, water and wine. Bring to a boil over high heat. Reduce the heat to medium-low and simmer, covered, for 15 minutes. Add the potatoes. Simmer, covered, until all the vegetables are very tender, about 15 minutes.

Stir in the trout, corn, cream and salt and pepper to taste. Cook, covered, over low heat for 5 minutes.

Stir in the parsley and lemon juice. Season to taste with more salt and pepper if necessary. Ladle into warm soup bowls. Serve garnished with celery leaves and a sprinkling of paprika.

Makes about 6 servings

ALMOND-CELERY SALAD

1 large bunch celery

⅓ cup ground, toasted, blanched almonds (see page 14)

2 tbsp fresh lemon juice

1 tsp dry mustard

1 ½ tsp finely chopped fresh tarragon or ½ tsp dried tarragon leaves

Salt and freshly ground black pepper to taste

⅓ cup olive oil

Lettuce leaves to serve

1 or 2 medium red onions, thinly sliced

A pretty salad that can be made ahead, like this one, is always handy if you're entertaining.

Keeping the stalks together, wash the bunch of celery carefully by running cold water in through the tops of the stalks. Drain well. Cut the whole bunch of celery, including the leaves, into thin crosswise slices, discarding the root end. Place the celery in a large glass bowl.

In a small bowl, combine the almonds, lemon juice, mustard, tarragon and salt and pepper to taste. Whisking continuously, add the olive oil until well combined.

Pour the dressing over the celery and stir gently to coat. Cover and refrigerate for at least 1 hour, stirring occasionally. (The salad can be prepared to this point and refrigerated, covered, for up to 3 days.)

To serve, line a round serving platter with lettuce leaves. Arrange the onion slices, overlapping, around the edge, leaving an outside border of lettuce. Mound the celery salad in the centre, just covering the inside edges of the onion slices.

Makes 6 servings

WALDORF SALAD

1 medium celeriac, peeled and diced

3 cups diced, unpeeled red apples

1 tbsp fresh lemon juice

½ cup diced celery (1 large stalk)

½ cup coarsely chopped walnuts or pecans

¼ cup seedless raisins

½ cup whipping cream (35% MF)

½ cup mayonnaise

½ tsp finely grated lemon zest

¼ tsp dry mustard

¼ tsp ground ginger

⅛ tsp mace

⅛ tsp ground cardamom

Salt to taste

Lettuce leaves to serve

Celery leaves for garnish

This crunchy salad with its creamy dressing is delicious with roast beef or chicken. For best results, do not dice the vegetables and fruit too finely. If celery root is unavailable, substitute an additional ½ cup diced celery.

In a large bowl, combine the celeriac and apples. Sprinkle with the lemon juice and toss well. Stir in the celery, nuts and raisins.

In a medium bowl, whip the cream until soft peaks form. Gently fold in the mayonnaise, lemon zest, mustard, ginger, mace, cardamom and salt to taste until well combined.

Add the dressing to the celeriac mixture and toss gently but thoroughly. Serve at once in individual lettuce cups or a large salad bowl lined with lettuce. Garnish with celery leaves.

Makes 8 servings

WALDORF SALAD WITH PEARS
Substitute diced, unpeeled pears for all or some of the apples.

1 tbsp lemon juice

6 large potatoes

4 small celeriac

1 small onion, chopped

¼ cup butter

⅓ cup milk, half-and-half cream (10% MF) or
    table cream (18% MF)

½ tsp freshly grated nutmeg

Salt and freshly ground white pepper to taste

2 tbsp chopped chives

PURÉE OF CELERIAC AND POTATOES

This creamy side dish is an excellent accompaniment to roast game.

Have ready a large saucepan containing 4 cups cold water and 1 tbsp lemon juice. Peel and quarter the potatoes and celeriac and place in the saucepan of water.

When ready to cook, drain well. Add the onion and a small amount of boiling water to the saucepan. Cover and cook until the vegetables are tender, 20 to 25 minutes. Drain well, then dry by placing the saucepan over low heat for a few seconds.

Mash the vegetables well or press through a food mill. (Do not use a food processor or the purée will be gluey.)

Add the butter, milk or cream, nutmeg and salt and pepper to taste. Whip the purée with a wooden spoon or a whisk until very smooth. Transfer to a warm serving dish and sprinkle with chives. Serve at once.

Makes 8 servings

SEE ALSO:

Celeriac Rémoulade   78
Old-Fashioned Chili Sauce   146

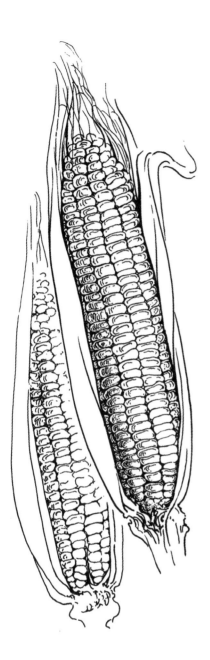

CORN

When Europeans came to Canada, the First Nations had long been growing corn, or maize to give it its original name. They valued it not only as a food, but as a form of currency, fuel, jewellery and a symbol in religious ceremonies.

The first settlers bartered with local aboriginals for seed and it was not unusual for them to grow corn even before they had their land cleared. From the First Nations people, too, they learned how to preserve corn by drying and grinding it. This versatile vegetable was part of the general foundation of settlers' meals. Fresh corn, dried corn and cornmeal were put to good use in countless ways to achieve some variety in an otherwise monotonous diet.

CHOOSING

This is one vegetable that should go straight from the garden to the pot. If you delay cooking sweet corn for even an hour, some of its sugar will have turned to starch. Even newer supersweet varieties are best cooked as soon as possible after picking.

Fresh sweet corn contains vitamins A and C and some phosphorus.

If you are lucky enough to have corn in your garden, it is ready to harvest when the end silks are brown and dry. The kernels will be plump and, if punctured with a fingernail, will secrete a milky substance. If immature, the substance will appear watery; if too old, it will be thick and doughy. Do not pull back the husks to check for ripeness since doing so reduces the corn's moisture; simply feel the size of the kernels from the outside of the husks.

When buying corn, select ears with fresh green husks, firm plump kernels and—most important—damp, pale green stems. Corn picked too long will have brown, dry stalks. One of the best tests is smell. Truly fresh corn has a unique fragrance that diminishes with age.

Commercially canned corn and frozen corn can be successfully used in recipes calling for cooked fresh corn kernels.

Two ears of fresh corn yield 1 serving. Two uncooked ears yield about 1 cup of kernels.

STORING

If you cannot cook the corn immediately, wrap unhusked ears in damp paper towels and refrigerate.

To freeze corn, blanch whole ears for 7 to 11 minutes and kernels for 4 minutes.

PREPARING

Remove the green husks and all the silk from around the kernels. If you are grilling or roasting the corn, pull down the husks, remove the silk and rewrap the ears in their husks.

To remove corn kernels before cooking, cut the corn kernels off the ears

A B C D E F G H I J K L M N O P Q R S T U V W X Y Z

about two-thirds the depth of the kernel, then scrape the ear with the blade of a knife to remove any remaining flesh and liquid. This way, you get none of the hard cob. If you want whole, distinct kernels, however, cut them off within ⅛ inch (3 mm) of the ear. An electric knife works well for either method.

COOKING

To boil, plunge husked ears into a large amount of boiling water. Cover and boil until tender-crisp, 3 to 6 minutes. A little sugar can be added to the water if you think the corn is old, but don't add salt.

To grill or roast, soak unhusked ears in water for 10 minutes, then grill for 15 to 20 minutes, turning often, or bake in a 375°F (190°C) oven for 20 to 30 minutes, turning often.

To microwave one or two ears, trim the stalks if extra long but leave the husks intact. Place in the microwave oven, leaving space between the ears if cooking two. Cook on high for 4 minutes per ear (i.e. 8 minutes for two ears). Immediately remove with oven mitts and slice off the end of the ear about 1 inch (2 ½ cm) from where the stalk starts, then pull the other end firmly to remove all the husks and silk.

Cut the kernels from leftover cooked ears of corn and use in salads, muffins, pancakes, stews and soups.

TINY CORN PANCAKES WITH SMOKED SALMON AND CRÈME FRAÎCHE

These lovely little pancakes, which disappear in no time, are well worth the short last-minute preparation they require. Make them in batches and keep them warm, but not hot or the crème fraîche will melt.

2 ears of corn

1 cup half-and-half cream (10% MF) or table cream (18% MF)

2 eggs

2 tbsp butter, melted

¼ tsp each salt and freshly ground black pepper

½ cup cornmeal

½ cup all-purpose flour

Canola oil for frying

¾ cup crème fraîche or good-quality sour cream

1 tsp fresh lemon juice

4 oz (125 g) thinly sliced smoked salmon or trout, cut into thin strips

Fresh dill sprigs for garnish

Cut the kernels from the corn to make 1 cup. Coarsely chop the kernels by hand or process in a food processor until coarsely chopped. Set aside.

In a blender, combine the cream, eggs, butter, salt and pepper and blend until smooth. Add the cornmeal and flour. Blend until smooth. Stir in the corn kernels. (The recipe can be prepared to this point and refrigerated, covered, for up to 1 day.)

Brush a large nonstick griddle or skillet with oil and heat over medium-high heat. Pour about 1 tbsp batter for each pancake onto the griddle. Cook until browned on the bottom, about 2 minutes. Flip and cook until browned on the other side, about 1 minute. Keep the pancakes warm. Repeat with the remaining batter, brushing the griddle with more oil before cooking each batch.

In a small bowl, stir together the crème fraîche and lemon juice. Arrange the pancakes in a single layer on a large warm serving platter. Top each with a dollop of crème fraîche. Arrange a strip of salmon over the top of each and garnish with a small sprig of dill. Garnish the platter with larger sprigs of dill, if desired.

Makes about 3 dozen appetizers

CORN CHOWDER

4 oz (125 g) salt pork, finely diced

1 medium onion, finely chopped

4 cups peeled, diced potato (about 5 large)

2 cups chicken or vegetable broth

1 tsp finely chopped fresh thyme or ¼ tsp dried thyme leaves

Freshly ground black pepper to taste

2 ½ cups cooked corn kernels (5 to 6 medium ears)

1 ¾ cups milk, divided

1 egg yolk

2 tbsp butter

Salt to taste

1 tbsp finely chopped parsley

When corn is not in season, use thawed and frozen or canned kernels for this classic soup.

In a large, heavy saucepan over medium heat, sauté the diced salt pork until crisp. Remove with a slotted spoon and drain on paper towels. Set aside.

Pour off all but 1 tbsp of the fat from the saucepan. Return the saucepan to medium heat. Add the onion and cook for 5 minutes.

Stir in the potatoes, broth, thyme and pepper to taste. Bring to a boil over medium-high heat. Reduce the heat to medium-low and simmer, covered, until the vegetables are soft, about 20 minutes. Remove 1 cup of the vegetables and purée, either using an immersion blender in a bowl or in a countertop blender. (If you use a food processor, process only briefly or the soup will be gluey.) Return the purée to the saucepan and stir well.

Stir in the corn, 1 ½ cups milk and the salt pork. Cook, stirring gently, until piping hot.

In a small bowl, whisk together the egg yolk and remaining milk. Stir the egg mixture into the soup. Stir in the butter until it melts. Do not boil. Season to taste with salt and pepper, if necessary. Pour into warm soup bowls and sprinkle each portion with parsley.

Makes 4 to 6 servings

CORN FRITTERS

2 cups uncooked corn kernels (4 to 5 medium ears)

2 egg yolks, well beaten

2 tbsp all-purpose flour

½ tsp salt

¼ tsp baking powder

⅛ tsp freshly ground black pepper

2 egg whites, stiffly beaten

2 tbsp butter or enough oil for deep-frying

Recipes for these fritters are found in many early Canadian cookbooks. They were often called Corn Oysters because they puff up like an oyster when fried.

Serve as a first course with tomato sauce (page 146), as a side dish or with sausages for breakfast.

In a large bowl, combine the corn and egg yolks. Stir in the flour, salt, baking powder and pepper. Gently fold in the egg whites.

In a large skillet, melt the butter over medium-high heat. Drop the corn mixture by large tablespoonfuls into the skillet. Fry, turning once, until golden brown on both sides, 5 to 7 minutes. Or deep-fry in 375°F (190°C) oil, turning once, until puffed and golden brown, about 3 minutes.

Makes 6 servings; about 18 fritters

GRILLED CORN WITH GARLIC BUTTER

⅓ cup butter, at room temperature

1 tbsp fresh lemon juice

2 tbsp finely chopped parsley

2 cloves garlic, minced

Salt and freshly ground black pepper to taste

8 freshly grilled ears of corn (see page 56)

Sometimes I like to marinate husked ears of corn in a little canola oil and some spices for a couple of hours in the refrigerator, then grill them. I cook the corn directly on the grill with the barbecue's lid down but turn them often, brushing them with any leftover marinade, until they are golden brown, 10 to 12 minutes. But, if I want an easier way to prep corn, I simply whip up a flavoured butter, like one of the ones in this recipe.

In a medium bowl, cream the butter well, then very gradually beat in the lemon juice. Stir in the parsley, garlic and season to taste with salt and pepper.

Pack into a small bowl or spoon onto a sheet of plastic wrap and shape the butter into a log. Cover or wrap tightly and refrigerate overnight. If packed in a small bowl, accompany with a spreader, or slice the log into rounds to serve with the corn.

Makes enough butter for 8 ears of corn

TARRAGON BUTTER
Substitute 2 tbsp finely chopped fresh tarragon for the parsley and garlic.

CURRY BUTTER
Substitute 1 tsp garam masala for the parsley.

LIME-CORIANDER BUTTER
Substitute fresh lime juice and ½ tsp finely grated lime zest for the lemon juice, and 2 tbsp finely chopped fresh coriander (cilantro) or mint for the parsley.

CREAMED SKILLET CORN

3 tbsp butter

2 cups uncooked corn kernels (4 to 5 medium ears)

¼ cup finely chopped shallots or mild onion

⅛ tsp granulated sugar

2 tbsp water

½ cup whipping cream (35% MF)

⅛ tsp freshly grated nutmeg

Salt and freshly ground black pepper to taste

When corn is in season, this easy side dish has all the good flavour of corn on the cob but is elegant enough for company.

In a large skillet, melt the butter over medium-high heat. Add the corn, shallots and sugar and cook, stirring, for 3 minutes.

Add the water and cover the skillet. Reduce the heat to low and cook until the corn is tender, 5 to 7 minutes.

Gradually stir in the cream. Increase the heat to medium and cook, uncovered, until the cream is reduced and coats the kernels, 3 to 5 minutes. Stir in the nutmeg, and salt and pepper to taste.

Makes 4 servings

CORN AND POTATO PANCAKES

2 baking potatoes (about 1 lb/500 g total),
   peeled and cut into small pieces

1 cup frozen and thawed or canned and drained
   corn kernels

3 eggs, separated

¼ cup sour cream

2 tbsp all-purpose flour

½ tsp freshly ground black pepper

¼ tsp baking powder

¼ tsp salt

2 tbsp vegetable oil (approx.)

Pancakes of any sort are homey and delicious but in a story I wrote on pancakes for *Homemaker's Magazine*, these were a particular hit. As the editor wrote, "These light-textured pancakes are positively addictive, as we found out when we sampled them in our test kitchen. While they're perfect alongside bacon and sausages, they also make a great vegetable accompaniment to roast chicken." If you have any leftover mashed potatoes from the night before, substitute 2 cups for the baking potatoes.

In a saucepan of boiling, salted water, cook the potatoes over medium-high heat until very tender, about 10 minutes. Drain well and transfer to a medium bowl.

Mash the potatoes roughly. With an electric mixer, beat the potatoes until smooth. Stir in the corn, egg yolks, sour cream, flour, pepper, baking powder and salt. In a separate bowl and using clean beaters, beat the egg whites until stiff peaks form. Gently fold the egg whites into the potato mixture until well combined.

In a large skillet, heat the oil over medium-high heat. Drop heaping tablespoonfuls of the batter into the skillet, spacing them well apart. Cook until bubbles appear on the surface, 3 to 4 minutes. Turn the pancakes and cook until well browned on the other side, about 3 minutes. Keep the pancakes warm. Repeat with remaining batter, adding more oil to the skillet as necessary.

Makes sixteen 3-inch (8 cm) pancakes

BAKED CORN PUDDING

¼ cup butter

2 cups uncooked corn kernels (4 to 5 medium ears)

¼ cup chopped onion

1 tbsp each, chopped sweet green and red pepper

2 tbsp all-purpose flour

1 cup half-and-half cream (10% MF) or table cream (18% MF)

½ cup shredded old cheddar cheese

2 eggs, lightly beaten

1 tsp granulated sugar

½ tsp salt

⅛ tsp freshly ground white pepper

⅛ tsp cayenne

½ cup finely crushed cracker crumbs

1 tbsp melted butter

This vegetarian main dish is a classic but still tastes as good today. Serve it with a crisp salad of greens for a company lunch.

Butter a shallow, 4-cup (1 L) baking dish with some of the butter.

In a medium saucepan, melt the remaining butter over medium heat. Add the corn, onion and green and red pepper. Cook, stirring, for 2 to 3 minutes. Reduce the heat to low. Cook, covered, for 5 minutes.

Blend in the flour and cook, stirring, for 1 minute. Gradually stir in the cream. Increase the heat to medium and cook, stirring constantly, until thickened. Stir in the cheese and remove the saucepan from the heat.

In a small bowl, stir together the eggs, sugar, salt, pepper and cayenne. Stir a little of the hot corn mixture into the egg mixture. Pour all the egg mixture back into the corn mixture and combine well. Pour into the prepared dish.

Stir together the cracker crumbs and melted butter. Sprinkle evenly over the pudding. (The pudding can be prepared to this point and refrigerated for up to 3 hours. If refrigerated, let stand at room temperature for 30 minutes before baking.)

To bake, preheat the oven to 350°F (180°C). Set the baking dish in a larger shallow pan and pour enough hot water into the pan to come two-thirds of the way up the sides of the dish. Bake, uncovered, until set, about 50 minutes.

Makes 4 servings

CORN RELISH

18 medium ears of corn, husked

4 large onions, coarsely chopped

1 medium head green cabbage, cored and quartered

2 large sweet green peppers, seeded and coarsely chopped

1 large sweet red pepper, seeded and coarsely chopped

4 cups granulated sugar

2 ½ cups cider vinegar

⅓ cup coarse pickling salt

1 tbsp dry mustard

1 tbsp all-purpose flour

1 tsp ground turmeric

½ tsp ground coriander

½ tsp ground cumin

Sometimes, the best recipes are shared by friends. An old favourite, this recipe comes from a friend's mother in Owen Sound, Ontario. For more detailed instructions on how to make pickles, see Preserving on page 9.

In a large saucepan of boiling water, blanch the ears of corn for 4 minutes. Drain and rinse under cold running water to cool. Cut the kernels from the ears (an electric knife works well) and place in a large, heavy saucepan.

In a food processor, process the onions, cabbage and green and red peppers, in batches, until finely chopped, adding each batch to the corn.

Stir in the sugar, vinegar, salt, mustard, flour, turmeric, coriander and cumin. Bring to a boil over high heat. Reduce the heat to medium and simmer, uncovered, until everything is well blended and the vegetables are tender, about 30 minutes.

Pour the hot relish into hot preserving jars, leaving a ½-inch (1 cm) headspace. Seal with prepared discs and rings. Boil in a boiling-water canner for 10 minutes. Remove the jars and let cool on a rack.

Makes about 10 cups

CORN MUFFINS

1 cup yellow cornmeal

½ cup all-purpose flour

2 tbsp granulated sugar

1 ½ tsp baking powder

¼ tsp baking soda

¼ tsp salt

½ cup buttermilk (see recipe introduction)

2 eggs, lightly beaten

¼ cup melted butter

½ cup uncooked corn kernels (about 1 large ear)

Cornbread, in many guises, is an old tradition in Canada. Here, it takes the form of a corn muffin studded with fresh corn kernels. Perfect served warm from the oven with butter, they're also delicious toasted the next day. If you don't have any buttermilk, put 1 tablespoonful fresh lemon juice or white vinegar in a 1-cup measure and add enough regular milk to yield ½ cup.

Preheat the oven to 400°F (200°C). Well grease ten 2 ½ inch (6 cm) muffin pan cups.

In a large bowl, stir together cornmeal, flour, sugar, baking powder, baking soda and salt.

In a small bowl, stir together buttermilk, eggs and butter. Stir buttermilk mixture into the dry ingredients just enough to blend them. Do not overmix. Stir in the corn.

Spoon the batter into the prepared muffin pan. Bake in the centre of the oven until a skewer inserted into the centre of a muffin comes out clean, about 20 minutes.

Makes ten 2 ½-inch (6 cm) muffins

SEE ALSO:
Corn-Stuffed Peppers — 110

Harvest Frittata — 166

Tarragon-Dressed Corn and Bean Salad — 17

A
B
C
D
E
F
G
H
I
J
K
L
M
N
O
P
Q
R
S
T
U
V
W
X
Y
Z

CUCUMBERS

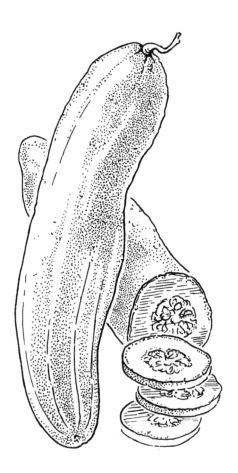

Originally from China, cucumbers have been refreshing palates for more than 3,000 years. They are now grown in all parts of the world and are used in many different cuisines.

Cucumbers are relatives of summer squash and watermelons. In Canada we can choose from the shorter, stubbier field cucumbers (grown outside) or the long, slender English cucumbers. The latter are grown in greenhouses and are virtually seedless. Cucumbers are ninety-five per cent water which gives them the crisp texture that's highly prized in pickled cucumbers.

Due to their water content, cucumbers contain very few calories but they are a source of vitamins A and C.

CHOOSING

Select firm, green, slender cucumbers. Cucumbers are sometimes coated with wax to protect them during transit; avoid these ones if you can.

For pickling, select very fresh, small, unwaxed cucumbers. Old cucumbers will be hollow once pickled.

Two medium field cucumbers or 1 large English cucumber yield 4 servings.

STORING

Store in perforated plastic bags in the crisper for up to 2 days.

Preparing Just wash and slice tender, young field cucumbers, or English cucumbers of any age. You can score the skins with the tines of a fork, if you like, for a decorative touch. Peel field cucumbers only if they have tough skins or have been waxed. The seeds of field cucumbers usually need to be removed, unless the cucumbers are very young. Simply cut the cucumber lengthwise and scoop out the seeds with a small spoon.

If you are using older cucumbers, which sometimes taste bitter, or wish to remove excess moisture, sprinkle sliced cucumbers lightly with salt and let them sit for 30 minutes. Pat dry before using.

COOKING

Although cucumbers are usually regarded as an ingredient for pickles or raw salads, they can also be surprisingly good when boiled, steamed or braised, or sautéed in butter and sprinkled with dill or other herbs.

THAI PICKLED CUCUMBER SLICES

1 large English cucumber or 2 medium field
  cucumbers

2 small shallots, thinly sliced

3 tbsp rice vinegar

3 tbsp fresh lime juice

1 tbsp fish sauce

1 tbsp granulated sugar

1 tsp seeded and minced hot red pepper

2 tbsp finely chopped fresh coriander (cilantro)
  or mint

This pretty salad is spicy and refreshing. To tame the heat a little, cut the top off the hot pepper, slice it in half down the centre and scrape out all the membranes and seeds before mincing it.

Score the cucumber by running the tines of a fork down its sides. Cut crosswise into very thin slices. Place the cucumber slices in a heatproof bowl, along with the shallots.

In a small saucepan, stir together the vinegar, lime juice, fish sauce, sugar and hot pepper. Bring to a boil, stirring constantly. Simmer for 2 minutes.

Pour the vinegar mixture over the cucumbers and toss to coat. Cover and refrigerate for at least 30 minutes and up to 6 hours, stirring occasionally.

With a slotted spoon, transfer to a small platter and sprinkle with coriander.

Makes 6 servings

DILLED CUCUMBER PICKLES

16 heads fresh dill

24 cups small cucumbers, washed and dried

8 cups water

8 cups white vinegar

1 cup granulated sugar

1 cup coarse pickling salt

2 ½ tbsp powdered alum

For best results, choose very fresh, firm cucumbers that are only 3 to 4 inches (8 to 10 cm) long for this classic pickle. Usually farmers' markets are the best places to buy fresh cucumbers and heads of dill. Alum is an edible chemical that helps keep pickles crisp; look for it in drug stores or the spice section of larger supermarkets. For more detailed instructions on how to preserve vegetables, see Preserving on page 9.

Place 1 head of dill in each of 8 hot, 4-cup (1 L) jars. Pack each jar with cucumbers and place another head of dill on top of each.

In a large stainless steel saucepan, stir together the water, vinegar, sugar, salt and alum. Stir over medium heat until the sugar and salt have dissolved. Bring just to a boil.

Pour the hot liquid into the jars, leaving a ½-inch (1 cm) headspace. Seal with the prepared discs and rings. Boil in a boiling-water canner for 10 minutes. Remove the jars and let cool on a rack.

Store in a dry, dark, cool place and allow 6 weeks for the flavours to develop before opening.

Makes eight 4-cup (1 L) jars

DILLED GREEN TOMATOES
Substitute tiny, firm green tomatoes for the cucumbers and proceed as for cucumber pickles.

DILLED PEPPERS
Substitute seeded, stemmed banana peppers for the cucumbers and proceed as for cucumber pickles.

CUCUMBER-HERB SALAD

1 small cucumber, thinly sliced

Salt to taste

¼ cup plain yogurt

1 tsp Dijon mustard

2 tbsp fresh lemon juice

2 tbsp finely chopped chives

1 tbsp finely chopped fresh dill or 1 tsp dried dill weed

Freshly ground white or black pepper to taste

Tomato wedges or sliced radishes for garnish

For best results, use an English cucumber for this refreshing salad.

Place cucumber slices in a large sieve and sprinkle them lightly with salt. Let sit for at least 30 minutes.

Meanwhile, whisk together the yogurt and mustard in a medium bowl. Slowly whisk in the lemon juice. Stir in the chives and dill and season to taste with pepper.

Just before serving, dry the cucumber slices well with paper towels. Add the cucumber to the sauce and stir gently. Transfer to a small glass serving bowl and garnish with tomato wedges or sliced radishes.

Makes 4 servings

CHILLED CUCUMBER SOUP WITH WALNUTS

3 medium field cucumbers (about 1 ½ lb/750 g total)

Salt to taste

2 cups buttermilk

1 small onion, chopped

¼ cup chopped parsley

2 cloves garlic, coarsely chopped

1 tbsp finely chopped chives

1 cup plain yogurt

1 cup low-fat sour cream

1 tbsp granulated sugar

1 tbsp fresh lemon juice

⅛ tsp cayenne

Freshly ground white pepper to taste

½ cup finely chopped toasted walnuts (see page 14)

Borage blossoms, chopped chives or parsley sprigs for garnish

This easy soup is a refreshing start to a summer meal. If you grow borage in your garden, the herb's purple-blue star-shaped flowers are the perfect garnish since they have a slight cucumber flavour.

Peel the cucumbers and slice in half lengthwise. With a teaspoon, scoop out the seeds and discard. Chop the cucumbers coarsely and place in a sieve. Sprinkle lightly with salt and let stand for 30 minutes.

Drain the cucumbers and pat dry. In a large bowl, combine the cucumbers, buttermilk, onion, parsley, garlic and chives. Purée the mixture in batches in a countertop blender (a blender, rather than a food processor, makes a smoother soup).

Pour the cucumber mixture back into the bowl. Stir in the yogurt, sour cream, sugar, lemon juice, cayenne and salt and pepper to taste. Stir in the walnuts. Cover and chill for at least 1 hour or for up to 2 days.

Serve in chilled bowls, garnished with borage blossoms.

Makes 6 servings

SEE ALSO:

Chilled Beet and Cucumber Soup   23

Gazpacho   148

EGGPLANT

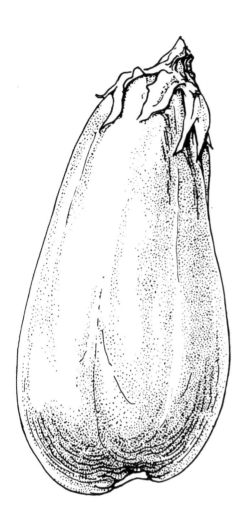

Eggplant belongs to the nightshade family and, like the tomato, is really a fruit. It was originally grown as an ornamental plant and considered poisonous. Now we know better.

The purple, pear-shaped eggplant is a native of Asia where it has been cultivated for centuries and was, in fact, first called "egg fruit." *Aubergine* is the French name for the vegetable but our name refers to the shape of some varieties.

Versatile and unique in flavour, eggplant is low in calories, but high in carbohydrates. Although it contains very little protein, eggplant is filling so is often used as a meat substitute in vegetarian dishes.

CHOOSING

Whether you are buying the larger, pear-shaped dark purple or variegated eggplant, the long slim Japanese variety or a little egg-shaped white eggplant, select fruits that are shiny and firm, tight in their skins and heavy for their size, with no soft or dark spots. Small ones will have fewer seeds and a firmer texture, but size does not affect their flavour.

One to 1 ½ pounds (500 to 750 g) of eggplant yield 4 servings.

STORING

Eggplant should be handled carefully to avoid bruising. Wrap in a plastic bag with some damp paper towel and store in the crisper.

PREPARING

Peeling or not depends entirely on the recipe, but trim off the stem end. If slicing larger eggplant, sprinkle the slices lightly with salt and let drain in a colander for 30 minutes (or place paper towels on top and weight with a board) to eliminate excessive moisture, any bitterness and to cut down on the amount of oil needed for frying. Rinse the eggplant and pat dry before using, and remember to add less salt than the recipe suggests.

Because eggplant contains a lot of water, it does not freeze well when raw, but casseroles containing partially cooked eggplant freeze well. Do not thaw before reheating.

COOKING

Sauté sliced or cubed eggplant in oil until browned, or prick the skin of a whole eggplant and bake in a 400°F (200°C) oven for about 30 minutes per pound (500 g). Steam a whole eggplant for about 25 minutes. Boil cubed eggplant for 1 to 2 minutes.

For one of the tastiest ways to make puréed eggplant, cut the eggplant in half, then broil or grill it, turning often, until the skin is charred and the flesh is tender. Scoop out the flesh, discarding the skin.

A B C D E F G H I J K L M N O P Q R S T U V W X Y Z

EGGPLANT CAPONATA

1 cup diced, peeled eggplant

½ tsp salt

2 tbsp olive oil (approx.), divided

1 onion, chopped

2 cloves garlic, minced

1 cup drained, canned whole tomatoes, chopped

⅓ cup chopped celery

½ cup seeded and chopped sweet red pepper

¼ cup chopped pitted black olives

2 tbsp well-drained capers

2 tbsp red wine vinegar

1 tbsp finely chopped parsley

1 tsp granulated sugar

¼ tsp each, dried basil and oregano leaves

Freshly ground black pepper to taste

Serve this soft vegetable mixture warm as a vegetable side dish or at room temperature as an appetizer in little toast cups (see sidebar) or purchased crisp mini tart shells.

Place the eggplant in a colander and sprinkle with the salt. Let drain for 30 minutes.

In a large skillet, heat half of the oil over medium-high heat. Add the onion and garlic and sauté for 5 minutes. Add the tomatoes and celery and cook, stirring occasionally, for 5 minutes. Remove the skillet from the heat and set aside.

Rinse the eggplant and pat dry. In a separate skillet, heat the remaining oil over medium-high heat. Add the eggplant and cook, stirring often, until golden on all sides, about 2 minutes. Remove the eggplant and drain on paper towels.

In the skillet you used to fry the eggplant, fry the red pepper over medium-high heat until wilted, adding a teaspoonful more oil, if needed.

Reduce the heat to low. Return the eggplant to the skillet, along with the tomato mixture, olives, capers, vinegar, parsley, sugar, basil, oregano and pepper to taste. Cook for 15 minutes, stirring occasionally, for flavours to blend. (The caponata can be cooled, covered and refrigerated for up to 3 days.)

Makes enough to fill 32 toast cups or 4 servings as a side dish

HOMEMADE TOAST CUPS

Cut the crusts from 8 thin slices of white bread. With a rolling pin, roll each slice of bread flat. Cut each slice into quarters. Press the pieces into greased miniature muffin cups. (Alternatively, roll out the bread, cut into rounds with a cookie cutter and fit into greased muffin or tart cups.) Brush lightly with olive oil and bake in a 350°F (180°C) oven until crisp and golden, 5 to 7 minutes. Let cool. (The cups can be stored in an airtight container at room temperature for several days.) Makes 32 cups.

GRILLED EGGPLANT DIP WITH GRILLED PITA TOASTS

6 small Asian or baby Italian eggplants (2 lb/1 kg total)

6 cloves garlic, thinly sliced

2 plum tomatoes

⅓ cups finely chopped fresh coriander (cilantro) or parsley

2 tbsp olive oil

2 tbsp fresh lemon juice

1 tsp ground cumin

Salt to taste

⅓ cup chopped toasted walnuts (see page 14); optional

Grilled Pita Toasts (recipe below)

I created a whole article for *Homemaker's Magazine* of snacks and appetizers cooked on the grill. This soft, smoky dip, perfect with garlicky crisp pita toasts (below), is one of my favourites.

Preheat the barbecue to medium-high. Cut deep slits in the eggplants and insert a slice of garlic in each slit. Place eggplants on greased grill and cook, turning occasionally, until charred and beginning to collapse, 20 to 30 minutes.

Grill the tomatoes, turning occasionally, until beginning to char, about 5 minutes.

Strip off and discard the eggplant skins. Finely chop the eggplant, and the garlic that was inserted into the slits. Place them in a bowl.

Peel, seed and chop the tomatoes. Add the tomatoes to the eggplant, along with the coriander, oil, lemon juice, cumin and salt to taste. (The dip can be prepared to this point, covered and refrigerated for up to 8 hours.)

Just before serving, stir in the walnuts (if using). Serve with grilled pita toasts.

Makes about 8 servings

GRILLED PITA TOASTS

4 pita breads (7 inches/18 cm)

¼ cup olive oil

2 cloves garlic, minced

1 tsp paprika

You can make pita toasts in the oven as well. Follow the recipe below but, before baking, cut each round into 8 wedges with scissors. Place the wedges in a single layer on baking sheets, then bake them in a 350°F (180°C) oven until golden brown and crisp, 7 to 9 minutes.

Preheat the barbecue to medium. Split each pita horizontally into 2 rounds. In a small saucepan on the edge of the grill, heat the oil with the garlic and paprika. Brush the oil lightly over both sides of each pita round.

Grill over medium-high heat until grill-marked and crisp, about 2 minutes, turning once. Cut or break each round into 4 wedges.

Makes 32 toasts

ROASTED EGGPLANT SOUP WITH MASCARPONE SWIRL

4 baby eggplants or 1 large eggplant

1 large baking potato

1 onion, chopped

¼ cup olive oil

4 cloves garlic, finely chopped

2 tsp finely chopped fresh oregano

Salt and freshly ground black pepper to taste

5 cups chicken broth, divided

¼ tsp saffron threads

MASCARPONE SWIRL

1 cup mascarpone cheese

2 tbsp finely chopped parsley

1 tbsp finely chopped fresh oregano

1 small clove garlic, minced

Salt and freshly ground black pepper to taste

For best texture, use a blender, not a food processor, to purée this silken soup.

Preheat the oven to 500°F (260°C). Cut unpeeled eggplants and potato into 1-inch (2 ½ cm) cubes.

In a large, greased, shallow roasting pan, toss the eggplant, potato, onion, olive oil, garlic and oregano. Spread out in a single layer and sprinkle with salt and pepper. Roast, uncovered and stirring occasionally, until soft, 20 to 30 minutes.

Purée the vegetables and a little of the broth, in batches, in a countertop blender (a blender, rather than a food processor, makes a smoother soup). Transfer to a medium saucepan, stir in the remaining broth and saffron, and bring to a simmer. Season to taste.

For the mascarpone swirl, blend together the mascarpone, parsley, oregano, garlic and salt and pepper to taste in a small bowl. Ladle the soup into warm soup bowls and swirl in some mascarpone mixture.

Makes 6 servings

RATATOUILLE SOUP

1 large eggplant (about 1 lb/500 g), cut in ½-inch (1 cm) pieces

2 zucchini (about 1 lb/500 g total), cut in ½-inch (1 cm) pieces

3 tbsp olive oil, divided

2 sweet red peppers, seeded and cut in ½-inch (1 cm) pieces

3 tomatoes, peeled and chopped

1 onion, chopped

3 cloves garlic, thinly sliced

¾ tsp herbes de Provence or dried thyme leaves

Salt and freshly ground black pepper to taste

6 cups vegetable or chicken broth

This delightful summer soup comes from Linda Stephen's beautiful cookbook *The Convection Oven Bible*. Many ovens today have a convection feature, but if yours does not, increase the temperature of your oven to 425°F (220°C); the cooking time will remain more or less the same. You can peel the eggplant if you wish, but it is not necessary. If you're not planning to purée the soup, use one green zucchini and one yellow summer squash for extra colour.

Garnish each serving with a spoonful of basil pesto (page 173) or some shredded fresh basil and accompany with Goat Cheese Toasts (see sidebar).

Preheat a convection oven set to roast to 400°F (200°C). Line two rimmed baking sheets with parchment paper (some vegetables might stick). On one sheet combine the eggplant, zucchini and 1 ½ tbsp oil. On the second sheet combine the red peppers, tomatoes, onion, garlic, herbs, remaining oil and salt and pepper to taste.

Convection roast, uncovered, stirring once or twice, until the vegetables are just tender, about 30 minutes.

Meanwhile, in a large saucepan, bring the broth to a boil. Add the roasted vegetables and juices. Bring back to a boil, reduce heat and simmer, uncovered, for 6 minutes.

If you prefer a creamy soup, use an immersion blender in the saucepan to blend the soup until smooth. Or purée the soup in batches in a countertop blender (a blender, rather than a food processor, makes a smoother soup). If necessary, pour the soup back into the rinsed-out saucepan. Reheat until piping hot.

GOAT CHEESE TOASTS

Cut twelve ½-inch (1 cm) thick slices from a narrow baguette. Spread with 4 oz (125 g) softened goat cheese. Place bread, cheese side up, on a parchment-paper-lined baking sheet. Convection roast in a 400° (200°C) oven (425°F/220°C in a regular oven) until hot, 2 to 3 minutes. Makes 12 toasts.

CHEESE-TOPPED EGGPLANT

1 lb (500 g) eggplant (1 medium or 3 small)
1 tsp salt
½ cup mayonnaise
¼ cup chopped parsley
1 tsp finely chopped fresh oregano or ¼ tsp dried oregano leaves
¼ cup dry bread crumbs
2 ½ tbsp freshly grated Parmesan cheese

A simple coating of crumbs and cheese provides a crunchy texture that contrasts with the soft cooked eggplant.

Peel the eggplant and cut crosswise in ½-inch (1 cm) slices. Place in a colander, sprinkle lightly with the salt and let stand for 30 minutes. Rinse the eggplant and pat dry.

Preheat the oven to 375°F (190°C). In a small bowl, stir together the mayonnaise, parsley and oregano. In a shallow bowl, stir together the bread crumbs and Parmesan cheese.

Spread some of the mayonnaise mixture on both sides of the eggplant slices. Dip slices in the crumb mixture to coat completely. Place the eggplant slices in a single layer on a greased baking sheet. Bake until tender, about 15 minutes.

Turn broiler to high. Broil eggplant about 3 ½ inches (9 cm) from the heat until golden brown, about 5 minutes.

Makes 4 servings

CHEESE-TOPPED TOMATOES

Substitute 4 to 5 medium tomatoes for the eggplant. Cut the tomatoes into ¾-inch (2 cm) slices. Do not sprinkle with salt. Spread the mayonnaise mixture on one side only of each tomato slice, then sprinkle with a thick coating of the crumb mixture. Bake, coated side up, in a 375°F (190°C) oven for 5 minutes, then broil for 5 minutes. Serve with grilled steak.

CURRIED EGGPLANT

3 small eggplants
1 tsp salt
¼ cup olive or canola oil
¼ cup seeded and finely chopped hot red
   pepper (or to taste)
1 cup finely chopped onion
1 large clove garlic, minced
½ tsp ground turmeric
¼ tsp ground cumin
¼ tsp ground coriander

This easy curried eggplant makes a quick, flavourful side dish for grilled lamb chops.

Trim eggplant and cut into ½-inch (1 cm) pieces (you should have about 3 cups). Place eggplant in a colander and add the salt. Let drain for 30 minutes. Rinse the eggplant and pat dry.

In a large skillet, heat the oil over medium-high heat. Add the eggplant and hot pepper. Sauté for 1 minute.

Reduce heat to medium-low and cook, covered, until the vegetables are barely tender, about 4 minutes. With a slotted spoon, remove vegetable mixture to a bowl and keep warm.

Increase the heat to medium. Add the onion, garlic, turmeric, cumin and coriander to the skillet. Cook, stirring often, until the onion is just golden, but not limp, 3 to 5 minutes. Return the eggplant and peppers to the skillet and heat through, stirring often. Serve hot or at room temperature.

Makes about 4 servings

SEE ALSO:

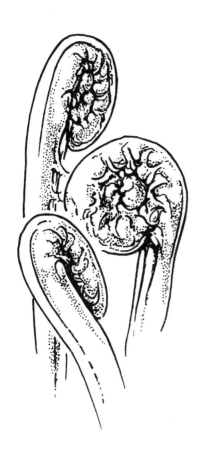

FIDDLEHEADS

When Queen Elizabeth II came to Canada in 1982 to give royal assent to the *Constitution Act*, she was served cream of fiddlehead soup at an official dinner.

Fiddleheads are indeed Canadian. They are actually unopened ferns rather than vegetables, but these and other greens from the woods supplied a much-needed supplement to the diet of early settlers. Native people had relied upon fiddleheads' nutrients (they are high in iron, potassium and vitamin C, and retain most of their nutrients even after cooking) and pointed them out to settlers who were grateful for this source of fresh food. In the 1830s, the author Catharine Parr Traill recorded eight varieties of ferns growing in the Peterborough, Ontario, area where she lived.

The edible frond of the ostrich fern is the most common and the only one you should harvest as food. It is still found in quantity along rivers and streams from New Brunswick to the Rockies.

You can buy frozen fiddleheads packaged in New Brunswick but fiddleheads are a treat to pick and enjoy while they are very fresh. Their unique flavour resembles a combination of asparagus and broccoli. I like to serve them quite simply during their brief season, usually in May, then freeze enough for Christmas dinner.

CHOOSING

Pick fiddleheads when they're very young with tightly curled heads and tender stalks. When harvesting, always leave one or two fronds on each plant.

In the supermarket or farmers' market, choose fresh-looking, bright green fiddleheads with tightly curled heads.

About 8 ounces (250 g) of fiddleheads yield 4 servings.

STORING

Store fiddleheads in a perforated plastic bag in the crisper and use within 1 or 2 days.

To freeze fiddleheads, blanch for about 3 minutes.

PREPARING

Pull out each stalk and head carefully, shake to remove the brown sheath and scales, then wash in several changes of lukewarm water. Soak in cold, salted water for 30 minutes to dislodge any insects.

COOKING

Cook, uncovered, in a large amount of boiling salted water for 5 to 7 minutes, or until the stalks are tender but still slightly crisp, or steam for 8 minutes. Serve hot, seasoned with butter, salt, pepper and fresh lemon juice. Low-fat hollandaise sauce (page 173) is also a good accompaniment. Or refresh under cold running water immediately after cooking, dry well and toss with lemon vinaigrette (page 170).

CREAM OF FIDDLEHEAD SOUP

2 tbsp butter

1 small onion, finely chopped or ¼ cup finely chopped shallots

10 oz (300 g) fresh or frozen fiddleheads

½ tsp finely chopped fresh thyme or ⅛ tsp dried thyme leaves

Salt and freshly ground black pepper to taste

3 cups chicken broth

1 medium potato, peeled and finely chopped

1 cup milk

½ cup cream (see recipe introduction)

1 tbsp fresh lemon juice

Croutons to serve

If you omit the lemon juice, this fresh-tasting soup can be prepared a day ahead and refrigerated. Add the lemon juice just before serving. Use whatever type of cream you have on hand.

In a large saucepan, melt the butter over low heat. Add the onion and cook, covered and stirring occasionally, for 10 minutes. Add the fiddleheads, thyme and salt and pepper to taste. Increase the heat to medium and bring to a simmer. Cover and simmer for 5 minutes, occasionally breaking up frozen fiddleheads with a wooden spoon.

Stir in the chicken broth and potato. Increase the heat to medium-high and bring to a boil. Reduce the heat to low and simmer, covered, until the potato is cooked, about 15 minutes. Let cool slightly.

Use an immersion blender in the saucepan to blend the soup until smooth. Or purée the soup in batches in a countertop blender (a blender, rather than a food processor, makes a smoother soup). If necessary, pour the soup back into the rinsed-out saucepan.

Stir in the milk and cream. Reheat but do not boil. Season to taste with salt and pepper. Add the lemon juice. Serve garnished with croutons.

Makes 4 servings

FIDDLEHEADS SAUTÉED WITH MORELS

10 oz (300 g) fresh fiddleheads, cleaned, or one 10 ½ oz (300 g) pkg frozen fiddleheads

¼ cup butter

1 lb (500 g) morels

2 tbsp fresh lemon juice

1 tsp finely chopped fresh tarragon or ¼ tsp dried tarragon leaves

Salt and freshly ground black pepper to taste

If you are not lucky enough to find the honeycombed wild mushrooms called morels, substitute cremini or oyster mushrooms. Even white button mushrooms will be delicious in this easy company side dish.

In a saucepan of boiling, salted water, blanch fiddleheads for 1 minute. If using frozen, thaw just enough to separate the fiddleheads.

In a large, heavy skillet, melt the butter over medium heat. Add the fiddleheads and morels and cook, stirring often, until tender, about 8 minutes.

Stir in the lemon juice, tarragon and salt and pepper to taste.

Makes 6 servings

STEAMED FIDDLEHEADS WITH LEMON BEURRE BLANC

10 oz (300 g) fresh fiddleheads or one 10 ½-oz (300 g) pkg frozen fiddleheads

1 small shallot, finely chopped

2 tbsp dry white wine

¼ cup cold unsalted butter, cut into small pieces

Finely grated zest of 1 lemon

Salt and freshly ground black pepper to taste

Every spring, my husband Kent goes out to his secret fiddlehead patch and brings home enough of the fronds that we can enjoy them while they are fresh and put some in our freezer for treats during the year. (I always save a bag of fiddleheads to serve at Christmas dinner.) This simple classic sauce uses flavours that go best with fresh fiddleheads— lemon, salt and pepper—to add the finishing touch.

Clean the fiddleheads and wash in several changes of water. Trim off any dark ends (caused by natural oxidization).

In a basket steamer or bamboo tray set over water in a wok, steam fresh or frozen (not thawed) fiddleheads until tender, 6 to 8 minutes. Drain well and transfer to a warm serving dish.

Meanwhile, in a small saucepan over medium heat, cook the shallot in the wine until the shallot is soft and the wine has almost evaporated, about 3 minutes.

Remove the saucepan from the heat and whisk in the butter, one piece at a time, until it's well blended. Whisk in the lemon zest and season to taste with salt and pepper. Spoon the sauce over the fiddleheads and serve at once.

Makes 4 servings

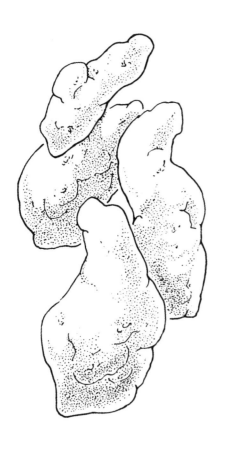

JERUSALEM ARTICHOKES

These knobby, brown tubers resembling fresh ginger are, oddly enough, neither from Jerusalem nor are they artichokes. One of our native vegetables, Jerusalem artichokes—also called sunchokes—were highly prized by the Huron who introduced them to French explorers in the seventeenth century. Samuel de Champlain learned of them from the Algonquin and described them as "roots with the taste of artichokes." They were subsequently cultivated in France, where they were called "Canadian potatoes."

Considered a relative of the sunflower—called *girasole* in France—they were also named "girasole artichokes." When introduced into England, girasole became Anglicized to "Jerusalem."

Jerusalem artichokes are tall, skinny plants with tiny, yellow flowers resembling daisies. They were a common sight in Canadian vegetable gardens and even at the back of perennial flower beds during the nineteenth century, but are now more popular throughout Europe than here.

Jerusalem artichokes are low in calories but rich in vitamins and minerals, particularly thiamin and potassium. They store carbohydrates in the form of inulin, rather than starch, and sugar as levulose, as do many fruits.

CHOOSING

Select roots or tubers that are firm and free from blemishes or mould. Jerusalem artichokes take on a sweet, nutty taste and crisp texture if left in the ground after a frost and can be harvested until the ground freezes.

One to 1 ½ pounds (500 g to 750 g) of Jerusalem artichokes yield 4 servings.

STORING

Because of their delicate skin, refrigeration is necessary to retard shrivelling. Store in a plastic bag in the crisper. Or bury Jerusalem artichokes in sand and keep near freezing point and they will remain crisp without sprouting.

PREPARING

Scrub with a brush and wash well. If you cook the tubers unpeeled, the flesh will remain white, and the skins rub or scrape off easily after cooking.

If you'd rather peel them before cooking, drop the peeled Jerusalem artichokes immediately in a container of cold water with a small amount of lemon juice added (acidulated water) to prevent them from turning dark.

COOKING

Because of their crisp texture, Jerusalem artichokes are good raw in salads or stir-fried in Chinese dishes as a substitute for water chestnuts or bamboo shoots. You can treat Jerusalem artichokes as you would potatoes: they can be baked, boiled and mashed with butter, sautéed or scalloped. They can also be ground and added to a meat loaf mixture.

To boil, cook Jerusalem artichokes, covered, in a small amount of salted water (or water mixed with a little milk), for 12 to 15 minutes, depending on size. Or steam them for about 12 to 20 minutes. Overcooking will make them mushy.

JERUSALEM ARTICHOKE AND OYSTER SOUP

2 tbsp fresh lemon juice
1 lb (500 g) Jerusalem artichokes
4 tbsp cold butter, divided
1 medium onion, chopped
2 stalks celery, diced
2 tbsp finely chopped shallots
2 tbsp all-purpose flour
4 cups chicken broth
1 cup shucked fresh oysters and their liquid
1 cup half-and-half cream (10% MF) or table cream (18% MF)
Salt and freshly ground white pepper to taste
Paprika for garnish

Rachel van Nostrand, who grew Jerusalem artichokes on her farm on Ontario's Niagara Peninsula, gave me this intriguing idea for a soup. For a very velvety finish, pass the purée through a fine-mesh sieve before adding the oysters and cream.

Add the lemon juice to a bowl of cold water. Wash, peel and coarsely dice the artichokes, dropping them in the bowl of water as you work.

In a large, heavy saucepan, melt 2 tbsp of the butter over low heat. Add the onion, celery and shallots and cook, stirring often, for 10 minutes. Increase the heat to medium. Add the flour and cook, stirring, for 3 minutes. Remove the saucepan from the heat. Gradually stir in the broth.

Drain the artichokes and add them to the saucepan. Bring to a boil, stirring often. Reduce the heat and simmer, covered, until the vegetables are tender, 15 to 20 minutes. Let cool slightly.

Use an immersion blender in the saucepan to blend the soup until smooth. Or purée the soup in batches in a countertop blender (a blender, rather than a food processor, makes a smoother soup). If necessary, pour the soup back into the rinsed-out saucepan.

Add the oysters and cream. Heat gently until the oysters curl around the edges, 3 to 5 minutes. Do not boil. Season to taste with salt and pepper.

Cut the remaining cold butter into small pieces. Serve the soup in hot bowls. Dot with pieces of butter and sprinkle with paprika.

Makes 6 to 8 servings

JERUSALEM ARTICHOKE AND ORANGE SALAD

1 lb (500 g) Jerusalem artichokes
1 tbsp fresh lemon juice
2 tbsp tarragon vinegar
¼ cup finely chopped green onions
¼ tsp Dijon mustard
Salt and freshly ground black pepper to taste
6 tbsp olive oil
Dark green lettuce leaves or watercress
1 large orange, peeled and thinly sliced

Serving Jerusalem artichokes raw, as in this pretty salad, brings out their interesting, nutty flavour.

Do not peel the artichokes, but scrub well and slice thinly into a small bowl. Sprinkle the artichokes with lemon juice as you work.

In a small pitcher, stir together the vinegar, green onions, mustard and salt and pepper to taste. Slowly whisk in the oil.

Add the dressing to the artichokes and refrigerate, covered, for at least 1 hour.

To serve, line a shallow serving dish or plate with lettuce leaves and overlap orange slices near the edge. Arrange the artichokes and their dressing in the centre.

Makes 6 to 8 servings

CRISP ARTICHOKE PANCAKES

Ice water
1 tbsp fresh lemon juice
8 oz (250 g) Jerusalem artichokes
3 medium potatoes
2 eggs
1 medium carrot, grated
¼ cup grated onion
1 tbsp finely chopped parsley
¼ cup all-purpose flour
1 tsp salt
½ tsp baking powder
⅛ tsp freshly grated nutmeg
Freshly ground black pepper to taste
¼ cup canola oil

Erna Heinitz, a vendor who used to sell Jerusalem artichokes at the Cambridge, Ontario, farmers' market, made these lacy pancakes for her family. They are delicious with sour cream or warm applesauce and served alongside sausages or smoked pork chops.

Pour ice water into a medium bowl and stir in the lemon juice. Using a food processor fitted with a steel blade, or a hand grater, finely grate the artichokes and potatoes and immediately place in the bowl of ice water.

In a large bowl, beat the eggs well and stir in the carrot, onion and parsley. In a small bowl, stir together the flour, salt, baking powder, nutmeg and pepper. Gradually add the flour mixture to the egg mixture, stirring well.

Drain the artichokes and potatoes in a sieve. Dry well by squeezing in a tea towel. Add to the egg mixture, stirring well.

Preheat the oven to 250°F (120°C). In a large, heavy skillet, heat half the oil over medium heat. For each pancake, spoon about 2 tbsp of the batter into the skillet, leaving at least 1 inch (2 ½ cm) between pancakes. Flatten each pancake with a spatula and cook until golden brown and crisp, 2 to 3 minutes on each side. As each batch is cooked, place on a hot platter and keep warm in the oven. Repeat with the remaining batter, adding more oil to the skillet as necessary.

Makes about 12 pancakes

CRISP POTATO PANCAKES

Substitute 3 medium potatoes for the artichokes and carrot. (You will use 6 medium potatoes in all.)

KOHLRABI

This unusual vegetable looks like a turnip but is, in fact, a member of the cabbage family with a swollen, turnip-shaped stem. A biennial herb, kohlrabi is becoming quite popular in markets here. Its taste is like a sweet turnip or mild radish.

Although its leaves and their stems can be eaten, the plant is grown primarily for its bulbous stem. Kohlrabi is rich in calcium and vitamin C.

CHOOSING

Kohlrabi is at its best when small (less than 2 inches/5 cm across), firm, with tender skins. Bigger bulbs can be woody or bitter.

One pound (500 g) of kohlrabi yields 3 to 4 servings.

STORING

Store in a perforated plastic bag in the crisper for up to 3 days. For longer storage, try layering the kohlrabi in sand in a root cellar.

Kohlrabi does not freeze well.

PREPARING

Peel kohlrabi if using raw but if cooking them, cook them whole and peel afterward.

COOKING

Small, young kohlrabi is best raw as part of a crudité tray or in a salad like Kohlrabi Rémoulade (page 78).

Cut into strips, kohlrabi is good stir-fried. Boil pieces or slices of kohlrabi, uncovered, in salted water for about 5 minutes. Whole bulbs might take 20 to 30 minutes. Steaming takes slightly longer than boiling.

One of the most popular ways of preparing kohlrabi is to peel and slice it, then boil briefly and combine with a rich cream sauce (page 172) flavoured with freshly grated nutmeg.

A
B
C
D
E
F
G
H
I
J
K
L
M
N
O
P
Q
R
S
T
U
V
W
X
Y
Z

KOHLRABI RÉMOULADE

SALAD

4 small kohlrabi (2 inches/5 cm)

6 tbsp canola or olive oil

2 tbsp white wine vinegar or fresh lemon juice

1 tsp granulated sugar

Salt and freshly ground black pepper to taste

DRESSING

1 raw egg*

½ tsp Dijon mustard

⅓ cup canola or olive oil

1 tbsp finely chopped chives

1 tsp finely chopped fresh dill or ¼ tsp dried dill
  weed

Lettuce and tomato wedges for garnish

This flavourful salad with its mayonnaise-type dressing, showcases kohlrabi at its best.

For the salad, peel the kohlrabi and slice into small julienne strips. In a medium glass bowl, whisk together the oil, vinegar, sugar and salt and pepper to taste. Add the kohlrabi and mix well. Cover and marinate at room temperature for 2 hours, stirring occasionally.

For the dressing, place the egg and mustard in a blender or food processor. Blend for 5 seconds. With the motor running, pour in the oil in a slow, steady stream and blend until thick. Blend in the chives and dill. Pour into a small pitcher, cover and refrigerate.

Just before serving, drain the kohlrabi, reserving the liquid to use as a dressing for another salad. Stir the chilled dressing into the kohlrabi and mix well but gently. Season to taste with salt and pepper if necessary.

Line a serving plate with lettuce leaves and pile the kohlrabi mixture on top. Garnish with tomato wedges.

Makes 4 to 6 servings

* When using raw eggs in a recipe, choose Canada Grade-A eggs within their best-before date; these eggs have been properly handled and graded by a registered farmer.

TURNIP OR RUTABAGA RÉMOULADE

Substitute 4 small turnips or 1 small rutabaga for the kohlrabi.

CELERIAC RÉMOULADE

Substitute 2 small celeriac for the kohlrabi.

PARSNIP RÉMOULADE

Substitute 4 small parsnips for the kohlrabi.

LEEKS

Cultivated in Egypt at the time of the Pharaohs, leeks have had intermittent success in various parts of the world since then. They have attained their highest status in Wales, where they are a national symbol.

The Roman emperor Nero used raw leeks to clear his voice for singing, and in the Middle Ages the juice and seeds of leeks were used as a toothpaste. And many a rural Canadian schoolboy saw great humour in entering the one-room school house on a fine spring morning having just eaten a raw wild leek. His pungent breath usually earned him a holiday.

If these members of the onion family are cooked, however, there is nothing sweeter nor more delicate in flavour.

Low in calories, leeks are high in vitamins A and E with a good amount of vitamin C.

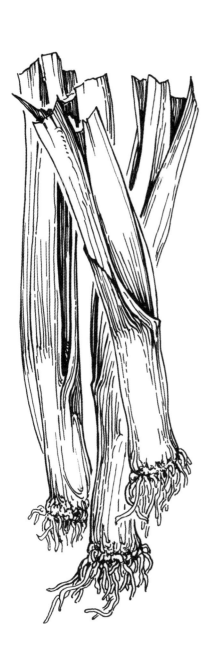

CHOOSING

If you grow your own, harvest leeks in the late fall when they are about 1 ½ inches (4 cm) in diameter. When you buy them, avoid large, woody leeks, which are often overpriced, and look for straight, firm, clean stalks with moist upper green leaves. Dried leaves indicate the leeks are old, and bulging bases might indicate they are woody.

Two pounds (1 kg) of leeks yield 4 servings.

STORING

Store leeks, unwashed and with their roots loosely wrapped, in the refrigerator for up to 2 weeks.

Leeks don't freeze well, but can be chopped and frozen for use in soup recipes.

PREPARING

Leeks are usually banked with soil during the growing period so there may be a large amount of sand and grit in among the leaves. To clean a leek, remove and discard any coarse outer leaves and trim away the roots and all but the white and light green parts. Split the leek from the top to about ½ inch (1 cm) from the bottom. Fan out the leaves and run cold water over them to wash away the sand and grit.

COOKING

Braising is an excellent way to cook leeks (see Leeks Braised with Tomatoes and Wine, page 80). You can also boil leeks in a small amount of salted water in a covered saucepan for about 10 minutes. Drain well before serving. Or steam them for a slightly longer time. Cooked leeks are good with a cream sauce (page 172) or cheese sauce (page 172).

A B C D E F G H I J K L M N O P Q R S T U V W X Y Z

CLASSIC VICHYSSOISE

2 tbsp unsalted butter

3 tbsp olive oil, divided

2 large leeks (white parts only), thinly sliced

4 cups vegetable or chicken broth

3 russet potatoes, peeled and cubed

Salt to taste

1 cup whipping cream (35% MF)

Freshly ground white pepper to taste

Finely chopped chives

There's nothing more refreshing on a hot summer day than this velvety soup.

In a large saucepan over medium heat, melt the butter with 2 tbsp of the oil. Add the leeks and cook, stirring often, until very soft but not coloured, about 10 minutes. Add the broth, potatoes and salt to taste. Bring to a boil. Reduce the heat to medium-low and simmer, covered, until the potatoes are tender, about 20 minutes. Let cool slightly.

Use an immersion blender in the saucepan to blend the soup until smooth. Or purée the soup in batches in a countertop blender (do not overblend or use a food processor as this will make the soup gluey). Pass the soup through a fine-mesh sieve. Let cool, then cover and refrigerate until very cold, preferably overnight.

Just before serving, whisk in the cream. Season to taste with pepper and more salt, if necessary.

Serve in large cool bowls. Drizzle each portion with some of the remaining olive oil and sprinkle with chives.

Makes 6 servings

LEEKS BRAISED WITH TOMATOES AND WINE

4 large leeks (1 ¾ lb/875 g total)

¼ cup olive oil

Salt and freshly ground black pepper to taste

4 ripe medium tomatoes, peeled, stem ends removed and quartered

½ cup dry white wine

2 large cloves garlic, minced

2 tbsp fresh lemon juice

1 tbsp finely chopped parsley

1 ½ tsp finely chopped fresh oregano or ½ tsp dried oregano leaves

½ tsp granulated sugar

1 bay leaf

This interesting and tasty side dish would be perfect as part of a buffet since it can be made ahead and is good served at room temperature.

Remove any coarse outer leaves from the leeks. Trim off the root ends and all the green tops. Cut each leek in quarters lengthwise. Wash well by running water down into each quarter. Dry and cut into 2-inch (5 cm) lengths.

In a large skillet, heat the oil over medium heat. Add the leeks and sauté until soft but not brown, about 3 minutes. Sprinkle with salt and pepper to taste.

Add the tomatoes, wine, garlic, lemon juice, parsley, oregano, sugar and bay leaf. Cover tightly and simmer until the leeks are barely tender, 6 to 8 minutes.

Increase heat to high and boil, uncovered, until the liquid has reduced, about 1 minute. Discard the bay leaf. Serve hot, cold, or at room temperature.

Makes 4 to 6 servings

LEEKS VINAIGRETTE

8 small or 4 large leeks (1 ¾ lb/875 g total)

3 cups chicken broth

1 bay leaf

Salt and freshly ground black pepper to taste

VINAIGRETTE

2 tbsp white wine vinegar

¼ tsp Dijon mustard

6 tbsp olive oil

1 tbsp well-drained capers

1 tbsp chopped chives or green onion tops

2 or 3 small radishes, washed but not trimmed

There is lots of flavour in this hearty salad. If you can find small leeks, leave them whole after you trim and clean them, but slice larger leeks for easier handling.

Trim the root ends and dark green tops from the leeks and clean them well. Cut into 2 inch lengths, if desired, and place in a wide saucepan. Add the broth and bay leaf and bring to a boil over high heat.

Reduce the heat to medium-low and simmer, covered, until tender, 8 to 10 minutes. Drain well and place on a shallow dish. Discard the bay leaf and sprinkle the leeks with salt and pepper.

For the vinaigrette, whisk together the vinegar and mustard in a small bowl. Slowly whisk in the oil until well blended. Pour the dressing over the warm leeks. (The leeks can be prepared to this point then covered and refrigerated for up to 3 days. Let stand at room temperature for 30 minutes and drain off some of the liquid if necessary before serving.)

Sprinkle with capers and chives. Garnish with radishes and serve warm or at room temperature.

Makes 4 to 6 servings

LEEKS IN MUSTARD CREAM

6 medium or 8 small leeks

½ cup whipping cream (35% MF)

¼ cup softened unsalted butter, cut into pieces

2 tsp Dijon mustard

¼ tsp ground cumin

Salt and freshly ground black pepper to taste

Finely chopped parsley for garnish

It's hard to resist this decadent vegetable dish that's a lovely accompaniment to chicken or salmon.

Trim the root ends and dark green tops from the leeks and clean them well. Place the whole leeks in a large skillet. Add enough salted water to just cover the leeks and bring to a simmer. Cook, covered, until tender, 8 to 10 minutes, depending on the size of the leeks.

Drain well. Cut each leek into 2 or 3 diagonal pieces and arrange in a warm shallow serving dish.

Meanwhile, heat the cream in a small saucepan over high heat until it boils. Stir in the butter and remove the saucepan from the heat. When the butter has melted, whisk in the mustard, cumin and salt and pepper to taste. Pour the cream mixture over the warm leeks and sprinkle with parsley.

Makes 6 to 8 servings

A
B
C
D
E
F
G
H
I
J
K
L
M
N
O
P
Q
R
S
T
U
V
W
X
Y
Z

LETTUCE

Most Canadian seed catalogues list about two dozen types of lettuce for home growing, including loose leaf, crisp headed, dark green or reddish varieties. There are new lettuces being developed all the time, but they all belong to four main categories: crisphead, butterhead, looseleaf and cos.

The most common crisphead lettuce is iceberg, while a popular, softer-leaved butterhead type is Boston. Looseleaf varieties include escarole, curly endive, oakleaf and nippy tasting arugula. Sturdy romaine is a cos lettuce. Look, too, for ready washed assorted baby leaves sometimes called spring mix.

All varieties of lettuce contain assorted minerals, plus vitamins A and C.

CHOOSING

Harvest lettuce the day you need it, but preferably while it is crisp in the early morning before the hot sun has had a chance to wilt it. If your homegrown lettuce is always bitter, investigate your soil; for best flavour, lettuce should be grown in fairly sandy soil.

Buy crisp, firm heads of lettuce that are heavy for their size, with no signs of wilt, decay or the brown spots called rust.

One pound (500 g) of lettuce yields 4 to 5 servings.

STORING

Unless the package states the leaves are ready washed, wash lettuce thoroughly but quickly as soon as possible after picking. Dry the leaves well. (A salad spinner is worth buying not only because it dries the lettuce well without bruising it, but it also is invaluable for drying cooled, blanched vegetables before packaging them for the freezer.) If storing in the crisper, place lettuce leaves in a plastic bag with paper towels between the layers to absorb excess moisture. Use within 2 days, replacing the towels after 1 day.

PREPARING

For salads, tear lettuce into bite-sized pieces as cutting the leaves will bruise and discolour them. Add a dressing just before serving since the leaves soon become soggy. For a variety of dressings, check out the Dressings and Sauces chapter on page 169.

For a tossed green salad, use a couple of varieties of lettuce and any combination of finely chopped fresh herbs. For a more substantial salad, add raw vegetables—thinly sliced cucumber, mushrooms, onion, zucchini, celery and radishes, cauliflower florets and tomato wedges—plus sliced hard-cooked egg and/or cheese. Edible flower petals like nasturtium make a spectacular garnish for any salad. Don't combine too many different ingredients in one salad—try to keep it simple.

COOKING

Lettuce can be braised, boiled, steamed and sautéed for a few minutes until tender.

LETTUCE-HERB SALAD

1 large or 2 small heads Boston lettuce

12 large mushrooms, sliced

6 green onions, sliced

½ cup finely chopped parsley

2 tbsp finely chopped chives

1 tbsp finely chopped fresh mint or 1 tsp dried
mint leaves

1 tsp finely chopped fresh oregano or ¼ tsp
dried oregano leaves

1 tsp finely chopped fresh thyme or ¼ tsp dried
thyme leaves

Onion-Honey Dressing (page 86)

This simple salad combines soft Boston lettuce with the contrasting texture of sliced mushrooms. For best flavour, use fresh herbs.

Wash and dry the lettuce carefully. Leave the small leaves whole but tear the remaining leaves into bite-sized pieces. Place the lettuce, vegetables and herbs in a large salad bowl.

Just before serving, toss the salad gently with some of the Onion-Honey Dressing (below).

Makes 6 to 8 servings

ONION-HONEY DRESSING

1 medium onion, finely chopped

1 large clove garlic, minced

⅓ cup liquid honey

⅓ cup tarragon vinegar

1 tbsp fresh lemon juice

1 tsp dry mustard

Salt and freshly ground black pepper to taste

½ cup canola oil

The tarragon vinegar goes especially well with the mushrooms in the Lettuce-Herb Salad (above). For another tarragon-mushroom combo, try Tarragon-Mushroom Vinaigrette on page 89.

In a food processor or mini chopper, process the onion and garlic until finely chopped. Add the honey, vinegar, lemon juice, mustard and salt and pepper to taste. Process until well combined. With the motor running, gradually add the oil through the feed tube and process until the dressing is well blended and creamy.

Store in a covered jar in the refrigerator overnight for flavours to blend. Shake well, then strain through a fine-mesh sieve. The dressing will keep for 3 to 4 days in the refrigerator.

Makes about 1 cup

BLUE CHEESE, PEAR AND RADICCHIO PIZZA

1 pear, unpeeled

1 tbsp butter

¼ tsp dried thyme leaves

Freshly ground black pepper to taste

Pizza dough (page 88)

¼ cup finely chopped pecans or walnuts

Cornmeal, as required

Canola oil, as required

4 oz (125 g) blue cheese, cut into ½-inch (1 cm) cubes

1 cup slivered radicchio

Pears, nuts and blue cheese go well together in a salad and the same trio makes a tasty topping for an easy pizza. A scattering of sliced radicchio just before serving adds a refreshing final touch. If you make your own pizza dough from scratch (page 84), prepare it just to the point where you punch it down. If you prefer to buy the pizza dough, you'll need 8 oz (250 g).

Preheat the oven to 500°F (260°C). Core and slice the pear. In a small skillet, melt the butter over medium heat and sauté the pear for 5 minutes. Sprinkle with thyme and pepper to taste and set aside.

Meanwhile, punch down the dough and knead in the pecans. Cover the dough with an upturned bowl and let stand for 10 minutes.

Pat or roll out the dough to a 12-inch (30 cm) round. Sprinkle a pizza pan with cornmeal, then press the dough into the pan. Brush the dough lightly with oil and scatter with the pear mixture.

Scatter the cheese evenly over the pizza. Drizzle lightly with a little more oil. Bake in the bottom third of the oven until the crust is golden brown, 12 to 15 minutes.

Just before serving, scatter with radicchio. Cut into wedges to serve..

Makes 2 to 3 main-course servings

PIZZA DOUGH

⅔ cup warm water

Pinch of granulated sugar

2 tsp active dry yeast

2 tbsp canola oil

1 ½ cups all-purpose flour (approx.)

½ tsp salt

This recipe doubles easily if you want to make two pizzas.

In a small bowl, combine the water and sugar. Sprinkle the yeast over the top and let stand in a warm place until bubbly and doubled in volume, about 5 minutes. Stir in the oil.

In a large bowl, whisk together the flour and salt. Make a well in the centre and pour in the yeast mixture. With a fork, gradually blend together the flour and yeast mixtures to form a dough.

With floured hands, gather the dough into a ball. Turn out onto a lightly floured surface and knead for about 5 minutes, adding just enough extra flour to make a soft, slightly sticky dough.

Place in a greased bowl, turning once to grease all over. Cover the bowl with greased wax paper and a tea towel. Let stand in a warm, draft-free place until tripled in size, 1 ½ to 3 hours.

Punch down the dough and form into a ball. Turn it out onto a lightly floured surface and cover with the upturned bowl. Let stand for 10 minutes. Roll out to a 12-inch (30 cm) round.

Makes enough dough for one 12-inch (30 cm) pizza crust

SPRING RISOTTO WITH ESCAROLE, MORELS AND PROSCIUTTO

4 cups chicken broth

1 oz (30 g) dried morels or other dried mushrooms

2 tbsp butter, divided

1 tbsp olive oil

1 onion, chopped

2 tsp finely chopped fresh thyme or ½ tsp dried thyme leaves

1 cup arborio rice

6 cups washed, dried and chopped escarole (1 small head)

½ cup freshly grated Parmesan cheese

2 oz (60 g) thinly sliced prosciutto, coarsely chopped

2 tbsp finely chopped chives or green onion tops

Freshly ground black pepper to taste

Additional freshly grated Parmesan cheese to serve

Escarole adds character and crunch to this comforting dish. Because the prosciutto and Parmesan are both salty, you may prefer using low-sodium chicken broth to reduce the sodium.

In a medium saucepan, bring the broth to a boil. Add the dried mushrooms. Remove the saucepan from the heat, cover and let stand for 30 minutes.

Remove the soaked mushrooms with a slotted spoon. When cool enough to handle, coarsely chop the mushrooms and set aside. Strain the broth through a cheesecloth- or a paper-towel-lined sieve. Return the broth to the saucepan and place over low heat.

In a large saucepan or deep skillet over medium heat, melt 1 tbsp butter with the olive oil. Add the onion and thyme and cook, stirring often, for 5 minutes. Add the soaked mushrooms and cook, stirring, for 2 minutes. Add the rice and cook, stirring, for 1 minute.

Keeping the rice at a brisk simmer, pour in ½ cup of the hot broth, stirring constantly, until the broth is mostly absorbed. Continue adding the broth ½ cup at a time, letting most of it be absorbed before adding more. The risotto should always be moist.

After 12 minutes, stir in the escarole. After 5 more minutes, taste the rice; it should be al dente (tender but firm to the bite). Some Italian cooks like the centre of the rice grains to be chalky but, if you don't like this texture, add more broth and cook for 5 more minutes, stirring constantly. Never cook until the rice grains are soft in the centre, as they will continue to cook after the risotto is removed from the heat.

Stir in the remaining butter, ½ cup cheese, prosciutto, chives, and pepper to taste. Serve immediately in warm shallow bowls, sprinkled with additional Parmesan cheese.

Makes 3 main-course or 6 to 8 appetizer servings

CREAMY LETTUCE AND PEA SOUP

6 large iceberg lettuce leaves

4 cups chicken or vegetable broth

3 cups fresh or frozen green peas

⅓ cup sliced green onions

5 sprigs fresh mint or 1 tsp dried mint leaves

1 tsp granulated sugar

Salt and freshly ground white pepper to taste

1 cup whipping cream (35% MF)

Fresh mint leaves for garnish

This lovely cold starter for a warm, early summer day features the classic combination of peas, lettuce and mint.

Line a large pot with the lettuce leaves. Add the chicken broth, peas, green onions and mint. Bring to a boil over medium-high heat. Reduce the heat to medium-low and simmer, covered, until the peas are tender, about 10 minutes. Let cool slightly.

Use an immersion blender in the pot to blend the soup until smooth. Or purée the soup in batches in a countertop blender (a blender, rather than a food processor, makes a smoother soup). If necessary, pour the soup back into the rinsed-out pot.

Stir in the sugar, and salt and pepper to taste. Let cool, then refrigerate, covered, for several hours.

Just before serving, stir in the cream. Season to taste with salt, if necessary. Pour into chilled bowls and garnish with mint leaves.

Makes 8 servings

MUSHROOMS

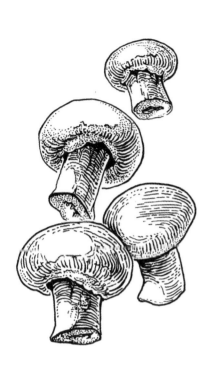

Once considered a luxury, mushrooms have become an increasingly popular part of our cuisine. Canadians seem to be particularly fond of the elegant touch mushrooms can give to a meal: the mushroom is now the third most valuable crop in the country, after the potato and tomato.

Of the many thousands of mushrooms growing on the planet, in Canada we still use more regular white button mushrooms than any other. However, we are steadily learning the wonderful flavours of different commercially cultivated and wild mushrooms. Here are a few of the more common varieties:

Creminis are much like the white button, but these brown mushrooms are meatier and more flavourful.

Portobello mushrooms are what creminis become when they grow up. Portobellos can be as large as 8 inches (20 cm) across. They are excellent for grilling or stuffing.

Shiitake mushrooms, originating in Asia and now grown here, have a nut-brown cap wider and more umbrella-shaped than creminis and buttons, and ivory flesh with an earthy, sometimes smoky flavour.

Oyster mushrooms are a soft grey or creamy colour and are slightly frilled with fragile flesh that has a delicate, nutty flavour.

Enoki mushrooms have tiny caps on long, thin stems. Enoki mushrooms are delicate and somewhat sweet in flavour with a touch of citrus. Because they are fragile, they are used more often as garnish since they toughen with overcooking.

Golden chanterelles, **morels** and **porcini** are wild mushrooms that are usually available only as dried mushrooms, although you may be able to find them fresh in some markets across the country.

There are numerous types of edible mushrooms that grow wild in Canada; morels grew in abundance in the countryside around Owen Sound, Ontario, where we used to live. But it's wise to let commercial growers provide you with this tasty fungus. Many wild varieties are poisonous and hard to distinguish from the edible ones unless you are very knowledgeable.

Low in calories, mushrooms are a fairly good source of protein, iron, and some B vitamins and minerals.

CHOOSING
Buy firm mushrooms that aren't discoloured or have any sign of moisture. Select the size appropriate to your recipe. Small button ones are good for pickling or salads. Large mushrooms are suitable for stuffing. All sizes have a similar flavour.

One pound (500 g) of mushrooms yields 4 to 6 servings.

STORING
Place unwashed mushrooms in an open container with a dampened towel draped over the top and refrigerate for up to 1 week.

A B C D E F G H I J K L M N O P Q R S T U V W X Y Z

To freeze mushrooms, sauté them in butter for 4 minutes then drain and pack in freezer bags.

PREPARING

Handle mushrooms gently because they bruise easily. Just before using, wipe with a damp cloth or wash quickly under cold running water and dry thoroughly. Because mushrooms have a high water content, they should not be soaked. Soaking will also cause them to lose nutrients and flavour.

Do not peel mushrooms or discard their stems since these parts contain most flavour.

Sprinkle with lemon juice to keep them from turning dark.

COOKING

Do not overcook mushrooms, and sauté only in nonreactive cookware. To retain moisture, sauté quickly in only enough fat to prevent the mushrooms from sticking to the saucepan. Make sure the mushrooms are dry and do not crowd too many in the saucepan at once. They should take only about 5 minutes or so, until they stop exuding liquid. Do not salt at the beginning, but add a sprinkling of salt, pepper and lemon juice at the end.

Large mushrooms are also good broiled. Brush well with oil and broil for 5 to 7 minutes per side, turning once and brushing with more oil.

Marinated or plain, raw mushrooms make a good addition to salads or an appetizer tray.

CLEAR MUSHROOM SOUP

Here's an elegant starter for your next company dinner party.

2 tbsp unsalted butter
2 tbsp finely chopped shallots
1 ½ lb (750 g) finely chopped white button or cremini mushrooms
6 cups chicken broth
1 ½ tsp fresh lemon juice
Salt and freshly ground black pepper to taste
1 lemon, thinly sliced

In a large saucepan, melt the butter over medium heat. Add the shallots and cook, stirring, until transparent, about 3 minutes. Add the mushrooms and cook, stirring occasionally, about 5 minutes.

Add the chicken broth and bring to a boil. Reduce the heat and simmer, uncovered, for 30 minutes. Let cool.

Strain the soup through a coarse-mesh sieve, pressing on the mushrooms firmly to extract all the liquid and allowing some specks of mushroom to go through the sieve.

Return the soup to the rinsed-out saucepan and reheat over medium heat. Stir in the lemon juice and season to taste with salt and pepper. Serve hot, garnished with thin slices of lemon.

Makes 6 servings

TARRAGON-MUSHROOM VINAIGRETTE

1 lb (500 g) white button mushrooms, cleaned

1 medium Spanish onion, thinly sliced into rings

TARRAGON VINAIGRETTE

⅔ cup tarragon vinegar

½ cup canola oil

2 tbsp water

1 tbsp granulated sugar

1 large clove garlic, crushed

Salt and freshly ground black pepper to taste

1 tbsp finely chopped parsley

This make-ahead salad is my daughter Anne Loxton's favourite recipe in this book.

Place the mushrooms in a large, nonreactive container. Separate the onion slices into rings and add to the mushrooms.

For the tarragon vinaigrette, stir together the vinegar, oil, water, sugar, garlic, and salt and pepper to taste in a small bowl until the sugar dissolves. Pour the vinegar mixture over the mushrooms and onion and gently stir together. Cover and refrigerate for at least 8 hours, stirring occasionally.

To serve, drain the mushrooms and onion, discarding the marinade. Place the mushroom mixture in a small serving bowl and sprinkle with parsley.

Makes 8 servings

WILD MUSHROOM, LEEK AND PROSCIUTTO STRATA

12 slices of bread cut from a day-old Italian loaf

4 cups half-and-half cream (10% MF) or table cream (18% MF), or 2 cups each, milk and cream

¼ cup butter, divided

4 leeks (white and 1 inch/2 ½ cm of pale green parts only), thinly sliced

8 oz (250 g) shiitake or portobello mushrooms, stemmed and cut into ¼-inch (6 mm) strips

8 oz (250 g) thinly sliced prosciutto, cut into ¼-inch (6 mm) strips

¼ cup finely chopped parsley, divided

2 tbsp finely chopped fresh thyme or marjoram, or a combination

2 cups shredded Gruyère cheese (about 8 oz/250 g)

6 eggs

2 tsp dry mustard

Freshly ground black pepper to taste

I love having a do-ahead casserole for brunches to just pop in the oven on the morning of the party. So-called "wild" or exotic mushrooms are readily available now in every supermarket. If you are lucky enough to find truly wild morel mushrooms, they would be exquisite in this dish.

Arrange the bread in a large shallow dish (it doesn't matter if some slices overlap) and pour the cream over the top. Set aside to soak.

In a large deep skillet, melt 3 tbsp of the butter over medium heat. Add the leeks and cook, stirring often, until softened, about 8 minutes. Add the mushrooms and cook, stirring often, for 5 minutes. Add the prosciutto and cook, stirring, for 2 or 3 minutes. Reserving 1 tbsp of the parsley, stir the remaining parsley and the thyme into the leek mixture. Set aside.

Gently squeeze any excess cream from the bread into a medium bowl. (Don't worry if the bread breaks up.)

In a greased, shallow 13- x 9-inch (3 L) baking dish, arrange one-third of the bread. Top with half of the leek mixture, spreading evenly, then with one-third of the cheese. Repeat the layers once. Arrange the remaining bread on top. (Don't worry if the bread doesn't cover each layer.)

To the reserved cream in the bowl, add the eggs, mustard and pepper to taste. Whisk until well combined. Pour the cream mixture into the dish. Sprinkle with the remaining cheese and dot with the remaining butter. Sprinkle with the remaining parsley. Cover tightly and refrigerate overnight.

When ready to bake, preheat the oven to 325°F (160°C). Bake the strata, uncovered, until the top is golden brown and a knife inserted in the centre comes out clean, 35 to 45 minutes.

Makes 8 servings

MIXED GREENS WITH ROASTED MUSHROOMS

1/4 cup white wine vinegar

1 tbsp Dijon mustard

2 cloves garlic, minced

1/4 tsp dried oregano leaves

Freshly ground black pepper to taste

1/2 cup olive oil

1 lb (500 g) large white button or cremini mushrooms, quartered

16 cups washed, dried and torn mixed greens

4 green onions, thickly sliced

Salt to taste

A garlicky mushroom mixture tops crisp greens in this interesting salad. Put the mushrooms in the oven to roast alongside a main dish. You can wash and dry the greens the day before, then layer them with paper towels and store in a plastic bag in the refrigerator.

In a glass measure, whisk together the vinegar, mustard, garlic, oregano and pepper to taste. Gradually whisk in the oil until the dressing is creamy. (The dressing can be covered and refrigerated for up to 24 hours. Let it stand at room temperature for 30 minutes, then whisk well before proceeding with the recipe.)

In a medium nonmetallic bowl, toss the mushrooms with 1/3 cup of the dressing, then let stand at room temperature for 30 minutes.

Meanwhile, preheat the oven to 400°F (200°C).

Spread the mushrooms out on a baking sheet and roast, uncovered and stirring once or twice, until browned, 25 to 30 minutes. Let cool completely.

Just before serving, toss the greens with the mushrooms and green onions in a large salad bowl. Season the remaining dressing with salt to taste and whisk well. Add the dressing to the greens and toss to coat well. Serve at once.

Makes 6 to 8 servings

MUSHROOMS IN WATERCRESS SAUCE

1 1/2 cups water

2 tbsp fresh lemon juice, divided

12 oz (375 g) white button mushrooms, sliced

1 medium onion, thinly sliced

WATERCRESS SAUCE

3/4 cup packed watercress leaves

1/4 cup packed parsley leaves

1 large clove garlic

3 tbsp olive oil

Salt and freshly ground black pepper to taste

Red lettuce leaves to serve

A tangy sauce provides a colourful dressing for earthy mushrooms in this unusual salad. If red lettuce is not available, use green lettuce and garnish the mushrooms with a thin border of shredded red cabbage or radish.

In a small saucepan, bring the water and 1 tbsp lemon juice to a boil. Add the mushrooms and onion and cover the saucepan. Reduce the heat to medium-low and simmer 2 minutes. Drain and pat dry. Place mushrooms and onion in a medium bowl.

For the watercress sauce, place the watercress, parsley, garlic and remaining lemon juice in a food processor or blender. With the motor running, slowly add the oil in a steady stream and process until thick. Season to taste with salt and pepper.

Pour the sauce over the mushroom and onion mixture and stir gently to combine. Cover and chill for at least 1 hour or overnight.

Line a serving platter with red lettuce leaves. Pile the mushroom mixture into the centre.

Makes 6 servings

MUSHROOMS AU GRATIN

2 tbsp butter

1 lb (500 g) small cremini or white button mushrooms, cleaned

1 ½ tbsp sliced green onion

⅓ cup sour cream

1 tbsp all-purpose flour

¼ tsp paprika

Salt and freshly ground black pepper to taste

½ cup shredded mild cheddar cheese

2 tbsp finely chopped parsley

An easy sour-cream sauce and a cheesy topping turn mushrooms into a do-ahead side or a lunch dish to serve with crusty bread and a tomato salad.

Preheat the oven to 425°F (220°C). In a large skillet, melt the butter over medium-high heat. Add the whole mushrooms and green onion and sauté until lightly browned, about 3 minutes. Cover the pan and cook for 2 minutes.

In a small bowl, blend together the sour cream, flour, paprika and salt and pepper to taste until smooth. Stir the sour cream mixture into the mushrooms and heat, stirring, until the mixture begins to boil. Transfer to a shallow 4-cup (1 L) baking dish. Sprinkle the cheese and parsley evenly over the top. (The dish can be prepared to this point, covered and refrigerated for up to 1 day.)

When ready to serve, bake, uncovered, until the mushrooms are heated and the cheese has melted, about 10 minutes (20 minutes if the dish was refrigerated).

Makes 4 servings

PICKLED MUSHROOMS

1 lb (500 g) tiny white button mushrooms, cleaned

3 cups boiling water

3 tbsp fresh lemon juice

1 bay leaf

1 tbsp thin pimento strips

1 cup white vinegar

2 large cloves garlic, halved

1 tbsp chopped parsley

2 tsp salt

1 ½ tsp finely chopped fresh thyme or ½ tsp dried thyme leaves

1 ½ tsp finely chopped fresh marjoram or ½ tsp dried marjoram leaves

1 tsp whole black peppercorns

½ cup canola oil

Ukrainians traditionally serve pickled mushrooms as part of their Christmas Eve meatless supper, but these flavorful little treats are good any time of the year. For more detailed instructions on how to prepare a sterilized jar, see Preserving on page 9.

Place the mushrooms in a stainless steel saucepan and add the boiling water, lemon juice and bay leaf. Bring to a boil. Reduce the heat to medium and simmer, uncovered and stirring often, for 2 minutes. Drain, discarding the bay leaf. Let cool.

When mushrooms are cool, pack them into a 3-cup (750 mL) sterilized jar. Top with the pimento.

Meanwhile, in a small saucepan, combine the vinegar, garlic, parsley, salt, thyme, marjoram and peppercorns. Bring to a simmer and simmer for 5 minutes.

Strain the hot vinegar mixture over the mushrooms. Pour in the canola oil. Cover tightly and refrigerate for 2 to 3 days before using. The mushrooms will keep for several weeks in the refrigerator.

Makes one 3-cup (750 mL) jar

MUSHROOM AND SWISS CHEESE STRUDEL

2 tbsp olive oil

1 onion, chopped

1 sweet red pepper, seeded and diced

2 cloves garlic, minced

1 lb (500 g) cremini mushrooms, sliced

½ tsp each, dried thyme, marjoram and oregano leaves

Salt and freshly ground black pepper to taste

8 sheets phyllo pastry

½ cup butter (preferably unsalted), melted

½ cup dry bread crumbs

2 cups shredded Swiss cheese

Serve this as a hearty appetizer or add a crisp green salad for a vegetarian main course. Use cremini mushrooms for best flavour.

In a large skillet, heat the oil over medium heat. Add the onion, red pepper and garlic and cook, stirring often, for 5 minutes. Add the mushrooms, thyme, marjoram, oregano and salt and pepper to taste. Increase the heat to high and cook, stirring often, until the liquid has evaporated, 3 to 5 minutes. Let cool.

Lightly dampen a tea towel. Lay 1 sheet of phyllo on the towel, keeping the rest well covered. Brush the sheet of phyllo with some of the melted butter and sprinkle lightly with bread crumbs. Top with another sheet of phyllo, brushing with butter and sprinkling with bread crumbs. Repeat with 2 more sheets of phyllo.

With a slotted spoon, arrange half of the mushroom mixture in a strip 2 inches (5 cm) from one long side, leaving a 2-inch (5 cm) border uncovered at the short sides. Sprinkle half of the cheese over the mushroom mixture.

Starting at the side with the filling and using the tea towel to start the rolling process, roll up the pastry halfway. Fold in the short sides and roll up completely to enclose the filling. Place, seam side down, on a buttered large baking sheet. Brush the top with butter.

Repeat with the remaining phyllo and filling. (The strudels can be prepared to this point, covered and refrigerated for up to 2 days.)

When ready to bake, preheat the oven to 400°F (200°C). Cut 7 slits in the top of each strudel. Bake in the bottom third of the oven until golden brown, 25 to 30 minutes. Cut into slices to serve.

Makes 8 appetizer or 4 to 6 main-course servings

BUTTER SAUTÉED MUSHROOMS

¼ cup butter

1 tbsp all-purpose flour

1 tsp paprika

1 ½ lb (750 g) small cremini or white button mushrooms, cleaned

1 tbsp fresh lemon juice

Salt and freshly ground black pepper to taste

This easy sauté make a delicious accompaniment for grilled or broiled steak.

In a medium saucepan over very low heat, melt the butter. Blend in the flour and cook, stirring, for 5 minutes. Remove from the heat and stir in the paprika.

Add the whole mushrooms and cook, uncovered, over very low heat, stirring often, until tender and browned, 10 minutes.

Remove from the heat, stir in the lemon juice and season to taste with salt and pepper. Serve hot.

Makes 6 to 8 servings

PORTOBELLO BURGERS WITH PESTO MAYONNAISE

4 portobello mushrooms (about 5 inches/12 cm across), stemmed

¼ cup olive oil

1 tbsp balsamic vinegar

1 clove garlic, minced

1 tsp each, dried basil and oregano leaves

⅓ cup mayonnaise

2 tbsp basil pesto (page 173)

4 thin slices provolone cheese

4 crusty hamburger buns, split

Lettuce leaves to serve

1 roasted red pepper, stemmed, seeded and quartered

Big, meaty and delicious, portobello mushrooms lend themselves to this vegetarian version of a burger. You can use a roasted pepper from a jar for this recipe, or roast your own (page 110).

If desired, remove the dark gills from the mushroom caps by scraping them off with a spoon. Place the mushroom caps, smooth side up, in a shallow dish. In a glass measure, whisk together the oil, vinegar, garlic, basil and oregano. Pour the oil mixture over the mushroom caps. Let stand at room temperature for 15 to 30 minutes.

Meanwhile, stir together the mayonnaise and pesto in a small bowl.

Preheat the barbecue to medium-high and brush the grill with some of the marinade. Grill the mushroom caps, smooth side down and with lid closed, for 8 minutes. Turn the mushroom caps and cook until they are very tender and no longer exuding liquid, 6 to 8 minutes.

Turn the mushroom caps smooth side down again. Top each mushroom with a slice of cheese and grill until the cheese melts, 1 to 2 minutes. Meanwhile, grill the buns, cut sides down, until golden.

Spread the pesto mayonnaise evenly over the cut sides of the buns. Line bottom half of each bun with lettuce leaves and top each with a red pepper quarter. Place a mushroom cap on each bun. Cover with the tops of the buns.

Makes 4 servings

GRILLED MUSHROOMS

1 lb (500 g) cremini or white button mushrooms, sliced

2 tbsp butter

1 tbsp dry sherry

Salt and freshly ground black pepper to taste

This easy side dish is absolutely the best accompaniment to barbecued steak.

Preheat the barbecue to medium-high. Place the mushrooms in the centre of a large sheet of heavy-duty aluminum foil. Dot the mushrooms with butter and sprinkle with sherry and salt and pepper. Fold the foil over the mushrooms, sealing the edges securely.

Place the package on the coolest part of the grill and cook, turning the package occasionally, until the mushrooms are tender, 15 to 20 minutes.

Makes about 4 servings

SEE ALSO:
Lettuce-Herb Salad   83

ONIONS

Onions have been around since before the days of the Old Testament. They're one of our most versatile vegetables and most widely used in every type of cuisine.

Members of the lily family, onions were one of the few staples available to Canada's early settlers. They are now grown extensively across the country and are the most important crop in the marsh areas of Ontario, south of Barrie.

Onions can be eaten raw or cooked and used to add flavour to countless dishes.

Fortunately there are several varieties of onion available to us all year round, including green spring onions, small white and yellow pickling or pearl onions, Spanish onions, red onions, white onions and—the most common—the yellow cooking onion.

Onions are low in calories, and contain vitamins A and C, calcium, phosphorous and iron.

CHOOSING

Select firm, well-shaped, solid onions with slim necks and dry skins that crackle. Avoid those with signs of moisture at the neck or wet patches on the skin.

About 1 ¼ pounds (625 g) of onions yield 4 servings.

STORING

Store onions, unwashed, in a cool, dry place in containers that allow good air circulation.

To freeze onions, peel and slice or chop them, then pack into freezer bags.

PREPARING

To avoid tears, hold onions under cold running water while you peel them. For easier peeling, particularly when preparing tiny onions, blanch them in a saucepan of boiling water for 1 minute, then plunge them into a bowl of cold water. An X cut in the root end of each onion will help prevent the layers separating when you are cooking whole onions.

COOKING

Raw or cooked, onions can provide interesting side and main dishes.

Tiny pearl or yellow onions are delicious if blanched until tender-crisp and dressed with a rich cream or cheese sauce (page 172). Large onions are excellent stuffed (Cheese-Stuffed Onions, page 97), or can be glazed or roasted with meat.

Boil onions, uncovered, in enough water to cover them for 10 to 20 minutes, depending on size. Steaming will take slightly longer. Bake in a 375°F (190°C) oven (or lower if roasting with meat) for 1 to 1 ½ hours.

If you are preparing onions for flavouring another dish, sautéing them quickly in butter is often sufficient.

When preparing a large quantity of sliced onions for a quiche or creamed dish, a long, slow braise in butter for 20 to 30 minutes will produce a very sweet result.

OTHER MEMBERS OF THE ONION FAMILY
CHIVES

This dwarf onion relative is a perennial herb popular for adding delicate onion flavour to a dish, or as a pretty garnish.

GARLIC

Fresh garlic is readily available and is one of my favourite seasonings. It has an interesting but potent flavour when used raw that becomes quite sweet when the garlic is cooked slowly. It stores well for a long time in a cool, dry, well-ventilated place. Don't store garlic in the refrigerator.

SHALLOTS

This sweet bulb has a flavour like a very mild onion with a touch of garlic.

LEEKS

See page 79.

BALSAMIC-GLAZED ONIONS

Balsamic vinegar adds a rich flavour to this simple little side dish.

2 pkgs (each 10 oz/238 g) pearl onions (about 4 ½ cups)

¼ cup balsamic vinegar

1 tbsp finely chopped fresh thyme or 1 tsp dried thyme leaves

1 tbsp butter

1 tbsp canola oil

½ tsp granulated sugar

Salt and freshly ground black pepper to taste

2 tbsp finely chopped parsley

Preheat the oven to 400°F (200°C). In a large saucepan of boiling, salted water, blanch the onions for 2 minutes. Drain well and immediately place the onions in a bowl of cold water. Drain well and peel the onions.

In a shallow 8-cup (2 L) baking dish, stir together the vinegar, thyme, butter, oil, sugar and salt and pepper to taste. Place the dish in the oven until the butter melts, 3 to 5 minutes.

Stir the vinegar mixture well to combine. Add the onions, tossing to coat with the vinegar mixture. Spread the onions out in a single layer in the dish. Bake, uncovered and stirring occasionally, until golden brown and tender, 35 to 40 minutes. Sprinkle with parsley to serve.

Makes 8 servings

MAKE-AHEAD

Bake the onions as above but omit the parsley. Refrigerate, covered, for up to 24 hours. Remove from the refrigerator 30 minutes before reheating. Reheat, covered, in a 350°F (180°C) oven until heated through, about 20 minutes. Sprinkle with parsley before serving.

COUNTRY GARLIC SOUP WITH POACHED EGGS

2 tbsp olive oil

6 cloves garlic, minced

4 slices of baguette

1 tsp paprika

5 cups chicken broth

4 eggs

Salt and freshly ground black pepper to taste

4 large sprigs parsley or fresh coriander (cilantro)

Our best vacations in Europe always include renting an apartment or house so I can pretend we live there, visiting all the local markets and cooking. September 2002 found us in an old farmhouse in Gard, in the Languedoc-Roussillon region of southern France.

Early one Sunday morning during our stay, fierce thunder, lightning and torrential rains set in and didn't let up until late Monday. The storm caused the worst flooding the area had seen for decades and twenty-seven people were killed as the swollen rivers angrily overshot their banks.

Fortunately our farmhouse was on a hill and although the little village below was hard hit, we were safe. The disaster did, however, curtail travel for a time, and since the restaurants were closed and many roads impassable, we were lucky we could cook our own meals.

A visit to the local market is always first on the list of activities when we settle into a place. Because we had arrived before the storm, we had managed to buy some vegetables, cheese, sausage, eggs and a good supply of local garlic.

On one of the days we couldn't travel out, I had to make do with such supplies and made this soul-warming, easy soup. It's similar to a soup found in Spain, but since there were eggs, garlic and part of a baguette on hand, I didn't think anyone would mind a cross-cultural lunch. This is a great soup to make when you are house-bound in any country.

Preheat the oven to 250°F (120°C). In a large deep skillet, heat the oil over low heat. Add the garlic and cook, stirring often, until light golden, about 8 minutes. Remove the garlic with a slotted spoon and set aside.

Increase the heat to medium and add the baguette slices to the skillet. Cook, turning once and moving the bread around in the skillet, until browned, about 4 minutes.

Place a baguette slice in each of 4 heatproof soup bowls, sprinkle each with some of the paprika and keep warm in the oven.

Add the broth and cooked garlic to the skillet and bring to a simmer. Break 1 egg into a cup and slip into the simmering broth. Repeat with the remaining eggs. Cover the skillet and poach the eggs at a bare simmer until the whites are firm but the yolks are still runny, 3 to 4 minutes.

With a slotted spoon, transfer eggs to the baguette slices and sprinkle with salt and pepper. Ladle the broth into the bowls and garnish with parsley. Serve at once.

Makes 4 servings

THE BEST POACHED EGGS

Pick the freshest eggs you can for poaching. Since the yolk membrane is stronger and the white is thicker in a very fresh egg, the yolk will stay together and the white will cling to it rather than dissipating in the poaching water.

HONEY-GLAZED ONIONS

20 small firm white onions (1 ½ inches/4 cm in
    diameter)
¼ cup butter
2 tbsp creamed honey
Salt to taste

For a real treat, serve this Prince Edward Island specialty with roast pork.

Preheat the oven to 350°F (180°C). Blanch the onions in a saucepan of boiling water for 1 minute. Drain and cool under cold, running water. Peel the onions and cut an X in the root end of each (this prevents the layers from separating). Place the onions in a greased shallow baking dish just large enough to hold them in a single layer.

In a small saucepan, melt the butter over medium heat. Add the honey and salt and stir until hot and the honey has melted.

Pour the butter mixture over the onions and stir to coat. Bake, uncovered and basting occasionally with the cooking juices, until the onions are tender and brown, about 45 minutes.

Makes 4 servings

CHEESE-STUFFED ONIONS

4 medium onions (3 inches/8 cm in diameter)
2 tbsp butter
1 cup toasted whole wheat bread crumbs
2 tbsp finely chopped parsley
¾ tsp finely chopped fresh thyme or ¼ tsp dried
    thyme leaves
Salt and freshly ground black pepper to taste
1 cup shredded old cheddar cheese
1 cup chicken broth
½ cup dry vermouth

These onions, with their rich cheddar filling, are wonderful served with a lamb stew.

Peel the onions and cut an X in the root end of each (this prevents the layers from separating). Scoop out the inside of each onion, leaving a ¼-inch (6 mm) thick shell. Chop the scooped-out onion finely and set aside.

In a saucepan of boiling water, cook the onion shells for 10 minutes. Drain upside down on a wire rack.

Preheat the oven to 325°F (160°C). In a large skillet, melt the butter over medium heat. Add the reserved chopped onion and sauté until golden. Add the crumbs and cook, stirring often, for 5 minutes. Stir in the parsley, thyme and salt and pepper to taste. Remove the skillet from the heat and stir in the cheese.

Sprinkle the inside of the onion shells lightly with salt and pepper. Stuff the onions with the cheese mixture, dividing evenly and mounding the tops. Place the onions in a greased, shallow baking dish just large enough to hold them. Pour the broth and vermouth around the onions. Bake, basting often, until tender and brown, about 1 hour.

Remove the onions to a warm serving platter. If your baking dish is flame-proof, put the dish over medium-high heat and boil the cooking liquid vigorously until it has reduced by about half. If your baking dish is not flame-proof, pour the liquid into a small saucepan before boiling. Pour the reduced liquid over the onions and serve.

Makes 4 servings

ONION-SAGE FOCACCIA

1 very small Spanish onion, thinly sliced

¼ cup white wine vinegar

2 tbsp liquid honey

Pizza dough (page 87)

¾ cup freshly grated Parmesan cheese

Cornmeal, as required

1 tbsp finely chopped fresh sage or 1 tsp
  crumbled dried sage leaves

2 tbsp canola oil

1 tsp cold water

I think onions are underrated as a vegetable. We use them to flavour soups and stews and the like but seldom think of them as the star of a dish. This simple flatbread allows the humble onion to take the spotlight. It's perfect as an appetizer to a light dinner or as an accompaniment to a main-course soup. If you make your own pizza dough from scratch (page 84), prepare it just to the point where you punch it down. If you prefer to buy the pizza dough, you'll need about 8 oz (250 g).

In a small bowl, combine the onion, vinegar and honey. Let stand at room temperature, stirring occasionally, for at least 30 minutes but no longer than 1 hour.

Punch down the pizza dough. Knead in ¼ cup of the cheese and form into a ball. Turn out onto a lightly floured surface and cover with an upturned bowl. Let stand for 10 minutes.

Preheat the oven to 425°F (220°C). Roll out the dough into a 10-inch (25 cm) round. Sprinkle a pizza pan or baking sheet lightly with cornmeal. Transfer the dough to the pan. Make indentations all over the dough with your fingertips.

Drain the onion and scatter evenly over the dough. Sprinkle with the remaining cheese, then the sage. Drizzle with the oil, then sprinkle all over with the water.

Bake in the bottom third of the oven until golden, 20 to 25 minutes. Cut into wedges and serve warm.

Makes 4 servings

CREAMY GARLIC-THYME CUSTARDS

2 whole heads garlic

2 tsp olive oil

2 tsp finely chopped fresh thyme or ½ tsp dried
  thyme leaves

Salt and freshly ground black pepper to taste

1 cup whipping cream (35% MF)

3 eggs

¼ tsp cayenne

4 small fresh thyme sprigs (optional)

When I developed this recipe for a Christmas 2000 menu I was doing for *Elm Street* magazine, my editor added these words to my lead: "These rich, velvety custards are the best thing to come out of a ramekin in years." High praise indeed. She also said the custards were the ultimate comfort food and she could sit down to eat all four without wasting a spoonful.

Make these in pretty little ramekins and serve as an appetizer, or as a side dish with roast beef or lamb, setting a ramekin on or beside each dinner plate.

Preheat the oven to 400°F (200°C). Cut the top off each garlic head to expose the cloves. Remove any loose outer skin. Place the garlic heads on a large piece of foil. Drizzle with the olive oil and sprinkle with the thyme, and salt and pepper to taste. Enclose in the foil, sealing the edges well. Roast until soft when the package is squeezed, about 45 minutes.

Unwrap and let cool. (Garlic can be roasted up to 1 day ahead, covered and refrigerated.)

Reduce the oven temperature to 275°F (140°C). In a blender, combine the whipping cream, eggs, ½ tsp salt, ¼ tsp black pepper and the cayenne. Turn the garlic heads upside down and gently squeeze the cloves out of the skins into the blender. Blend the mixture until smooth.

Pour the cream mixture into four buttered ¾-cup (175 mL) ramekins or custard cups. (Unbaked custards can be covered and refrigerated for up to 4 hours. Stir each gently before baking.)

Place the ramekins in a shallow pan just large enough to hold them and pour boiling water into the pan to come half-way up the sides of the ramekins. Bake until the centres of the custards are firm to the touch, about 1 hour to 1 hour, 10 minutes. (The custards can sit at room temperature for up to 2 hours before serving. To reheat, place the ramekins on a rack in a large skillet containing about 1 inch of simmering water. Cover the skillet, then simmer for about 10 minutes or until custards are hot throughout.)

Serve at once, garnished with fresh thyme sprigs (if using).

Makes 4 servings

PARSNIPS

Parsnips have generally been greatly underrated and have, consequently, suffered abuse or been neglected for years. In sixteenth-century Europe they were considered suitable only as animal fodder, but they finally achieved some popularity in England and were subsequently introduced to North America.

Here they suffered from the myth they were poisonous and our nasty habit of overcooking them. When properly prepared, parsnips have a delicious nutty flavour.

Parsnips are best if harvested in the spring as soon as the ground can be dug. Freezing changes the carbohydrates to sugar, giving them a sweet, delicate flavour, but recent varieties of parsnips are good year round.

Parsnips are a good source of potassium and a very good source of dietary fibre and vitamin C.

CHOOSING

Select small to medium parsnips that are smooth, firm, well-shaped and free from brown spots.

About 1 ½ pounds (750 g) of parsnips yield 4 servings.

STORING

Leave homegrown parsnips in the ground until needed. Store bought parsnips in a perforated plastic bag in the crisper for up to 4 weeks. If stored in a root cellar, cover parsnips with moist sand.

To freeze parsnips, peel and cut them into slices or strips, then blanch for 1 minute.

PREPARING

Scrub parsnips well and peel if desired, although they can be peeled after cooking. Cut the woody core from the centre of large parsnips, if necessary.

COOKING

Boil chopped parsnips, covered, in a small amount of boiling, salted water for 5 to 10 minutes. If you wish to purée parsnips, cook them a little longer. Steaming will take slightly longer than boiling. Bake chunks of parsnips in a covered baking dish with 2 tbsp liquid in a 325°F (160°C) oven for about 45 minutes.

Parsnips are also delicious boiled until barely tender, then breaded and sautéed or deep-fried.

ROASTED PARSNIP SOUP WITH TURMERIC SWIRL

2 lb (1 kg) parsnips (about 6), peeled, trimmed and cut into 1- x ½-inch (2.5 x 1 cm) pieces

2 tbsp canola oil, divided

Salt and freshly ground black pepper to taste

1 onion, finely chopped

2 cloves garlic, minced

1 tsp curry powder (mild or medium)

6 to 7 cups chicken broth

1 tsp turmeric

½ cup plain yogurt

¼ cup finely chopped fresh coriander (cilantro)

6 sprigs fresh coriander (cilantro)

My good friend the food writer and editor Julia Aitken shared this delightful soup recipe from her cookbook *125 Best Entertaining Recipes*. Roasting parsnips brings out their natural sweetness which, in turn, teams well with spicy flavours. There's just a touch of curry in this creamy soup, so it's not too hot, just wonderfully comforting. Toasting the turmeric before adding it to the yogurt eliminates any raw taste the spice might have.

Preheat the oven to 400°F (200°C). In a large shallow roasting pan, toss together the parsnips, 1 tbsp oil, and salt and pepper to taste. Roast, uncovered and stirring occasionally, until the parsnips are tender and golden brown, 40 to 45 minutes.

In a large saucepan or Dutch oven, heat the remaining oil over medium-high heat. Add the onion and cook, stirring often, until soft but not brown, 3 to 5 minutes. Add the garlic and curry powder and cook, stirring, until fragrant, 2 to 3 minutes. (Do not let the garlic brown.)

Add the parsnips, 6 cups of broth and salt and pepper to taste. Bring to a boil over high heat. Reduce the heat to medium-low and simmer, covered, until all the vegetables are tender, 20 to 30 minutes.

Meanwhile, in a small dry skillet, toast the turmeric over medium heat, stirring often, until it darkens slightly, smells aromatic and starts to smoke, 1 to 2 minutes. Remove the skillet from the heat. Scrape the turmeric into a bowl and let cool completely. Add the yogurt and stir well. Set aside.

Use an immersion blender in the saucepan to blend the soup until smooth. Or purée the soup in batches in a countertop a blender (a blender, rather than a food processor, makes a smoother soup).

If necessary, pour the soup back into the rinsed-out saucepan. If the soup is too thick, add the remaining 1 cup broth. Stir in the chopped coriander. (The soup can be cooled, covered and refrigerated for up to 3 days.)

Reheat the soup over medium heat until piping hot, but not boiling. Season to taste with salt and pepper if necessary. Ladle into warm soup bowls. Swirl a spoonful of turmeric-flavoured yogurt into each serving. Garnish with coriander sprigs.

Makes 6 servings

PARSNIP PATTIES

1 ½ lb (750 g) parsnips (about 5)
⅓ cup butter, divided
1 small onion, finely chopped
1 egg
Salt and freshly ground black pepper to taste
2 tbsp all-purpose flour

These crisp patties, a specialty of Nova Scotia, are terrific with broiled pork chops and a crisp green salad.

Scrub and trim the parsnips but leave them whole. Cook the parsnips in a small amount of boiling water in a covered saucepan until tender, about 25 minutes. Peel the parsnips. In a medium bowl, mash them until smooth.

Meanwhile, melt ¼ cup of the butter in a large skillet over medium heat. Add the onion and sauté for 2 or 3 minutes.

Remove the skillet from the heat and stir the onion into the mashed parsnips. Add the egg, and salt and pepper to taste. Let cool slightly.

As soon as the mixture is cool enough to handle, shape it into flat patties, each about 3 inches (8 cm) in diameter. Sprinkle the patties on both sides with flour.

In the same skillet, melt the remaining butter over medium-high heat. Fry the patties, in batches, until golden brown on both sides, about 2 or 3 minutes per side. Serve immediately.

Makes 4 servings

POTATO PATTIES
Substitute 1 ½ lb (750 g) potatoes for the parsnips.

RUTABAGA-POTATO PATTIES
Substitute 12 oz (375 g) each, rutabaga and potatoes for the parsnips.

BAKED PARSNIP PURÉE

½ cup water
2 lb (1 kg) parsnips (about 6), peeled, trimmed
  and cut into thick slices
1 tbsp fresh lemon juice
¼ cup melted butter
3 tbsp whipping cream (35% MF)
1 tsp granulated sugar
1 tsp finely grated lemon zest
⅛ tsp freshly grated nutmeg
Salt to taste
1 tbsp cold butter
2 tbsp finely chopped walnuts or pecans or dry
  bread crumbs

This make-ahead purée goes well with roast pork or poultry. Cook the parsnips a little bit longer than you usually would so the purée will be smooth.

Bring the water to a boil in a medium saucepan. Add the parsnips and lemon juice. Reduce the heat to medium-low and simmer, covered, until the parsnips are very tender, about 20 minutes. Drain well.

In a food processor or blender, purée the parsnips until smooth. Add the melted butter, cream, sugar, lemon zest, nutmeg and salt to taste. Process until very smooth.

Scrape the mixture into a buttered 4-cup (1 L) baking dish. Dot with the cold butter and sprinkle with nuts or crumbs. (The dish can be prepared to this point, covered and refrigerated for up to 1 day. Let stand at room temperature for 30 minutes before baking.)

When ready to bake, preheat the oven to 350°F (180°C). Bake the purée, uncovered, until heated through, 20 to 30 minutes.

Makes 6 servings

GLAZED ROSEMARY PARSNIPS

These sweet, herb-flecked parsnips are delicious with roast lamb.

¼ cup unsalted butter

1 ½ lb (750 g) parsnips (about 5), peeled, trimmed and cut into 2- x 1-inch (5 x 2.5 cm) pieces

2 tbsp packed brown sugar

1 tsp finely chopped fresh rosemary or ¼ tsp crushed dried rosemary leaves

Salt and freshly ground black pepper to taste

1 tbsp finely chopped parsley

Cut a round of waxed paper the same diameter as your large, heavy skillet. Butter one side of the paper.

In the skillet, melt the ¼ cup butter over low heat. Add the parsnips. Cover with the waxed paper, butter side down, and a lid. Steam over low heat until the parsnips are just tender when pierced with a sharp knife, 7 to 10 minutes.

Remove the lid and paper. Sprinkle the parsnips with the sugar, rosemary, and salt and pepper to taste. Increase the heat to medium and cook, stirring often, until the parsnips are glazed, about 2 minutes. Serve garnished with parsley.

Makes 4 servings

GLAZED GINGER CARROTS
Substitute 1 ½ lb (750 g) carrots for the parsnips and ¼ tsp ground ginger for the rosemary.

GLAZED GINGER TURNIPS
Substitute 1 ½ lb (750 g) turnips for the parsnips and ¼ tsp ground ginger for the rosemary.

GLAZED GINGER RUTABAGA
Substitute 1 ½ lb (750 g) rutabaga for the parsnips and ¼ tsp ground ginger for the rosemary.

THYME-BREADED PARSNIPS

2 lb (1 kg) parsnips (about 6), peeled, trimmed and cut into 2- x 1-inch (5 x 2.5 cm) pieces

¼ cup each, all-purpose flour and dry bread crumbs

2 tsp crumbled dried thyme leaves

Salt and freshly ground black pepper to taste

¼ cup butter (approx.)

I always think of parsnips as spring vegetables because on the farm where I grew up, we would leave them in the garden all winter and dig them up in the spring before they started to sprout and were particularly sweet. A crunchy herb coating makes these parsnips an excellent side dish for roast poultry or meat.

In a covered saucepan of boiling, salted water, cook the parsnips until almost tender, about 5 minutes. Drain well.

In a shallow bowl, whisk together the flour, bread crumbs, thyme and salt and pepper to taste.

Using tongs, roll the hot parsnips in the crumb mixture to coat well, setting them on a waxed-paper-lined tray as you work. (The recipe can be prepared to this point, cooled, covered and left at room temperature for 2 hours, or refrigerated up to 24 hours.)

In a large skillet (or 2 smaller skillets), melt the butter over medium heat. Add the breaded parsnips and cook, turning often, until golden brown on all sides, about 10 minutes. Add a little more butter to the skillet, if necessary.

Makes 6 to 8 servings

SEE ALSO:

PEAS

Peas have long been one of the most popular vegetables. Easily dried and stored, they have been a defense against cold winters and periods of famine for centuries.

Introduced to Canada by early settlers, dried peas became an important part of the diet of voyageurs and French-Canadian bateau men because they were easily transported. Until the latter part of the seventeenth century when fresh, shelled green peas became fashionable in the French court, dried peas were actually far more popular.

Fresh peas are not only more flavourful than dried, they have more texture, nutrient value and sugar. Like corn, peas' sugar content begins to change to starch from the moment they are picked.

Peas with edible pods, known as *mange-tout* (literally "eat all") in French, like snow peas and sugar snaps (which combine the best attributes of regular and snow peas), are very popular and delicious eaten raw. Try them as part of a crudité platter and serve both raw shelled peas and the edible-pod strains in salads.

Peas are high in A and B vitamins.

CHOOSING

If you rub a handful of peas-in-the-pod between your hands and they squeak, the peas are fresh. The pods should be bright green, shiny and well filled. Avoid limp pods or those that appear too full.

Two pounds (1 kg) of peas-in-the-pod or 1 pound (500 g) edible-pod peas yield 4 servings.

STORING

Store peas, still in their pods but not covered, in the coldest part of the refrigerator.

To freeze peas, shell them, remove the strings (see Preparing, below) from sugar snap or snow peas, then blanch for 2 minutes.

PREPARING

Just before cooking, shell regular peas, but do not wash them after shelling. Wash edible-pod varieties, then snap off the stem tip of each, pulling it down toward the flat side of the pod to remove the strings on both sides of the pod.

COOKING

To boil, bring a large amount of salted water to a boil, drop in the peas and cook uncovered, for about 2 minutes for shelled peas, 1 minute for sugar snap or snow peas. For shelled peas, a pod or two or a couple of sprigs of fresh mint added to the cooking water will add flavour. Steaming takes a minute longer. Shelled peas braised in butter are also delicious, and edible-pod peas make a colourful, crisp addition to stir-fried dishes.

OLD-FASHIONED SPLIT PEA SOUP

1 lb (500 g) dry green split peas (about
  2 ¼ cups)

10 cups water

1 meaty ham bone

1 cup chopped onion

1 large clove garlic, minced

1 ½ tsp finely chopped fresh marjoram or ½ tsp
  dried marjoram leaves, crushed

Freshly ground black pepper to taste

1 cup finely chopped celery with leaves

1 cup grated carrot

2 tbsp finely chopped parsley

Salt to taste

Croutons for garnish

This hearty soup has long been a family favourite. Since dried peas were easy to carry, they played an important part in the diet of voyageurs who combined them with salt pork and water to make a hearty soup. Depending on the type of peas you use, you may have to soak them overnight; check the package for instructions.

In a large pot, combine the peas with enough cold water to cover them.

Add the ham bone, onion, garlic, marjoram and pepper to taste. Bring to a boil over high heat. Reduce the heat to medium-low and simmer, covered and stirring occasionally, for 2 hours.

Remove the ham bone and cut off any meat, discarding the bone. Dice the meat and add back to the pot, along with the celery, carrot and parsley. Bring back to a simmer and cook, covered and stirring occasionally, for 45 minutes. (The soup taste even better if cooled, covered and refrigerated for up to 1 day. It also freezes well.)

When ready to serve, reheat the soup and season to taste with salt. Serve hot garnished with croutons.

Makes 8 to 10 servings

GREEN PEA AND ORANGE SALAD

4 cups shelled green peas

2 seedless oranges

1 small mild onion (or ½ Spanish onion)

¼ cup pecan halves

⅔ cup Basic Vinaigrette (page 170)

⅛ tsp cayenne

Shredded lettuce leaves (optional)

This pretty, refreshing salad will be a hit on a buffet table.

In a saucepan of boiling, salted water, cook the peas just until tender. Drain well and set aside in a large bowl.

Peel the oranges and remove as much of the white pith and membrane as you can. Cut the orange into 1-inch (2 ½ cm) pieces. Add to the peas.

Slice the onion thinly and separate it into rings. Add to the peas, along with the pecans. Stir gently together.

Whisk together the vinaigrette and cayenne. Pour over the salad and stir gently to coat everything with the vinaigrette.

Cover and let sit in a cool place for 1 to 2 hours for the flavours to blend, but do not leave overnight since the peas will discolour.

Line a serving platter with lettuce leaves (if using). Drain the salad well and spoon onto the platter.

Makes about 6 servings

MINTED NEW PEAS

2 cups freshly shelled peas

2 or 3 empty pea pods

¼ cup unsalted butter

1 ½ tbsp finely chopped fresh mint or 1 tsp dried mint leaves

⅛ tsp granulated sugar

Salt and freshly ground black pepper to taste

Peas and mint are a classic combination and this simple recipe shows why.

In a saucepan of boiling, salted water, cook the peas and pods until tender, 2 to 4 minutes. Drain well, discarding the pods.

In a large skillet, melt the butter over medium heat. Add the peas, mint, sugar and salt and pepper to taste. Sauté until the peas are heated through.

Makes 4 to 6 servings

MINTED SUGAR SNAP PEAS

Substitute 1 lb (500 g) sugar snap peas for the shelled peas and cook in boiling water for just 1 minute before proceeding with the recipe.

PURÉE OF PEAS

3 tbsp butter

2 green onions, chopped

¼ cup water

1 tsp granulated sugar

Salt to taste

4 cups freshly shelled peas

2 or 3 empty pea pods

3 tbsp whipping cream (35% MF)

2 tbsp butter

1 tsp finely chopped fresh chervil or ¼ tsp dried chervil leaves

Freshly ground white pepper to taste

Spoon this creamy purée into a warm serving bowl, or pipe it into sautéed large mushroom caps and serve as a garnish for grilled lamb chops.

In a medium saucepan over medium heat, melt the butter. Add the green onions and cook, stirring, for 5 minutes. Add the water, sugar and salt to taste and bring to a boil.

Add the peas and pea pods and bring back to a boil. Reduce the heat to medium-low and simmer, tightly covered, until the peas are tender, 5 to 8 minutes. Discard the pods and let cool slightly.

Use an immersion blender in the saucepan to blend the peas until smooth. Or purée the peas in batches in a countertop blender (a blender, rather than a food processor, makes a smoother purée).

Transfer the purée to the top of a double boiler or a stainless steel bowl. (The purée can be prepared ahead to this point and kept at room temperature for up to 2 hours.)

Just before serving, beat the cream, butter, chervil and pepper to taste into the purée. Season to taste with salt, if necessary. Set the purée over simmering water, stirring occasionally, until heated through.

Makes 6 servings

1 lb (500 g) snow peas or sugar snap peas
2 tbsp peanut or canola oil
3 large cloves garlic, minced
1 tbsp soy sauce
1 tsp granulated sugar
Freshly ground black pepper to taste

STIR-FRIED SNOW PEAS

This easy stir-fry side dish takes just minutes to prep. Serve with lemon-marinated roast chicken thighs.

Pull the strings from the peas (see page 105).

In a wok or large skillet heat the oil over medium-high heat. Add the garlic and stir-fry until golden.

Add the peas and stir-fry until the peas are tender but still slightly crisp and bright green, 2 to 3 minutes. Add the soy sauce, sugar and pepper to taste. Serve at once.

Makes 4 servings

STIR-FRIED SNOW PEAS AND SHRIMP
Add 4 oz (125 g) shelled raw small or chopped shrimp with the peas.

SEE ALSO:
Hodge Podge   168

PEPPERS

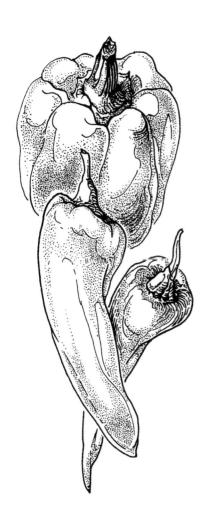

The sweet peppers we use as vegetables and their hotter relatives we use to spice up some dishes are all natives of Mexico and Latin America. They're members of the capsicum family but not related to the peppercorns we use as everyday seasoning.

Both sweet and hot peppers were cultivated by the Aztecs and later introduced to Europe by explorers. In Canada, there are several varieties of sweet peppers available, as well as many more choices of hot peppers.

Once, it was hard to find anything but green sweet peppers in the market but now there's a rainbow of colours: yellow, orange, red, white, purple and even black. Called bell peppers south of the border because of their shape, these sweet peppers now are joined by other sweet peppers, like the Italian sheppard that's tapered to a point, and mildly flavoured cubanelles which are also tapered but lack the shoulders of the sheppard. Sweet banana peppers are pale yellow, tapered peppers with square shoulders at the stem. They can be very sweet and are good for salads and sandwiches.

Hot peppers (chili peppers) contain a higher amount of capsaicin, an alkaloid found in their veins and seeds. This powerful oil can burn the eyes and mouth if handled carelessly. Either wear disposable gloves when preparing hot peppers, or be sure to scrub your hands, knife and cutting board with hot, soapy water immediately afterward.

Most hot peppers don't grow well in our climate, but I have seen baskets of local jalapeño peppers in our farmers' market lately, as well as little, round, red cherry hot peppers. And many supermarkets import several varieties of hot peppers from elsewhere.

The most widely used hot pepper in the Caribbean is the scotch bonnet, a squashed little fellow which can be red, green, orange or yellow. Tiny bird's-eye peppers are usually less than 1 inch (2 ½ cm) long and add heat to Thai dishes.

Peppers are very high in vitamin C and if green peppers are allowed to turn red before picking, the vitamin C content is even greater. However, red peppers don't keep as long as green. In our northern climate, it is not always possible to have all peppers ripen in the garden, but I have known people to successfully take a plant (which has attractive foliage in itself) indoors and harvest red peppers at Christmas.

CHOOSING

Select peppers that are thick-fleshed, glossy and heavy for their size. They should be firm with no soft spots.

Two large or 4 small sweet peppers yield 4 servings.

STORING

Keep unwashed peppers in a plastic bag in the crisper up to 5 days. For longer storage, peppers freeze well (but lose their crunchy texture) and are one of the few vegetables that don't require blanching first. Prepare as

A B C D E F G H I J K L M N O P Q R S T U V W X Y Z

below, without peeling, and spread out in a single layer on a baking sheet. Freeze until firm, then store in a freezer bag; you can pick out as many as you need at one time for stews or sauces.

PREPARING

For sweet peppers, wash them well, cut in half and remove cores, seeds and membranes or ribs. For most recipes, peeling is not required, but peeled, roasted peppers give a finer texture to certain dishes, like soups and sauces (see below for roasting and peeling instructions).

COOKING

Sweet peppers are delicious sautéed, or stuffed and baked and are ideal for a crudité tray or raw in salads.

To roast peppers, place on a foil-lined baking sheet 4 inches (10 cm) from the hot broiler. Broil until blackened and blistered on all sides, about 15 minutes. Or place the peppers on a baking sheet and roast, turning occasionally, in a 500°F (260°C) oven, until evenly charred, about 20 minutes. Invert a large bowl over the peppers or seal in a paper bag. Let sit until cool enough to handle, about 10 minutes. Peel away the skin and remove the stem, seeds and membrane.

CORN-STUFFED PEPPERS

This interesting combination of summer vegetables would make a nice lunch with whole wheat rolls and a green salad. Well-shaped sweet peppers that stand upright are best for stuffing.

4 medium sweet green peppers
2 tbsp butter
1 small onion, chopped
1 stalk celery, finely chopped
2 eggs
¼ cup whipping cream (35% MF)
1 ½ cups shredded old cheddar cheese
1 cup cooked corn kernels
1 tsp finely chopped fresh thyme or ¼ tsp dried thyme leaves
⅛ tsp cayenne
Salt and freshly ground black pepper to taste
Paprika, as required

Preheat the oven to 350°F (180°C). Cut a slice from the stem end of each pepper and remove the seeds and membranes from the inside. Chop any flesh from the slice you cut, and set aside. In a large saucepan of boiling water, parboil the peppers for 3 minutes. Drain well.

In a small skillet, melt the butter over medium heat. Add the onion, celery and reserved chopped pepper and cook, stirring often, until the onion is transparent and begins to brown, about 5 minutes. Remove the skillet from the heat and set aside.

In a large bowl, lightly beat the eggs and cream together. Stir in the onion mixture, cheese, corn, thyme, cayenne and salt and pepper to taste.

Stuff the peppers with the cheese mixture, dividing evenly. Place the peppers, upright, in a shallow greased baking dish just large enough to hold them. Sprinkle the stuffing liberally with paprika. Bake until the stuffing is hot when a slim, sharp knife is inserted into one of the peppers, about 20 minutes.

Makes 4 servings

RED PEPPER SOUP

4 large sweet red peppers (2 lb/1 kg), roasted (see page 111)
1 tbsp butter
2 onions, chopped
1 cup water
2 cloves garlic, minced
5 cups chicken broth
2 tsp paprika
1 tsp granulated sugar
2 tbsp fresh lemon juice
¼ tsp cayenne
Salt and freshly ground black pepper to taste

If you wish, garnish small bowls of this pretty and intensely flavoured soup with garlic croutons or a little sour cream.

Working over a bowl, remove as much skin as possible from the peppers, reserving any juice but discarding the stems and seeds. Cut the peppers into 1-inch (2 ½ cm) strips.

In a large saucepan, melt the butter over medium-low heat. Add the onions and cook, stirring often, until softened but not browned, about 10 minutes. Add the peppers and their juices, water and garlic and cook, uncovered, for 10 minutes.

Stir in the broth, paprika and sugar. Bring to a boil over medium-high heat. Reduce the heat to medium-low and simmer, uncovered, for 20 minutes.

Use an immersion blender in the saucepan to blend the soup until smooth. Or purée the soup in batches in a countertop blender (a blender, rather than a food processor, makes a smoother soup). Strain the soup through a sieve, if you wish, or leave it unstrained for more texture.

Pour the soup back into the rinsed-out saucepan, if necessary. Stir in the lemon juice and cayenne, and season to taste with salt and pepper. (The soup can be prepared ahead. Refrigerate, covered, for up to 24 hours.)

When ready to serve, reheat the soup gently. Taste and adjust the seasoning, if necessary, before serving.

Makes 8 servings

RAINBOW PEPPER SALAD

2 tbsp olive oil
1 each, sweet red, yellow, orange and green pepper, seeded and cut into strips
3 cloves garlic, minced
1 to 2 tsp seeded and minced hot pepper, such as jalapeño
1 tbsp balsamic vinegar
Salt and freshly ground black pepper to taste

Don't overcook the peppers for this easy and colourful dish since they should still have a touch of crunch to them. Team the salad with grilled beef or lamb.

In a very large skillet, heat the oil over medium-high heat. Add the sweet peppers and cook, tossing constantly, until tender-crisp, 6 to 8 minutes.

Sprinkle the peppers with the garlic and hot pepper. Cook, stirring often, for 2 minutes.

Toss with the vinegar and salt and pepper to taste and serve hot or at room temperature.

Makes 6 servings

TAPENADE OF SWEET PEPPERS AND SUN-DRIED TOMATOES

1 cup dry-pack sun-dried tomatoes
3 sweet red peppers, roasted, stemmed, seeded and peeled (see page 111)
1 tbsp fruity olive oil
2 ripe tomatoes, peeled, stem ends removed and chopped
1 medium onion, chopped
3 to 4 cloves garlic, minced or crushed
1 tbsp finely chopped fresh oregano or 1 tsp dried oregano leaves
1 tbsp balsamic vinegar
2 tbsp anchovy paste (optional)
1 cup pitted black olives, finely chopped
½ cup finely chopped parsley
Salt and coarsely ground black pepper to taste

Tapenade is a Provençal condiment usually made with olives, capers and anchovies, but my friend Judy Shultz, a food and travel writer in Edmonton, adds sweet peppers and sun-dried tomatoes. Judy serves this as a spread for baguette toasts or a topping for a pizza. It would also be good added to a muffuletta sandwich.

Instead of roasting and peeling your own peppers, you can buy roasted peppers packed in oil, but be sure there are tiny bits of charred skin visible to show they have, indeed, been roasted.

In a small bowl, cover the sun-dried tomatoes with hot water and set aside for about 5 minutes. Drain well, then chop coarsely or snip into pieces with kitchen scissors. Cut the peppers into chunks.

In a large skillet, heat the oil over medium heat. Add the sun-dried tomatoes, peppers, tomatoes, onion and garlic and cook, stirring, for about 2 minutes.

Stir in the oregano and vinegar. Increase the heat to high and cook, stirring often, until most of the liquid has evaporated, about 5 minutes.

Remove the skillet from the heat and stir in the anchovy paste (if using). Let cool slightly. Spoon the tomato mixture into a food processor and pulse until a coarse purée forms.

Scrape the purée into a large bowl and stir in the olives, parsley and salt and pepper to taste.

Spoon into glass jars or airtight containers, cover and refrigerate for up to 2 weeks or freeze for longer storage.

Makes 3 cups

SEE ALSO:

Black Bean Chili	162
Corn Relish	60
Dilled Peppers	63
Gazpacho	148
Old-Fashioned Chili Sauce	146
Ratatouille	160
Ratatouille Gratin	160
Ratatouille Soup	76
Spicy Zucchini Relish	156
Sweet Potato Vichyssoise with Red Pepper Purée	135
Two-Cheese Baked Penne with Roasted Vegetables	159

POTATOES

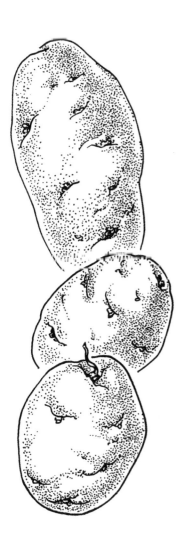

Potatoes are Canada's most important vegetable crop. There are fifty varieties grown here and, although each province boasts of producing tons of the vegetable each year, the Maritime provinces lead the way. New Brunswick and Prince Edward Island must receive special mention, for the great quantity produced in New Brunswick and for the research and development going on in Prince Edward Island. The Elite Seed Farm, owned by PEI's potato producers, is the sole source of disease-free seed for the island and an important source of seed for export to other parts of the world.

Since it first travelled from Peru to Europe in the sixteenth century, the potato has been a staple in many other countries, too. The tuber has played a prominent role in Canada since it was first cultivated in Port Royal, Nova Scotia, in 1623.

In her 1836 book *The Backwoods of Canada*, the author Catharine Parr Traill wrote, "The 'potatoe' is indeed a great blessing here; new settlers would otherwise be often greatly distressed, and the poor man and his family who are without resources, without the 'potatoe' must starve."

Pioneers planted them as soon as they could and relied on them as more than a vegetable. Potatoes were used to make yeast for bread, mixed with flour to save money, and starch squeezed from their pulp even found its way into the family laundry. They were used to sooth headaches, and small pieces of raw potato made good corks for bottles. Even in French Canada, where potatoes were at first referred to disparagingly as "roots," and eaten only when times were desperate, they gradually started showing up at every meal.

Potatoes contribute a great deal to our daily diet. They contain a large amount of vitamin C, iron and many of the B vitamins, but contain no fat and only 100 calories per medium potato.

CHOOSING

Buy firm, clean graded potatoes that are free from cuts or bruises, well shaped and with shallow eyes. Avoid any green potatoes. Although each variety of potato lends itself to a specific cooking method, the variety is not always noted on the bag.

Kennebecs, Netted Gems or other elongated potatoes are good for baking, mashing and deep-frying.

For potato salad (see Old-Fashioned Potato Salad, page 115), waxy potatoes are best. Choose any shape, red or white, when they are new, but with older potatoes, pick the round red varieties since they hold their shape when boiled, are moist and not as starchy as long potatoes.

The Yukon Gold, developed in Canada, is an all-purpose potato with yellowish flesh and skin, a medium-dry, firm texture and buttery flavour.

Other exotic varieties are Purple Viking or Peruvian Purple that are all-purpose and, as their names suggest, purple. Fingerlings are the size and shape of fingers with a sweet flavour and crisp texture, are best cooked whole and unpeeled and are particularly good roasted.

One to 1 ¼ pounds (500 to 625 g) of potatoes yield 4 servings.

STORING

New or early potatoes do not store well. Buy only in small amounts and handle them gently. Store later varieties for up to 1 month in a cool (about 50°F/10°C), dark place with good air circulation. Do not refrigerate since this affects the potatoes' flavour. Do not store with onions since they give off a gas that will spoil potatoes.

Potatoes do not freeze well if baked or boiled. Water- or oil-blanched potatoes, however, can be frozen for deep-frying.

PREPARING

When necessary, peel just before cooking, dropping the potatoes into cold water as you work so they don't darken. Whenever possible, cook potatoes in their skins so they retain most of their nutrients.

If kept in cold storage, transfer potatoes to room temperature a day or two before cooking. Scrub, then cut away any green or damaged sections. Except when making fries (see Crisp Deep-Fried Potatoes, page 116), avoid soaking uncooked potatoes in water.

COOKING

To boil potatoes, cook them in a small amount of boiling water in a covered saucepan until tender, about 20 minutes (the time will depend on the size of the pieces of potato, the variety used and whether the potatoes are "new" or stored, older ones). Drain immediately. Steaming will take slightly longer.

If serving the potatoes mashed, mash them or pass through a potato ricer while they're still warm, then whisk in butter, milk or cream and seasonings. Don't use a food processor to purée potatoes since the heat it produces will cause the potatoes to be gluey.

Roasting is another good method, especially if you arrange the potatoes around meat to be roasted. Turn the potatoes often to brown them; they should cook in about 1 hour. You can parboil the potatoes first to reduce the roasting time.

Pan-frying in oil is a quick, easy method. Boiled potatoes are delicious pan-fried in butter or deep-fried in oil. And see also the recipe for Baked Potatoes (page 117).

OLD-FASHIONED POTATO SALAD

2 ½ lb (1 ¼ kg) potatoes (6 to 8), peeled and quartered

2 tbsp white wine vinegar

1 tsp granulated sugar

Salt and freshly ground black pepper to taste

3 hard-cooked eggs, shelled and chopped

8 large radishes, sliced

½ cup drained, chopped dill pickle

4 green onions, sliced

¼ cup diced celery

¾ cup light mayonnaise

¼ cup low-fat sour cream

1 tbsp Dijon mustard

⅛ tsp cayenne

I could make a whole meal of this potato salad, but it does go awfully well with ribs or barbecued chicken, too.

In a saucepan of boiling, salted water, cook the potatoes until tender, about 20 minutes. Drain well and chop coarsely.

Place the potatoes in a large bowl and, while they're still hot, add the vinegar, sugar and salt and pepper to taste. Toss well. Add the eggs, radishes, dill pickle, green onions and celery. Toss gently.

In a small bowl, whisk together the mayonnaise, sour cream, Dijon mustard and cayenne. Add the mayonnaise mixture to the potato salad and stir gently to coat well. Taste and add more salt and pepper if necessary. Serve immediately, or refrigerate for up to 8 hours. If refrigerated, let stand at room temperature for 30 minutes before serving.

Makes 6 servings

BAKED GERMAN POTATO SALAD

16 small red potatoes, scrubbed but not peeled

4 oz (125 g) side bacon, diced (about 1 cup)

2 stalks celery, sliced

1 onion, chopped

2 tbsp all-purpose flour

½ tsp dry mustard

Salt and freshly ground black pepper to taste

½ cup cider vinegar

⅓ cup granulated sugar

1 cup water

¼ cup finely chopped parsley

A version of this robust hot salad is often found in older cookbooks written in the Waterloo, Ontario, region where I live. This is how one of those authors, Edna Staebler, described the area's salad: "If you have ever tasted the warm, buttery yellow potato salad made in Waterloo County you'll never again be satisfied with the stiff white blobs they (sometimes) call potato salad everywhere else." Edna's dressing was made with butter, sour cream and raw eggs. My version is lighter in calories but I do like to add some side bacon for extra flavour.

In a saucepan of boiling, salted water, cook the potatoes until barely tender when pierced with the tip of a knife (do not overcook). Drain well. When cool enough to handle, peel the potatoes and cut into ¼-inch (6 mm) slices. Place the potato slices in a greased, shallow, 8-cup (2 L) baking dish.

In a large skillet over medium heat, fry the bacon until crisp. Remove with a slotted spoon and drain on paper towels.

Add the celery and onion to the fat remaining in the skillet and cook over medium heat for 3 minutes. Stir in the flour, mustard and salt and pepper to taste. Cook, stirring, for 2 minutes.

Stir in the vinegar, sugar, then the water all at once. Bring to a boil, stirring constantly, and cook for 1 minute. Stir in the parsley and bacon.

Pour the bacon mixture over the potatoes and toss gently to coat. (The potatoes can be prepared to this point, covered and refrigerated for up to 6 hours. Remove from the refrigerator 30 minutes before baking.)

When ready to bake, preheat the oven to 375°F (190°C). Bake the potatoes, uncovered, until bubbly, about 45 minutes. Serve hot or warm.

Makes 6 servings

WHIPPED POTATO CASSEROLE

10 to 12 medium potatoes, peeled

¼ cup butter

1 pkg (250 g) brick cream cheese, cubed

1 cup sour cream

Salt and freshly ground black pepper to taste

¼ cup fine, fresh bread crumbs

¼ cup finely chopped parsley

2 tbsp butter, melted

This make-ahead mashed potato casserole is a traditional Christmas side dish in our family. If you wish, use light cream cheese and low-fat sour cream.

Cook the potatoes in boiling, salted water in a covered saucepan until tender, 20 to 30 minutes. Drain well, return to the saucepan and place over low heat briefly to dry the potatoes.

Mash the potatoes with the butter. Add the cream cheese, sour cream and salt and pepper to taste. Beat until creamy. Spoon the mashed potatoes into a greased, 8-cup (2 L) baking dish.

In a small bowl, stir together the bread crumbs, parsley and butter. Sprinkle evenly over the potatoes. (Potatoes can be prepared to this point, cooled, covered tightly and refrigerated for up to 2 days. Remove from the refrigerator 30 minutes before reheating.)

When ready to bake preheat the oven to 350°F (180°C). Bake the potatoes, covered, for 20 minutes. Uncover and bake until hot throughout, about 10 minutes.

Makes 10 servings

PÂTÉ AUX PATATES

4 medium potatoes (about 1 lb/500 g)

6 medium onions (about 1 lb/500 g)

1 cup shredded Gruyère cheese (about 4 oz/125 g)

¼ cup butter

⅓ cup milk, divided

¼ tsp dried savory leaves

Salt and freshly ground black pepper to taste

Pastry for a double-crust 9-inch (23 cm) pie

This potato, cheese and onion pie is traditionally served in Quebec at Christmas time. DuBarry Campeau, a Canadian broadcaster, sent me the idea.

Peel the potatoes and onions, then cut them into quarters. In a large saucepan of boiling, salted water, cook the potatoes for 15 minutes. Add the onions and cook until the potatoes and onions are tender, 15 to 20 minutes. Drain well and mash until fairly smooth. Stir in the cheese, butter, ¼ cup of the milk, the savory and salt and pepper to taste.

Preheat the oven to 425°F (220°C). Roll out half the pastry and use to line a greased 9-inch (23 cm) pie plate. Spoon the vegetable mixture into the pie. Roll out the remaining pastry and cover the pie, sealing and fluting the edge. Cut several slits in the top of the pie to allow the steam to escape. Brush the top of the pie with the remaining milk.

Bake the pie in the bottom third of the oven for 10 minutes. Reduce the heat to 350°F (180°C) and bake until the pie is golden brown, 30 to 35 minutes. Serve hot or warm.

Makes 6 to 8 servings

BAKED POTATOES

4 medium long potatoes
¼ cup butter
½ tsp coarse salt

This method of baking produces a tender, crisp skin and sweet, fluffy interior, which is far superior to potatoes baked in foil. Serve the potatoes hot with butter, salt and pepper. Plain yogurt or sour cream also make delicious toppings.

Preheat the oven to 425°F (220°C). Scrub the potatoes clean under cold, running water. Dry well, then prick two or three times with a fork or sharp knife.

In a shallow roasting pan just large enough to hold the potatoes, melt the butter over medium heat. Place the potatoes in the pan, rolling to coat them with the butter. Sprinkle with salt.

Bake, uncovered and turning once, until tender, about 1 hour or more, depending on the size and variety of the potatoes.

Makes 4 servings

SPEEDIER BAKED POTATOES
To bake potatoes in half the time, start them in a microwave oven. Prick as for the recipe for Baked Potatoes, then microwave them on high for 2 minutes per potato. Let them stand for 15 minutes, then bake as above for just 30 minutes.

CRISP POTATO SKINS
For a tasty snack, cut the leftover skins of baked potatoes into 1 inch (2 ½ cm) strips and place them on a baking sheet. Brush generously with butter, sprinkle with salt to taste. Bake in a 475°F (240°C) oven until crisp, about 8 minutes.

COLCANNON

5 medium potatoes (1 ¼ lb/625 g), peeled and cut into large pieces
½ small rutabaga (1 ¼ lb/625 g), peeled and cut into large pieces
½ small head cabbage (1 ¼ lb/625 g), coarsely shredded
1 leek (white and pale green parts only), cleaned and coarsely chopped, or 1 small onion, coarsely chopped
⅓ cup butter
⅛ tsp ground mace
Salt and freshly ground black pepper to taste

Kohl cannon, call cannon, caulcannon: there are almost as many versions of this hearty dish as there are spellings of its name. A favourite of Irish, German and Scottish settlers in Newfoundland and the Maritimes, it was customarily eaten for the first time each year on Halloween.

In a large saucepan, cook the potatoes and rutabaga in a small amount of boiling, salted water until almost tender, 10 to 20 minutes. Add the cabbage and leek and cook until tender, about 10 minutes.

Drain the vegetables well in a colander. Return to the saucepan and mash well. Stir in the butter, mace and salt and pepper to taste. Spoon into a warm serving dish.

Makes about 6 servings

CRISP DEEP-FRIED POTATOES

6 to 8 medium potatoes
Ice water
Oil for deep-frying
Salt to taste

Soaking raw fries in ice water removes the excess starch that would otherwise absorb the oil and make the fries soggy. The double-frying method not only ensures crispness, but is convenient for serving since you can cook the fries partially ahead. For the best fries, use only older, baking potatoes.

Peel the potatoes and cut into ¼- x ¼-inch (6 x 6 mm) lengths, dropping the pieces into a bowl of ice water as you work. Set the potatoes aside to soak until you are ready to cook them. Just before cooking, drain the potatoes well, spread out on a tea towel and pat dry thoroughly.

Pour enough oil into a deep-fryer or large pot to come to 3 to 4 inches (8 to 10 cm) up the sides. For the first frying, heat the oil until the deep-fryer or a candy thermometer registers 370°F (188°C). Place the potatoes, only a few at a time, in the frying basket and immerse in the hot oil. Fry until any sputtering stops and the potatoes are a pale golden brown, about 2 minutes. Remove the potatoes from the hot oil and drain well on a double thickness of paper towel. The potatoes can sit at room temperature for up to 1 hour before refrying and serving.

Just before serving, reheat the oil until the deep-fryer or a candy thermometer registers 385°F (196°C). Fry the potatoes until they are crisp and brown, about 1 minute. (The cooking time depends on the size of the strips and the variety of potato. Watch carefully and go more by appearance than time.)

Drain the fries well on paper towels and transfer to a heated serving dish. Sprinkle with salt to taste and serve at once.

Makes 4 to 6 servings

GERMAN POTATO CAKE

4 cups peeled, grated potatoes (3 to 4 large potatoes)

3 eggs
1 small onion, grated
¼ cup all-purpose flour
¼ cup canola oil
½ tsp baking powder
½ tsp salt
¼ tsp freshly ground black pepper
¼ tsp freshly grated nutmeg

Known as potato kugel in its native Germany, this hearty dish is delicious with sausage and warm applesauce.

Preheat the oven to 350°F (180°C). Wrap the potatoes in a clean tea towel and twist to wring out the moisture. Set aside.

In a large bowl, beat the eggs until thick and light. Add the potatoes and onion to the eggs.

Stir in the flour, oil, baking powder, salt, pepper and nutmeg. Scrape the potato mixture into a greased 4- to 6-cup (1 to 1 ½ L) baking dish. Bake, uncovered, until golden brown, about 1 hour. Serve at once.

Makes 6 servings

NEW POTATOES ROASTED WITH OLIVE OIL AND GARLIC

12 small new potatoes (about 2 lb/1 kg), unpeeled

4 cloves garlic, crushed

2 tbsp olive oil

2 tsp finely chopped fresh rosemary or thyme or ½ tsp dried rosemary or thyme leaves

1 tsp paprika

Salt and freshly ground black pepper to taste

When I can buy waxy little new potatoes at my local farmers' market, I love to toss them with olive oil, garlic and herbs, then roast them until they're tender inside and crusty on the outside.

Preheat the oven to 375°F (190°C). Scrub the potatoes and dry them well. In a small roasting pan, toss together the potatoes, garlic, oil, rosemary and paprika.

Roast, covered and stirring occasionally, until tender, 30 to 40 minutes. Season to taste with salt and pepper before serving.

Makes about 4 servings

PUMPKIN

The pumpkin is a winter squash native to North America. Long a staple of Canada's First Nations, settlers followed their example and grew pumpkins in their cornfields, then sliced and dried them to keep over the winter.

In Canada, we are more apt to use this member of the squash family just as a jack-o'-lantern or in desserts, although it is considered a vegetable elsewhere in the world, and makes a wonderful, creamy soup.

CHOOSING

Buy pumpkins with hard, blemish-free, bright-coloured rind. Look for those that are heavy for their size. Small, sweet pie pumpkins are best for pie since they don't have the sinewy, stringy flesh of the big Halloween pumpkins. Calabazas or Jamaican pumpkins (with green-grey rinds) also have fine-textured, sweet, moist bright orange flesh that's fine for pies and soup. You can substitute puréed pumpkin for squash in any soup.

One pound (500 g) of pumpkin yields 2 cups of cooked pumpkin purée.

STORING

Wash pumpkins well, especially the side that rested on the ground. Dry thoroughly and store in a single layer in a dry, cool place.

Cooked pumpkin freezes well.

PREPARING

Peel the pumpkin, discard the seeds and cut into large pieces.

COOKING

Steam pumpkin pieces for 15 to 20 minutes. Drain well and purée in a blender or food processor until smooth. Or cut a pie pumpkin in half lengthwise, dig out the seeds and any stringy pulp, then place cut sides down on a parchment-paper-lined baking sheet and bake in a 400°F (200°C) oven for 40 to 60 minutes.

1 cup canned evaporated milk

3 eggs, separated

¾ cup firmly packed brown sugar

¼ tsp salt

¼ cup brandy

1 ½ cups cooked pumpkin purée (not pie filling; 12 oz/375 g raw pumpkin)

1 tsp cinnamon

½ tsp ground ginger

¼ tsp ground cloves

⅛ tsp freshly grated nutmeg

One 10-inch (25 cm) unbaked pie shell

GARNISH

½ cup whipping cream (35% MF)

1 tbsp icing sugar

1 tbsp brandy

1 tbsp slivered candied ginger

BRANDIED PUMPKIN PIE

Canada's United Empire Loyalists were the first to come up with the idea for pumpkin pie. This recipe, with its touch of candied ginger, makes a nice big pie for a family dinner. The alcohol in the brandy added to the pie itself will bake off in the oven, but omit the brandy in the garnish if there are kids around your Thanksgiving table.

Preheat the oven to 425°F (220°C). Scald the milk in the top of a double boiler or in a stainless steel bowl over a saucepan of simmering water.

In a small bowl, beat the egg yolks lightly. Pour the hot milk into the yolks, stirring constantly. Blend in the brown sugar and salt. Return the mixture to the top of the double boiler. Cook over simmering water, stirring constantly, until the mixture coats a spoon, about 4 minutes. Remove from the heat and stir in the brandy.

In a medium bowl, stir together the pumpkin, cinnamon, ginger, cloves and nutmeg. Fold the pumpkin mixture into the milk mixture, blending until smooth.

In a separate clean bowl, beat the egg whites until stiff but still moist. Fold the egg whites into the pumpkin mixture.

Pour the pumpkin mixture into the pie shell. Bake in the bottom third of the oven for 15 minutes. Reduce the temperature to 350°F (180°C) and bake until the filling is set, 30 to 35 minutes. Let cool on a wire rack.

Just before serving, make the garnish. In a chilled bowl, whip the cream until it starts to thicken. Add the icing sugar and continue whipping until the cream is thick and fairly stiff. Whip in the brandy.

Pipe the cream decoratively around the edge of the cooled pie and garnish with ginger slivers. Or spoon the whipped cream onto each serving and scatter with candied ginger.

Makes 8 servings

BRANDIED CARROT PIE
Substitute 1 ½ cups cooked carrot purée for the pumpkin.

BRANDIED SQUASH PIE
Substitute 1 ½ cups cooked winter squash purée for the pumpkin.

BRANDIED RUTABAGA PIE
Substitute 1 ½ cups cooked rutabaga purée for the pumpkin, and increase the brown sugar to 1 cup.

CARAMELIZED ONION AND PUMPKIN VARENYKY

FILLING

1 large onion

2 tbsp olive oil

½ tsp salt

1 ½ cups cooked pumpkin purée (not pie filling;
   12 oz/375 g raw pumpkin)

¾ tsp crumbled dried sage

½ tsp each, dried thyme leaves and freshly
   ground black pepper

DOUGH

2 cups all-purpose flour

1 tsp salt

1 egg

½ cup cold water (approx.)

1 tbsp canola oil

These filled dumplings—called varenyky by Ukrainians, perogies by the Polish—came to Canada with European settlers and are still made by their descendants, many of whom live on the Prairies or in Thunder Bay, Ontario. Fillings might include mushrooms, potato and cheese, sauerkraut, cabbage or even fruit, like plums or blueberries. My friend Sharon Boyd, who is of Ukrainian descent, and I experimented with this new idea for a filling and everyone loved it.

For the filling, cut the onion in half and slice each half thinly. In a large skillet, heat the oil over medium heat. Add the onion and salt, stirring to coat the onion well with the oil. Cook, covered, until softened, about 5 minutes. Uncover, reduce the heat to medium-low and cook, stirring often, until the onion is well browned, about 20 minutes.

Meanwhile, place the pumpkin in a sieve and drain well, especially if you're using fresh pumpkin purée.

Add the pumpkin to the onions, along with the sage, thyme, pepper and more salt, if necessary. Cook over medium heat, stirring often, until any liquid evaporates, about 5 minutes. Remove the skillet from the heat and let cool.

For the dough, whisk the flour and salt together in a deep bowl. In a small bowl, beat the egg with a fork and stir in the water and oil.

Add the egg mixture to the flour mixture and stir gently to make a soft dough. (You may need a few more drops of water but do not make the dough sticky.)

On a lightly floured counter, knead the dough only until smooth (too much kneading will toughen it). Divide the dough in half, cover and let rest for 10 minutes.

Keeping the remaining dough covered to prevent it drying out, roll out half the dough very thinly on a lightly floured counter. Cut rounds with a 3-inch (8 cm) cookie cutter or the rim of a drinking glass. Place a scant teaspoonful of the filling on each round. Stretch the dough slightly and fold over to form a half-circle, pressing the edges together with your fingers. (The edges should be free of any filling so they will seal properly.)

As you fill the dumplings, place them in a single layer on a tea-towel-lined baking sheet and cover with another tea towel. Do not crowd the dumplings to prevent them sticking together. Repeat with the remaining dough and filling. (Cover any scraps of dough and let rest for 10 minutes before rerolling.)

Bring a large pot of salted water to a rapid boil. Cook the dumplings, a few at a time, in the boiling water. The dumplings will float to the top when they are cooked, about 2 minutes, depending on thickness of dough. (The dumplings can be made ahead and frozen uncooked. Cook them straight from the freezer as above.)

Makes 36 dumplings

PUMPKIN BRÛLÉES

2 cups whipping cream (35% MF)

5 egg yolks

⅓ cup granulated sugar

¾ cup thick pumpkin purée (not pie filling; about 6 oz/175 g raw pumpkin)

½ tsp cinnamon

⅛ tsp salt

2 tsp vanilla

½ cup packed brown sugar

The finale to many fall suppers is often a smooth, rich pumpkin pie. Here, I've used all the same flavours in easy brûlées. Serve the ramekins on dessert plates alongside small bunches of grapes or a crisp cookie. Be sure to start the recipe at least 8 hours before serving. If you use canned pumpkin purée for this recipe, spoon the rest of the can into an airtight container and freeze it for up to 3 months.

Preheat the oven to 325°F (160°C). In a small, heavy saucepan, heat the cream over medium-high heat just until tiny bubbles appear around the edge. Remove the saucepan from the heat.

In a large bowl, whisk together the egg yolks and granulated sugar until just combined. Stir in the pumpkin purée, cinnamon and salt. Slowly whisk in the hot cream, then stir in the vanilla.

Pour the mixture into eight ½-cup (125 mL) ramekins or custard cups. Place the ramekins in a metal baking pan just large enough to hold them, then pour hot water into the pan to come two-thirds of the way up the sides of ramekins. Cover the pan with foil.

Bake until the custards are just set but the centres still jiggle, 25 to 30 minutes (do not overcook). Remove ramekins to a wire rack and let cool. Refrigerate, covered, for at least 6 hours or up to 2 days, until very cold.

One to 2 hours before serving, place the ramekins on a baking sheet. Sieve the brown sugar to remove any lumps, then sprinkle the sugar evenly over custards. Broil as close as possible to the element of a preheated broiler until the sugar caramelizes, 2 to 3 minutes. (Alternatively, you can caramelize the sugar with a small blowtorch made for kitchen use.) Let cool and serve within 2 hours.

Makes 8 servings

RADISHES

Radishes were cultivated in Europe as long ago as pre-Roman times. It is believed they were part of the daily diet of the slaves building the pyramids in Egypt. Today radishes are a popular vegetable grown throughout the world.

Many varieties of radish are available in Canada. The small, round Red Globe radish, sometimes called Cherry Belle, is the most common in Canada. White Icicles are milder-tasting, long, tapered radishes. French Breakfast are elongated with red shoulders and a white tip, and also milder than Red Globes. The black Spanish radish has white flesh and is the spiciest radishes available here. Native to Asia, daikon radishes are large, carrot-shaped radishes with juicier, hotter flesh than Red Globes, although they're not as pungent as Black Spanish.

Also, look for colourful varieties like Watermelon and red, pink, white or purple Easter Egg radishes that are similar in taste and texture to Red Globe.

With only 23 calories per 1 cup of sliced raw radishes, they're low in calories and, despite their crunchiness, low in fibre. Radishes are high in vitamin C and a source of folate and potassium.

CHOOSING

When buying red radishes, skip the prebagged ones and select bunches with perky looking green leaves. The radishes should be firm and brightly coloured with smooth, unblemished surfaces. Choose smaller radishes since larger ones might be pithy. Daikon radishes should be well shaped, firm and glossy.

ONE LARGE BUNCH OF RED RADISHES YIELDS ABOUT 4 SERVINGS. STORING

Radish tops, like carrot tops, draw nutrients and moisture from the roots so remove the tops as soon as possible, but reserve the tops if they're fresh-looking as they're good in salads and can be cooked (see below). Keep radishes in a perforated plastic bag in the crisper; most will keep for a week or two. Radishes don't freeze well.

PREPARING

Trim off the stem and root ends, then scrub radishes well and dry thoroughly before storing or cooking. If you wish to serve them raw with butter and salt (see below) or a dip of some kind, leave on the root end and a little of the top to use as a handle, cleaning around this with the tip of a paring knife.

COOKING

More commonly eaten raw as crunchy salad vegetables, radishes are also delicious lightly steamed or sautéed.

The French let raw radishes be the star in snacks and appetizers, serving sliced red radishes on crusty bread lavishly spread with cold unsalted butter, or dipping whole red radishes in softened unsalted butter and coarse salt.

For a quick appetizer, cut large red radishes in half lengthwise and spread the cut sides with soft goat cheese, then sprinkle with toasted cumin seeds and arrange on a platter of radish leaves.

If your radish tops are fresh and unblemished, they're good added to salads or sautéed or steamed just enough to wilt them.

MARLEN CHASE'S SMOKED SALMON AND RADISH SPREAD

¾ cup sour cream
½ cup low-fat pressed cottage cheese
½ cup softened cream cheese
Salt and freshly ground black pepper to taste
4 oz (125 g) smoked salmon, finely chopped
½ cup finely chopped red radishes
⅓ cup finely chopped red onion
2 tbsp chopped chives

My friend, the food writer and gallery owner Andrew Chase, has always loved radishes. Perhaps it was this delicious spread of his mother's that first hooked him. Enjoy this as a spread on baguette slices, spoon it onto endive leaves, or use to fill tiny tart shells like those made by Siljans.

In a medium bowl, beat together the sour cream, cottage cheese, cream cheese, and salt and pepper to taste until smooth.
Stir in the salmon, radishes, red onion and chives.

Makes about 2 ½ cups; 8 to 10 servings

RADISH AND CHEESE SALAD

8 large red radishes with leaves
1 large shallot, thinly sliced
3 tbsp olive oil
1 tbsp each, fresh lemon juice and red wine vinegar
2 tsp liquid honey
Salt and freshly ground black pepper to taste
4 oz (125 g) burrata, torn into pieces

Radishes were so adored by the ancient Romans that golden replicas of them were offered to the sun god Apollo. This salad is certainly pretty enough to offer to a god. Burrata is a fresh Italian cheese made with mozzarella and cream. If you can't find it, substitute bocconcini.

Cut the stem and root ends from the radishes, reserving the best leaves. Wash and dry the leaves well and set aside. Thinly slice the radishes and place in a medium bowl. Add the shallot.
In a small bowl, whisk together the olive oil, lemon juice, vinegar, honey,and salt and pepper to taste. Pour the oil mixture over the radish mixture and toss to coat well. Let stand at room temperature for 30 minutes.
To serve, arrange the radish leaves in a circle on a platter. Mound the radish mixture on top and scatter with the cheese.

Makes 4 servings

HOT BUTTERED RADISHES

1 large bunch red radishes (about 12 oz/375 g), trimmed)

Fresh, unblemished radish leaves (optional)

1 tbsp each, butter and olive oil

2 tbsp packed brown sugar

2 tbsp cider vinegar

Salt and freshly ground black pepper to taste

This easy skillet side dish illustrates how delicious cooked radishes can be. Serve alongside grilled or pan-fried lamb or pork chops.

Cut the stem and root ends from the radishes. Cut the radishes in half (or in quarters if very large). Wash radish leaves and set aside (if using).

In a large skillet, melt the butter with the oil over medium heat. Add the radishes and cook, tossing occasionally, until the white sides start to colour, 8 to 10 minutes.

Add the sugar and toss to coat the radishes. Averting your face (the vinegar will sizzle), add the vinegar and salt and pepper to taste.

Cook, shaking the skillet, until the radishes are glazed. Add the radish leaves (if using) and cook, stirring, until wilted.

Makes 4 servings

SPINACH

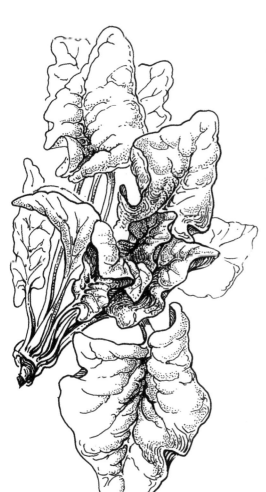

Developed by Persians in the sixth century, spinach found its way soon after to China, later to Europe and sometime early in the nineteenth century to Canada when it was, strangely enough, considered a cure for insomnia.

Properly cooked, spinach can be one of the most delicious and versatile of our leafy vegetables. It is a good source of vitamins A and C, calcium, iron, potassium and other minerals.

CHOOSING

Look for dark green, fresh-looking, crisp, whole leaves.

About 2 ½ pounds (1 ¼ kg) of fresh spinach yield 4 servings (the leaves reduce dramatically in volume when cooked).

STORING

If you buy a 10-ounce (284 g) package of spinach, open the bag and remove any damaged leaves before storing. Bunched spinach is usually cheaper and fresher. Baby spinach packaged in a clamshell is good for salads but tends to be more expensive. Store fresh spinach in a plastic bag in the crisper for up to 4 days.

To freeze spinach, blanch it for 2 minutes then drain well.

PREPARING

Separate a bunch of spinach, trim off the roots and place the leaves in a sink of lukewarm water. Remove and repeat with a sink of cold water. Very sandy spinach might need several washings, but spinach from a bag should require only one. Baby spinach packaged in a clamshell is usually prewashed.

Check all leaves carefully. Remove any coarse stems by folding the leaf in half lengthwise, with the stem on the outside, then ripping off the stem. This is important if you are using the spinach raw in a salad.

COOKING

Place washed spinach in a heavy, stainless steel saucepan and cook, covered, with just the water clinging to its leaves after washing. Cook just until wilted, 2 to 5 minutes. Drain well in a sieve. Butter, lemon juice or vinegar, and salt and pepper are good seasonings. Freshly grated nutmeg also helps to bring out the flavour of cooked spinach.

Steaming takes longer, the time depending on the amount of spinach being cooked. Sautéing is another excellent method of cooking (see Sautéed Spinach, page 129).

A B C D E F G H I J K L M N O P Q R S T U V W X Y Z

SPINACH VICHYSSOISE

¼ cup butter

2 cups sliced leeks (white parts only of 3 large leeks)

¼ cup finely chopped celery and leaves

2 cloves garlic, minced

5 cups chicken broth

4 cups sliced, peeled potatoes (4 medium)

2 tbsp fresh lemon juice

Salt and freshly ground white pepper to taste

1 lb (500 g) fresh spinach

2 cups half-and-half cream (10% MF) or table cream (18% MF)

Thin lemon slices for garnish

About ten years ago my daughter Anne Loxton told me she had a delicious soup at an Easter dinner party in Bermuda. When she said her hostess told her it was from *The Recipes Only Cookbook*, published in 1989, I realized it was my recipe and felt happy people were still enjoying my fresh-tasting twist on a classic.

In a large saucepan, melt the butter over medium heat. Add the leeks, celery and garlic. Reduce the heat to low and cook, stirring often, until softened but not brown, about 20 minutes.

Stir in the broth, potatoes, lemon juice, and salt and pepper to taste. Bring to a boil over medium-high heat. Reduce the heat to medium-low and simmer, covered, until the potatoes can be pierced easily with a fork, about 10 minutes.

Stir in spinach. Bring back to a boil and simmer for 5 minutes.

Use an immersion blender in the saucepan to blend the soup until smooth. Or purée the soup in batches in a countertop blender (a blender, rather than a food processor, makes a smoother soup).

Pour into a large bowl and let cool. Stir in the cream and add more salt, white pepper and lemon juice to taste, if necessary. Cover and refrigerate for several hours or overnight.

After chilling, taste and adjust seasoning again, if necessary. If the soup is too thick, stir in a little more cream or broth. Serve in chilled bowls or glasses and float thin slices of lemon on each serving

Makes 8 to 10 servings

SPINACH CAESAR

3 tbsp light mayonnaise

2 tbsp fresh lemon juice

2 cloves garlic, minced

2 tsp Dijon mustard

2 tsp anchovy paste

½ tsp Worcestershire sauce

Salt and freshly ground black pepper to taste

3 tbsp olive oil

⅓ cup freshly grated Parmesan cheese

8 cups lightly packed baby spinach

4 slices bacon, cooked until crisp, then crumbled

½ cup toasted pine nuts or slivered almonds (see page 16)

I created this tasty variation on an old-favourite for *Homemaker's Magazine*. Baby spinach costs a bit more than regular spinach, but it's worth it. If using regular spinach, wash and drain it well, remove any larger stems and tear the leaves into bite-sized pieces. If you wish, you can reduce the saturated fat in the salad by replacing the bacon with ¼ cup finely chopped sun-dried tomatoes.

In a small bowl, whisk together the mayonnaise, lemon juice, garlic, mustard, anchovy paste, Worcestershire sauce, and salt and pepper to taste. Gradually whisk in the oil. Stir in the cheese. Season to taste with more salt and pepper, if necessary.

In a large bowl, toss the spinach with half of the bacon and half of the pine nuts.

Toss the salad with just enough dressing to coat the spinach (Leftover dressing can be covered and refrigerated for several days.) Sprinkle with the remaining bacon and pine nuts.

Makes 6 to 8 servings

SPINACH QUICHE

One 10-inch (25 cm) unbaked pie shell

2 tbsp butter

1 small onion, chopped

½ cup sliced mushrooms

1 large clove garlic, minced

1 pkg (10 oz/284 g) fresh spinach, tough stems removed and leaves washed, or 1 pkg (300 g) frozen spinach

3 eggs

1 ½ cups shredded old cheddar cheese

1 cup milk

1 tbsp finely chopped fresh basil or 1 tsp dried basil leaves

½ tsp celery salt

1 tbsp dry bread crumbs

1 tbsp freshly grated Parmesan cheese

1 tbsp melted butter

The combination of spinach and mushrooms is a winning one for a quiche filling. Serve with tomato salad and French bread.

Preheat the oven to 400°F (200°C). Prick the bottom of the pie shell all over with a fork. Press a piece of foil or parchment paper into the pie shell and fill with uncooked dry white beans or rice. Bake in the bottom third of the oven until the edges of the pastry are pale golden, 15 minutes. Reduce the oven temperature to 375°F (190°C).

Remove the beans and foil and prick the pie shell all over with a fork. Return to the bottom third of the oven and bake until the pastry is pale golden, about 15 minutes. Let cool. Leave the oven on.

In a small skillet melt the butter over medium heat. Add the onion, mushrooms and garlic and sauté until softened, about 5 minutes.

Meanwhile, place the fresh spinach in a heavy, stainless steel saucepan and cook, covered, with just the water clinging to its leaves after washing. Cook just until wilted, 2 to 5 minutes. Drain well and chop. If using frozen spinach, cook it according to the instructions on the package. Drain well.

In a large bowl, beat eggs. Stir in the mushroom mixture, cooked spinach, cheese, milk, basil, and celery salt. Pour the egg mixture into the baked pie shell. Bake in the bottom third of the oven until the filling is almost set, about 20 minutes.

In a small bowl, stir together the bread crumbs, Parmesan cheese and melted butter. Sprinkle the crumb mixture evenly over the top of the quiche. Bake until lightly browned on top, 5 to 10 minutes. (The quiche can be kept warm in the switched-off oven for 10 minutes or more.)

Makes 6 servings

SAUTÉED SPINACH

2 tbsp olive or canola oil

1 pkg (10 oz/284 g) fresh spinach, chopped

2 tbsp dry sherry

1 large clove garlic, minced

Salt and freshly ground black pepper to taste

This quick way with spinach tastes great and prevents the spinach from being watery.

In a large skillet, heat the oil over medium heat. Add the spinach, sherry and garlic and sauté until the spinach is tender and well-flavoured with garlic, about 6 minutes. Season to taste with salt and pepper.

Makes 3 to 4 servings

SEE ALSO:
Vegetable Strudel 161

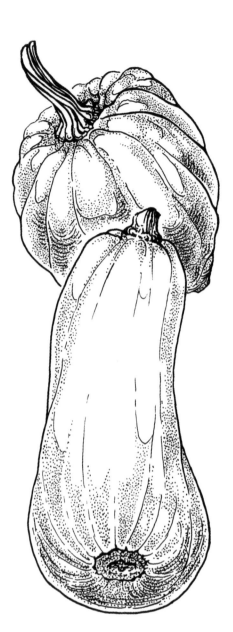

SQUASH

Native to North America, squash are members of the cucurbitaceae group, which includes cucumbers, summer squash (see pages 62 and 153), winter squash, watermelons, gourds and pumpkins (see page 120), a family of vegetables—fruits, really—in a multitude of shapes and colours.

Early settlers found Canada's First Nations growing pumpkins and readily adopted these and other winter squash as staples in their diet.

Hardy winter squash, with their bright orange flesh, are one of fall's great delights. They're harvested as soon as they're ripe, and provide a taste of summer through many cold months. If you travel around Canada in the fall, each farmers' market offers a different variety. Hubbard, acorn or pepper, buttercup and butternut are the most familiar. Look also for sweet potato, turban, banana, peanut and some miniature varieties that are starting to appear. (Don't, however, try to cook ornamental gourds; they're inedible.) Spaghetti squash falls between winter and summer types, but has the hard rind of a winter squash. The sweetest squash is the sweet potato, while the meatiest is the butternut.

Winter squash has a high vitamin A content and some vitamin C; neither vitamin diminishes during storage. The thick, heavy skin of winter squash means it keeps well.

CHOOSING

Buy winter squash with hard, blemish-free, bright-coloured rind. Look for those that are heavy for their size.

Two to 3 pounds (1 to 1 ½ kg) of winter squash yield 4 servings. One pound (500 g) of winter squash yields 2 cups of cooked squash purée.

STORING

Wash winter squash well, especially the side that rested on the ground. Dry thoroughly and store in a single layer in a dry place between 40 and 50°F (4 to 10°C). Most varieties of winter squash should keep for many months under these conditions.

To freeze butternut squash, simply blanch the flesh for 2 minutes. Other varieties need to be cooked completely before freezing.

PREPARING

Unless cooking it whole (see below), peel the squash, discard the seeds and cut into large pieces.

COOKING

To bake winter squash whole, cut a slit or two in the rind and bake in a 350°F (180°C) oven for about 1 hour for a 2 lb (1 kg) squash. When cool enough to handle, cut in half and remove and discard the seeds. Scoop out the flesh, mash well, then season with butter, salt and pepper.

To steam winter squash, peel and cut into large pieces, then steam for 15 to 20 minutes. Avoid boiling squash because the texture of boiled squash is unappetizing.

A microwave oven does an excellent job of cooking squash. Microwave 3 cups of peeled, cubed squash, covered, on high for 7 to 9 minutes, stirring once. Let stand, covered for 2 minutes, then drain.

ROASTED SQUASH SOUP WITH SAGE AND PANCETTA

Pancetta is salt-cured, unsmoked Italian bacon. The deli departments of most large supermarkets sell it.

1 butternut squash (about 2 ¾ lb/1 ⅖ kg)

4 oz (125 g) coarsely chopped pancetta

2 onions, coarsely chopped

2 cloves garlic, minced

1 ½ tbsp finely chopped fresh sage or 1 ½ tsp crumbled dried sage leaves

¼ tsp hot pepper flakes (or to taste)

6 cups chicken broth

Salt and freshly ground black pepper to taste

Sour cream for garnish

1 large ripe tomato, diced

8 to 10 fresh or dried sage leaves (optional)

Preheat the oven to 400°F (200°C). Cut the squash in half and remove the seeds. Place, cut sides down and covered with foil, on a greased or parchment-paper lined shallow roasting pan. Roast until tender, about 45 minutes. When cool enough to handle, scrape the flesh from the rind and set aside.

In a large saucepan, cook the pancetta over medium heat until crisp, about 5 minutes. Remove with a slotted spoon and drain on paper towels.

Reduce the heat to medium-low. Add the onions, garlic, chopped sage and hot pepper flakes to the fat remaining in the saucepan. Cook, stirring occasionally, until very soft, about 10 minutes.

Add the roasted squash, broth and salt and pepper to taste. Bring to a boil over medium-high heat. Reduce the heat to medium-low and simmer, covered, for 20 minutes for flavours to blend.

Use an immersion blender in the saucepan to blend the soup until smooth. Or purée the soup in batches in a countertop blender (a blender, rather than a food processor, makes a smoother soup). (The soup can be prepared to this point, cooled, covered and refrigerated for up to 3 days.)

When ready to serve, reheat the soup gently. Season with more salt and pepper to taste, if necessary. Serve in heated bowls and garnish each portion with a dollop of sour cream, a sprinkle of diced tomato and reserved pancetta and a sage leaf (if using).

Makes 8 to 10 servings

BAKED RUM SQUASH

2 large acorn squash
Salt and freshly ground black pepper to taste
4 tbsp butter
4 tsp light brown sugar
4 tsp dark rum
Freshly grated nutmeg to taste
1 tbsp slivered candied ginger
4 tbsp coarsely chopped walnuts

Put these sweet squash halves in the oven, along with a dish of scalloped potatoes, while you are roasting pork or ham and dinner's done.

Preheat the oven to 350°F (180°C). Cut each squash in half lengthwise and scoop out the seeds. Place, cut sides up, in a shallow baking dish and sprinkle with salt and pepper.

Place 1 tbsp butter in each half, then sprinkle each with 1 tsp of the brown sugar and rum and a pinch of nutmeg. Sprinkle evenly with the candied ginger and walnuts.

Cover the dish loosely with foil and bake until the squash is tender, 45 minutes to 1 hour.

Makes 4 servings

ACORN SQUASH WITH RICE STUFFING

4 medium acorn squash (about 1 ½ lb/750 g each), halved and seeded
¼ cup unsalted butter, divided
2 tbsp maple syrup
¼ tsp ground allspice
⅛ tsp freshly grated nutmeg
Salt and freshly ground black pepper to taste
4 stalks celery, finely chopped
2 medium shallots, finely chopped
1 clove garlic, minced
1 tbsp fresh thyme leaves, chopped, or 1 tsp dried thyme leaves
2 tbsp olive oil
1 ½ tbsp cider vinegar
2 tsp grainy Dijon mustard
1 ½ tsp liquid honey
1 ¼ cups cooked basmati or long grain rice
1 cup cooked wild rice
⅔ cup coarsely chopped, toasted pecans (see page 16)
½ cup dried cranberries, chopped

When the Toronto chef Hannah Pahuta caters an event, vegan diners might be lucky enough to enjoy something like this main dish. Hannah adds some cheddar, Gruyère or fontina to the rice mixture for vegetarians.

Preheat the oven to 400°F (200°C). Place squash halves, cut sides up, on a parchment-paper-lined baking sheet.

In a small bowl and using the microwave, melt 2 tbsp of the butter. Whisk in the maple syrup, allspice, nutmeg and salt and pepper to taste. Brush the butter mixture all over the flesh of the squash halves. Roast, uncovered, until just fork tender, 30 to 40 minutes.

Meanwhile, melt the remaining butter in a large skillet over medium heat. Add the celery, shallots, garlic, and salt and pepper to taste. Cook, stirring occasionally, until just softened, about 6 minutes. Stir in the thyme and cook until fragrant, about 1 minute.

In a large bowl, whisk together olive oil, vinegar, mustard and honey. Add the long grain and wild rice and mix well. Stir in the celery mixture, pecans and cranberries. Season generously with salt and pepper to taste.

Divide the rice filling among the roasted squash halves, using a mounded ½ cup for each. (The squash can be prepared to this point and left at room temperature for up to 1 hour. Roast as described below, adding an extra 5 minutes or so to the roasting time.)

Return the squash to the oven and roast until the squash is completely fork tender, the edges have started to brown, and the filling is heated through, 20 to 25 minutes.

Makes 8 servings

ACORN SQUASH WITH SAUSAGE STUFFING

2 medium acorn squash or sweet potato squash

1 lb (500 g) bulk sausage

1 medium onion, chopped

1 clove garlic, minced

1 large tart apple, peeled and finely chopped

3 tbsp finely chopped parsley

1 ½ tsp finely chopped fresh thyme or ½ tsp dried thyme leaves

1 tsp finely chopped fresh sage or ¼ tsp dried sage leaves

Salt and freshly ground black pepper to taste

This is the ultimate one-dish meal—especially when you can eat the "dish."

Preheat the oven to 350°F (180°C). Cut each squash in half lengthwise and scoop out the seeds. Place, cut sides down, in a baking dish just large enough to hold the squash halves. Add enough hot water to the dish to come 1 ½ inches (4 cm) up the sides. Bake, uncovered, for 30 minutes.

Meanwhile, brown the sausage meat in a large, heavy skillet over medium-high heat, breaking it up with a spoon. Add the onion and garlic and sauté until translucent.

Pour off any excess fat. Stir in the apple, parsley, thyme, sage, and salt and pepper to taste.

Drain the squash. Turn the squash halves cut sides up and sprinkle with salt and pepper to taste.

Fill the squash halves with the sausage mixture, dividing evenly. Return to the oven and bake, uncovered, until the squash is tender, about 30 minutes.

Makes 4 servings

SEE ALSO:

Brandied Squash Pie	121
Curried Harvest Vegetables with Lentils	157
Squash and Bean Stew with Chipotle Cream	167

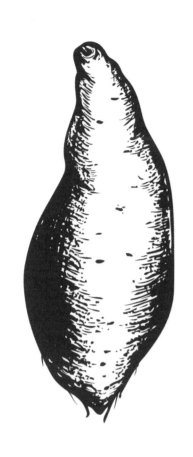

SWEET POTATOES

Although often mislabeled "yams," true sweet potatoes, which grow in Canada, are botanically related to neither yams nor regular potatoes. Sweet potatoes have pointier ends than regular potatoes and skin colour that varies according to the variety from light pink through orange to red. Their flesh can be yellow-orange to red-orange.

Sweet potatoes are fairly low in calories and a good source of fibre, as well as vitamins A and C. They also contain vitamin E, folate, potassium and iron, and an abundance of antioxidant vitamins, especially beta carotene.

CHOOSING

Look for unblemished, firm sweet potatoes with no soft spots or bruises.

One pound (500 g) of sweet potatoes yields about 1 ¼ cups of cooked sweet potato purée.

STORING

Do not store in the refrigerator but in a well-ventilated, cool place that's about 55°F (12°C).

Cooked and mashed sweet potatoes freeze well.

PREPARING

Sweet potatoes need only a good washing before cooking. Bake them unpeeled for best flavour. They can be wrapped in foil and cooked on the barbecue. If you do steam them, drop them in water immediately after peeling to prevent them turning brown.

COOKING

Rarely eaten raw because they're difficult to digest uncooked, sweet potatoes can be roasted in their skins after piercing (and are more nutritious cooked this way) or peeled, then steamed, boiled or grilled.

GINGERED SWEET POTATOES

6 medium sweet potatoes
2 tbsp butter
2 tbsp sour cream
¾ tsp ground ginger (or more to taste)
Salt and freshly ground black pepper to taste

Roasting the potatoes for this brightly coloured side gives the dish an extra layer of flavour but you can, if you prefer, steam or boil them.

Preheat the oven to 400°F (200°C). Scrub the potatoes but do not peel. Pierce them in several places and arrange on a baking sheet. Roast until tender, about 1 hour. Reduce the oven temperature to 350°F (180°C).

When the potatoes have cooled just enough to handle them but are still hot, remove the peel.

In a large bowl and using an electric mixer, beat the potatoes until smooth. Add the butter, sour cream, ginger and salt and pepper to taste. Beat until well combined. Taste and add more ginger, if necessary.

Spoon the potatoes into a greased, 6-cup (1 ½ L) baking dish. (Potatoes can be cooled, covered and refrigerated for up to 1 day. Bring to room temperature before reheating.)

Bake, covered, until hot throughout, about 30 minutes.

Makes 8 to 10 servings

SWEET POTATO FRIES

2 medium sweet potatoes
2 tsp canola oil
½ tsp chili powder
Salt to taste

Roasting sweet potato fries in a tiny bit of oil produces a low-fat version of this addictive snack. The recipe doubles easily.

Preheat the oven to 400°F (200°C). Peel the potatoes and cut each lengthwise into six 1-inch (2 ½ cm) wedges.

In a large bowl, toss the wedges with the oil, chili powder and salt to taste. Spread them out in a single layer on a large baking sheet.

Roast, turning every 10 minutes, until tender, about 35 minutes.

Makes 3 servings

SWEET POTATO VICHYSSOISE WITH RED PEPPER PURÉE

8 cups chicken or vegetable broth
4 large sweet potatoes (about 2 lb/1 kg), peeled and quartered
1 tbsp minced fresh ginger
4 tsp ground cumin
3 leeks (white and pale green parts only), cleaned and cut into 1-inch (2 ½ cm) pieces
1 apple, peeled, cored and cut into 8 wedges
Salt to taste
Sour cream (optional)
1 sweet red pepper, roasted, stemmed and seeded (see page 111)

My good friend the food writer, author and nutritionist Monda Rosenberg shared this easy soup recipe. A low-fat and low-calorie hot version of the classic chilled potato and leek soup, it contains no cream but is loaded with beta carotene. If you prefer, buy a jar of roasted peppers and purée one large one in the food processor for the garnish.

In a large saucepan, bring the broth to a boil over high heat. Add the sweet potatoes, ginger and cumin. Bring back to a boil. Reduce the heat to medium-low and simmer, covered and stirring occasionally, 10 minutes.

Add the leeks and apple to the broth. Simmer the soup, covered and stirring often, until the potatoes are very tender, about 45 minutes.

Use an immersion blender in the saucepan to blend the soup until smooth. Or purée the soup in batches in a countertop blender (a blender, rather than a food processor, makes a smoother soup).

Return the soup to the rinsed-out saucepan, if necessary. Season to taste with salt, if necessary. (The soup can cooled, covered and refrigerated for up to 1 day.)

When ready to serve, reheat the soup over medium heat, stirring often. For a creamier texture, stir in sour cream, ¼ cup at a time, until the soup is to your liking (do not boil).

Meanwhile, purée the roasted pepper in a food processor until smooth. Serve the soup in large bowls with swirls of red pepper purée and additional sour cream (if using).

Makes 8 to 10 servings

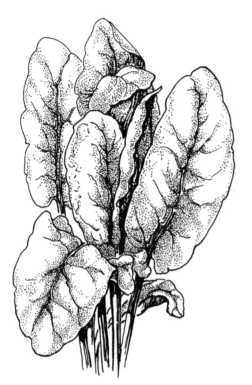

SWISS CHARD AND OTHER HEARTY GREENS

Swiss chard, with its colourful leaves, was a staple in our farm kitchen garden when I was a child. Early Canadian gardens all seemed to have this easy to grow vegetable, and now we see it more often in supermarkets. Swiss chard is actually a member of the beet family and is often grown in Canadian gardens instead of spinach because the leaves continue to sprout throughout the summer even after continual cutting.

A good source of vitamins and minerals, Swiss chard's lower acid content makes it slightly milder than spinach.

CHOOSING
Look for dark green, fresh-looking, crisp, whole leaves.

About 2 ½ pounds (1 ¼ kg) of Swiss chard yields 4 servings (the leaves reduce dramatically in volume when cooked).

STORING
Store Swiss chard, unwashed, in a perforated plastic bag in the crisper for up to 4 days.

To freeze Swiss chard, blanch it for 2 minutes.

PREPARING
Wash Swiss chard well. Leave any tiny leaves on their stems but cut the stems out of larger leaves and chop them before cooking.

COOKING
Place washed Swiss chard in a heavy, stainless steel saucepan and cook, covered, with just the water clinging to its leaves after washing. Cook just until wilted, 2 to 5 minutes. Drain well in a sieve. Butter, lemon juice or vinegar, and salt and pepper are good seasonings. Freshly grated nutmeg also helps to bring out the flavour of cooked Swiss chard.

Steaming takes longer, the time depending on the amount of Swiss chard being cooked. Sautéing is another excellent method of cooking (see Sautéed Spinach, page 129, and substitute Swiss chard). You can use Swiss chard in any recipe calling for spinach.

OTHER HEARTY GREENS
As immigrants from other parts of the world started to settle in Canada, they brought with them their own favourite leafy greens. Kale came with the Dutch, collard greens with the Portuguese and myriad different greens with the Asian community.

KALE

A member of the brassica family, which includes cabbage, mustard, broccoli and cauliflower, kale is one of the most nutritious vegetables. It has powerful antioxidant properties, is anti-inflammatory and also high in beta carotene, vitamins A, C and K, and reasonably rich in iron and calcium.

A little peppery and sweet with a slightly bitter edge, kale is best after chilly fall weather makes it mellower, even after a frost for the sturdier varieties. Fresh, tender smaller leaves can be enjoyed raw in salads, but the bigger curly, Italian lacinato (also known as Tuscan, black or cavolo nero) or Red Russian varieties need a good 15 to 20 minutes cooking to make the kale tender.

To prepare kale, cut out and remove the centre ribs of the leaves (the stems can be left on baby kale).

COLLARDS

Collards taste a bit like cabbage with a smoky hint that is more pronounced when the vegetable is paired with ham or sausage. Another vegetable bursting with nutrients, collards are low in calories but high in folate and vitamin C, a good source of vitamins A and E, high in calcium and potassium with some iron and riboflavin.

As with kale, cut out and discard the centre ribs and stalks before cooking.

ASIAN GREENS

Bok choy is probably the most familiar Asian green now grown in Canada. There are three types of bok choy: regular and baby bok choy both have white stems, dark green, flat leaves and a bulbous base; Shanghai bok choy is green all over and about 12 inches (30 cm) long. Baby bok choy is only 3 to 6 inches (8 to 15 cm) long, while regular bok choy falls somewhere between Shanghai and baby bok choy in size. All types may have flowers but avoid any with opened blooms, and choose those with crisp stalks and fresh-looking leaves.

The list of other Asian greens seems endless and many Asian produce stores will have dozens of different ones on display. Gai lan (Chinese broccoli) is described in the Broccoli chapter (page 28). It's a cousin of regular broccoli, but has thin stalks, large, deep green leaves and, instead of big flowering heads, a few unopened flower buds.

All Asian greens should be eaten as soon as possible after purchase. To store for a few days, place in a perforated plastic bag in the crisper. Wash thoroughly before use and if you are using them in a stir-fry, cut them into uniform size for even cooking. Garlic and fresh ginger work well as flavourings. Add any of the greens to stir-fried noodles, stir-fried rice or clear soups.

Asian greens are all members of the cabbage family. They contain high levels of beta carotene and vitamin C, which are both powerful antioxidants. They are also low in calories but a source of folate and vitamin A, calcium, iron, magnesium and potassium.

HOT SWISS CHARD SALAD

6 cups washed and torn Swiss chard leaves

8 slices lean bacon

½ cup thinly sliced onion

3 large cloves garlic, minced

4 tsp granulated sugar

2 tsp all-purpose flour

Salt to taste

⅓ cup chicken broth

¼ cup red wine vinegar

3 hard-cooked eggs, shelled and sliced

This warm salad has an interesting sweet-sour flavour.

In a large pot of boiling water, blanch the Swiss chard for 2 minutes. Drain well. Squeeze out the excess moisture and place the Swiss chard in a warm, large serving bowl.

In a large skillet over medium heat, cook the bacon until crisp. Drain on paper towels, then crumble and set aside.

Pour off all but ¼ cup fat from the skillet. Reduce the heat to low. Add the onion and garlic to the skillet and cook, stirring often, until softened, 2 to 3 minutes.

Blend in the sugar, flour and salt to taste. Gradually stir in the broth and vinegar. Cook, stirring, until thickened and smooth.

Pour the hot onion mixture over the Swiss chard, tossing to coat. Sprinkle with crumbled bacon. Arrange the sliced hard-cooked eggs on top. Serve at once.

Makes 4 to 6 servings

TUSCAN KALE AND WHITE BEAN SOUP

2 tbsp olive oil

1 onion, chopped

2 carrots, diced

2 stalks celery, diced

1 sweet red pepper, seeded and diced

1 small zucchini, diced

2 tbsp tomato paste

3 cloves garlic, minced

2 tsp finely chopped fresh rosemary or 1 tsp crumbed dried rosemary leaves

¼ tsp hot pepper flakes

6 cups vegetable or chicken broth

4 cups chopped kale leaves (stems removed)

1 can (19 oz/540 mL) white kidney beans, drained and rinsed

A 2-inch (5 cm) piece Parmesan rind (optional)

1 tsp balsamic vinegar

Salt and freshly ground black pepper to taste

Additional olive oil for drizzling (optional)

Tuscan kale is the most appropriate for this Italian soup, but any kale will work. It's hearty enough to make a nourishing main course with crusty bread. I always keep the leftover hard rinds of Parmesan cheese to add to either soups like this or pasta sauce.

In a large saucepan, heat the oil over medium heat. Add the onion, carrots, celery, red pepper and zucchini and cook, stirring often, until softened, about 5 minutes. Add the tomato paste, garlic, rosemary and hot pepper flakes and cook, stirring, for 1 minute.

Stir in the broth, kale, beans and Parmesan rind (if using). Bring to a boil over medium-high heat. Reduce the heat to medium low and simmer, uncovered, until all the vegetables are tender, about 15 minutes.

Stir in the vinegar and season to taste with salt and pepper. (The soup can be cooled, covered and refrigerated for up to 1 day.)

When ready to serve, reheat over medium heat. Discard the Parmesan rind and serve in wide soup bowls, drizzled with a little olive oil (if using).

Makes 4 servings

CALDO VERDE (CREAMY POTATO PURÉE AND GREENS)

8 cups chicken broth

1 ½ lb (750 g) potatoes, peeled and halved (4 to 5 potatoes)

2 large onions, quartered

8 oz (250 g) cured chorizo

¼ cup olive oil, divided

3 cloves garlic, minced

2 tsp salt, divided

4 cups water

2 cups finely shredded collard leaves

Freshly ground black pepper to taste

This quintessential Portuguese recipe appears in Carla Azevedo's beautiful book *Pimentos & Piri Piri: Portuguese Comfort Cooking*. Many Portuguese families grow collard greens in their backyards and, in Portugal, grocery stores often have a manual shredder used only to prepare collard greens for recipes like this. To shred your own collard greens, wash the leaves, trim off the stalks and cut the leaves in half lengthwise. Stack a few leaves together, roll into a tight cigar shape, then slice as thinly as possible.

In a large saucepan, combine the broth, potatoes, onions, chorizo, 2 tbsp of the oil, the garlic and 1 tsp of the salt. Bring to a boil over medium-high heat. Reduce the heat to medium and cook, covered, until the potatoes are very tender, 25 to 30 minutes.

In a separate large saucepan, combine the water, collard greens and remaining salt. Bring to a boil over medium heat and simmer, uncovered, until the collard greens are bright green and tender, 5 to 7 minutes. Drain well and return to the saucepan. Set aside and cover to keep warm.

When the potatoes are tender, use a slotted spoon to remove the chorizo to a cutting board. Slice it thinly, then cut the slices into slivers and set aside.

Use an immersion blender in the saucepan to blend the potato mixture until smooth. Or purée it in batches in a countertop blender (a blender, rather than a food processor, makes a smoother purée).

Add the potato purée to the collard greens, stir well to combine and reheat if necessary. Season to taste with more salt and pepper.

To serve, ladle into bowls and garnish with a few slivers of chorizo. Drizzle each portion with about 1 tsp of the remaining olive oil.

Makes 8 to 10 servings

HOT AND SWEET BOK CHOY

8 heads baby bok choy

2 tbsp sweet chili sauce

1 tbsp slivered fresh ginger

1 tbsp each, soy sauce and oyster sauce

¼ tsp hot pepper flakes

I often double the chili sauce mixture in this simple recipe and use half of it, without microwaving it, to marinate salmon fillets before roasting them to serve alongside the bok choy. Sweet chili sauce is a Thai sweet-sour sauce used on grilled foods and for dipping.

Cut the bok choy in half lengthwise. Steam it over a saucepan of simmering water until tender but still bright green and crisp, 2 to 3 minutes.

In a microwave-safe dish, stir together the chili sauce, ginger, soy sauce, oyster sauce and hot pepper flakes. Heat in the microwave on high until bubbly, about 30 seconds. Drizzle over the bok choy and serve at once.

Makes 4 servings

KALE CAESAR SALAD

My thanks to Meghan Collins, in acquisitions at Formac Lorimer Books, for this kale salad recipe with its punchy anchovy dressing.

DRESSING

1 can (50 g) anchovies, drained
¼ cup olive oil
2 tbsp fresh lemon juice
1 clove garlic, minced
1 tsp Dijon mustard

SALAD

5 cups baby kale or 5 oz (150 g) mature curly
  kale leaves, trimmed and chopped
1 hard cooked egg, shelled
¼ cup freshly grated Parmesan cheese (approx.)

For the dressing, mince the anchovies in a mini chopper or by hand. In a small bowl, stir together the anchovies, olive oil, lemon juice, garlic and mustard until well combined.

For the salad, place the kale in a large bowl. Grate the egg over the top and sprinkle with cheese.

Toss the kale with enough of the dressing to just coat the leaves (do not add too much; any leftover dressing will keep in the refrigerator for about 1 week). Sprinkle more cheese on top, if necessary.

Makes 4 servings

KALE AND SMOKED HAM FRITTATA

Use any of the kale varieties for this quick lunch dish.

2 tbsp olive oil, divided
1 small onion, chopped
½ cup chopped smoked ham
½ cup diced sweet red pepper
4 eggs
⅓ cup half-and-half cream (10% MF) or table
  cream (18% MF)
Salt and freshly ground black pepper to taste
4 oz (125 g) kale, ribs removed and leaves
  coarsely chopped
½ cup shredded Swiss cheese

Preheat the oven to 350°F (180°C). In an 8-inch (20 cm) ovenproof skillet, heat half of the oil over medium heat. Add the onion, ham and red pepper and cook, stirring occasionally, until the onion is softened. Remove the skillet from the heat and let cool slightly.

In a medium bowl, whisk the eggs, cream and salt and pepper to taste. Fold in the onion mixture, then the kale and cheese.

Wipe out the skillet, add the remaining oil and heat over medium heat. Add the egg mixture and reduce the heat to low. Cook, covered, until the egg mixture is set around the edges of the skillet, about 9 minutes. Uncover the skillet and transfer to the oven. Bake until puffed and completely set, about 15 minutes. Let stand for a few minutes before cutting into wedges.

Makes 2 to 3 servings

KALE CHIPS

As a registered massage therapist, my friend Nancy Brent is very health-conscious. She cooks quite a few vegetarian meals for her family, and understands the nutritional power of vegetables like kale. Her favourite way of enjoying it is in a black bean taco. She sautés the kale with olive oil and garlic and puts it on top of the cooked black bean mixture. As well, Nancy often makes kale chips for snacking.

Although any kind will work, the flat Tuscan variety is best for chips, but watch it carefully while it roasts since it can be quite thin in spots and will scorch quickly.

Wash and dry the leaves well. Cut out and discard the centre ribs, then cut the leaves into bite-sized pieces. Lay them out in a single layer on baking sheets and brush both sides liberally with olive oil and sprinkle them with coarse salt. Roast in a 400°F (200°C) oven until crisp-looking, about 10 minutes. Watch carefully in case the leaves scorch. Let cool on wire racks (the leaves will become crisper as they cool).

DUTCH KALE AND POTATOES

2 lb (1 kg) potatoes (about 6), peeled and quartered

A 1 lb (500 g) piece smoked sausage, such as kielbasa

¼ cup butter

1 onion, chopped

2 lb (1 kg) curly kale, stems removed and leaves finely chopped

½ cup half-and-half cream (10% MF) or table cream (18% MF), warmed

Salt and freshly ground black pepper to taste

Cider vinegar to taste

One of my favourite vendors at our Cambridge, Ontario, farmers' market, Corrie Burke, fondly remembers her mother making this comforting, traditional Dutch dish of mashed potatoes, garden kale and smoked sausage.

Place the potatoes and sausage in a large saucepan of salted water. Bring to a boil over high heat. Reduce the heat to medium-low and simmer, covered, until very tender, about 20 minutes.

Meanwhile, in a large, deep skillet, melt the butter over medium heat. Add the onion and cook, stirring often, for 5 to 8 minutes. Add the kale and sauté until very tender, 20 to 30 minutes, adding a little water to the skillet if the mixture sticks.

When the kale is cooked, remove the sausage from the potatoes and set on top of the kale. Cover the skillet and keep warm.

When the potatoes are cooked, drain well. Add the warm cream and salt and pepper to taste. Mash until smooth.

Transfer the sausage to a cutting board and cut into slices. Stir the kale mixture into the mashed potato. Spoon the mashed potato mixture onto warm dinner plates and top with the sausage. Sprinkle each serving with vinegar to taste.

Makes 4 to 6 servings

TOMATOES

Peruvians were cultivating tomatoes long before the arrival of Christopher Columbus. Transported from Peru to Italy in the fifteenth century, the tomato was introduced to Canada sometime during the nineteenth century. The tomato is really a fruit and was originally called love apple or golden apple. The word tomato derives from the Mexican *tomatl*.

A relative of eggplant, potato, petunia and tobacco, the tomato is a member of the deadly nightshade family and was for centuries considered to be inedible, if not downright poisonous. Before the 1860s, tomatoes were grown here as a decorative garden plant. Canadians eventually discovered the tomato was edible and now it's one of our most popular vegetables.

Ripe red tomatoes have a high vitamin C content and some vitamin A. Orange-coloured varieties are high in vitamin A. Green tomatoes have less vitamin A and more calories and carbohydrates.

CHOOSING

For highest vitamin content, pick tomatoes when they're evenly coloured but not soft. Out of season, try to find local, greenhouse tomatoes or substitute good-quality canned tomatoes rather than hard, tasteless imported substitutes.

About 2 pounds (1 kg) of tomatoes yield 4 servings.

STORING

Store tomatoes at cool room temperature for best flavour since storing them in the refrigerator robs them of flavour. Overripe tomatoes can be kept in the refrigerator.

For longer storage of tomatoes that are not overly ripe, lay them out on a flat surface so they are not touching each other. Mature green tomatoes will ripen if laid out in a single layer at room temperature but away from direct sunlight.

Although they lose all their texture, tomatoes can be frozen without blanching. Either peel them and stew slightly, or cut out the stem ends and freeze the tomatoes whole on a baking sheet. When solid, pack them in freezer bags. This latter method takes up more room. In either case, the tomatoes are good for soups or stews.

PREPARING

If using tomatoes raw, wash, core and slice them just before serving.

To peel and de-seed tomatoes to use in cooked dishes, plunge them into boiling water for about 30 seconds, then drain and cool. Cut out the stem ends and slip off the skins. Cut each tomato in half crosswise, then gently squeeze each half to remove the seeds and juice.

To peel tomatoes to use raw, place them on a wire rack in the kitchen sink. Pour boiling water over them. Turn the tomatoes over and pour boiling water over them again. Transfer to a bowl of ice water. When cool enough to handle, remove the peel.

TOMATO-VEGETABLE SOUP

For best flavour, be sure the tomatoes are nice and ripe for this velvety soup.

3 tbsp unsalted butter

2 tbsp olive oil

3 medium onions, sliced

2 leeks (white and pale green parts only), cleaned and sliced

2 large cloves garlic, minced

2 carrots, sliced

2 stalks celery with leaves, sliced

1 tbsp finely chopped fresh basil or 1 tsp dried basil leaves

3 or 4 sprigs parsley, finely chopped

1 tsp brown sugar

⅛ tsp cayenne

2 bay leaves

Salt and freshly ground white pepper to taste

¼ cup all-purpose flour

6 cups boiling chicken broth

12 ripe medium tomatoes (about 4 lb/1 ⅘ kg) stem ends removed and coarsely chopped

Additional finely chopped fresh basil or parsley

In a large saucepan, melt the butter with the oil over low heat. Add the onions and cook, stirring constantly, for 1 or 2 minutes. Cook, covered, until softened, about 5 minutes.

Add the leeks and garlic. Cook, covered, for 3 minutes. Add the carrots, celery, basil, parsley, sugar, cayenne, bay leaves and salt and pepper to taste. Cook, covered, for 5 minutes.

Stir in the flour and cook, stirring, for 3 minutes. Gradually add the boiling broth, stirring constantly. Add the tomatoes and bring to a boil over medium-high heat. Reduce the heat to medium-low and simmer, covered, until all the vegetables are tender and the tomatoes have broken up, about 35 minutes. Discard the bay leaves.

Pass the soup through a food mill or rub through a fine-mesh sieve into a clean saucepan. Reheat over medium heat. Season to taste with salt, pepper and sugar, if necessary. Serve in heated bowls and garnish with a sprinkling of finely chopped fresh basil or parsley.

Makes 8 to 10 servings

OVEN-ROASTED TOMATO SOUP WITH AVOCADO PURÉE

3 lb (1 ½ kg) ripe plum tomatoes (16 to 20 tomatoes)

1 tbsp finely chopped parsley

2 cloves garlic, minced

2 tsp dried basil leaves

Salt and freshly ground black pepper to taste

¼ cup olive oil

4 cups chicken broth

1 tsp each, ground coriander and cumin

⅛ tsp cayenne

AVOCADO PURÉE

1 large ripe avocado

2 tsp finely chopped fresh coriander (cilantro)

1 tsp fresh lime juice

Salt to taste

Fresh coriander (cilantro) sprigs for garnish

This vibrant soup can be served hot or chilled but, either way, ladle it into shallow bowls so the green avocado purée is visible. To check if an avocado is ripe, cradle it in your hand; it should yield to gentle pressure. For avocados with knobby, hard skins, the darkest ones are the ripest.

Preheat the oven to 250°F (120°C). Cut the tomatoes in half lengthwise and, with a small sharp knife, cut out the stem ends of each. Arrange the tomatoes, cut sides up, on a large baking sheet. Sprinkle evenly with the parsley, garlic, basil and salt and pepper to taste. Drizzle with the oil. Bake, uncovered, until the tomatoes have shrunk slightly, about 2 hours.

In a blender or a food processor, blend the tomatoes and any juices on the baking sheet, in batches, until smooth. Transfer each batch to a large saucepan.

Stir in the broth, ground coriander, cumin, cayenne, and salt and pepper to taste. Bring to a boil over high heat. Reduce the heat to medium-low and simmer, covered, for 20 minutes. Rub the soup through a fine-mesh sieve into a large bowl to remove tomato skins.

To serve the soup cold, refrigerate it, covered, until thoroughly chilled. To serve hot, heat through gently until hot. In either case, season to taste with salt and pepper before serving.

Just before serving, make the avocado purée. Cut the avocado in half and remove the pit. Scoop out the flesh into a small bowl and mash with a fork until smooth. Stir in coriander, lime juice and a pinch of salt.

Ladle the soup into shallow bowls and place a spoonful of avocado purée in the centre of each. Garnish with coriander sprigs.

Makes 6 servings

FRESH TOMATO SAUCE

1 ½ lb (750 g) firm, ripe tomatoes (about 4 medium tomatoes)

3 tbsp sherry vinegar

1 tsp granulated sugar

¼ cup olive oil

Salt and freshly ground black pepper to taste

This uncooked sauce is fabulous tossed with fresh pasta.

Peel the tomatoes using the second method on page 142. Cut out the stem ends from the tomatoes, then cut each in half crosswise and gently squeeze to eliminate as many seeds and as much extra juice as possible.

In a food processor or a blender, combine the tomatoes, vinegar and sugar. Process for a few seconds until the tomatoes are coarsely chopped. Add the oil, and salt and pepper to taste. Process just until combined, about 15 seconds.

Makes about 6 servings

TOMATO ICE

2 lb (1 kg) ripe tomatoes (about 6 medium)

1 ¼ cups granulated sugar

1 cup water

2 tbsp fresh lemon juice

1 tsp dry vermouth

Salt to taste

Fresh basil sprigs or celery leaves for garnish

Add scoops of this refreshing savoury ice to a platter of cold seafood, or serve between courses as a palate-cleanser.

Peel the tomatoes using the second method on page 142. Cut out the stem ends from the tomatoes. In a food processor or blender purée the tomatoes, in batches if necessary. Strain the tomatoes through a fine-mesh sieve or pass through a food mill to remove all the seeds.

Process again in the food processor or blender, then strain through a fine-mesh sieve a second time to make a very smooth purée. You should have about 2 cups.

In a medium saucepan, stir together the sugar and water. Bring to a boil and boil, without stirring, for 3 minutes. Remove the saucepan from the heat and let cool.

Add the tomato purée to the cooled syrup. Stir in the lemon juice, vermouth and salt to taste. Pour into a shallow, metal container, cover with foil and freeze until almost firm, about 4 hours.

Return the partially frozen tomato mixture to the food processor or blender and process until mushy. Pour back into the container, cover and freeze again until firm, at least 4 hours or overnight, stirring two or three times. (Alternatively, freeze in an ice-cream maker according to the manufacturer's instructions.)

Thirty minutes before serving, transfer the ice to the refrigerator to soften slightly. Scoop into individual frosted glass dishes. Garnish with basil or celery leaves.

Makes about 3 ½ cups; about 8 servings

CHILLED TOMATO SOUP

12 very ripe medium tomatoes, peeled, stem ends removed, seeded and chopped (see page 143)

1 small onion, chopped

⅓ cup mayonnaise

1 tbsp finely chopped fresh basil or 1 tsp dried basil leaves

1 tsp curry powder

⅛ tsp granulated sugar

Salt and freshly ground black pepper to taste

Sour cream for garnish

Finely chopped fresh basil or thin slices of lime for garnish

This soup is a cinch to make but has a real taste of summer. It would be a lovely way to start an August dinner party.

Place the tomatoes, onion, mayonnaise, basil, curry powder, sugar, and salt and pepper to taste in a food processor or blender and process until smooth (you may have to do this in batches).

Pour the soup into a large bowl and refrigerate, covered, for at least 4 hours or overnight.

Serve very cold in chilled soup bowls, garnished with a dollop of sour cream and basil or lime slices.

Makes 4 servings

COOKED TOMATO SAUCE

12 ripe medium tomatoes, peeled, stem ends removed, seeded and chopped (see page 143) or 3 ¾ cups drained, canned whole tomatoes

2 tbsp olive oil

1 can (5 ½ oz/156 mL) tomato paste

1 tbsp finely chopped fresh basil or 1 tsp dried basil leaves

2 large cloves garlic, crushed

2 tsp granulated sugar

1 ½ tsp finely chopped fresh oregano or ½ tsp dried oregano leaves

Salt and freshly ground black pepper to taste

Use this flavourful tomato sauce as an accompaniment to other vegetables or as a base for a homemade pasta or pizza sauce.

If using canned tomatoes, chop them coarsely but do not drain. In a large stainless steel saucepan, heat the olive oil over medium heat. Add the tomatoes (and their liquid, if canned), the tomato paste, basil, garlic, sugar, oregano, and salt and pepper to taste. Bring to a boil over medium-high heat.

Reduce the heat to very low and simmer, uncovered and stirring occasionally, until thick and fairly smooth, about 1 hour. Remove the saucepan from the heat. Season to taste with salt, pepper and more sugar, if necessary. For a smoother sauce, pass through a food mill or rub through a fine-mesh sieve.

Makes about 3 cups

OLD-FASHIONED CHILI SAUCE

6 quarts very ripe tomatoes (about 10 lb/4 ½ kg)

8 medium onions, chopped

5 medium sweet red peppers, seeded and chopped

3 cups chopped celery

1 cup cider vinegar

¼ cup seeded and finely chopped hot red pepper

2 tbsp coarse pickling salt

1 tsp freshly ground black pepper

1 tsp ground cloves

1 tsp ground allspice

1 tsp ground ginger

1 tsp cinnamon

1 tsp freshly grated nutmeg

1 tsp celery seeds

2 cups firmly packed brown sugar

This was my mother's recipe for chili sauce and the one I've made for many years. Now my daughter-in-law Cherrie makes it as well, often joining me for a chili-sauce-making marathon. In Ontario, we still find tomatoes in baskets (quarts and litres), but in parts of Canada tomatoes are sold by weight. Use your food processor, if you have one, to speed up the chopping of the onions, sweet peppers and celery. For more detailed instructions on how to make preserves, see Preserving on page 9.

Peel the tomatoes using the first method of page 142. Cut out the stem ends and chop the tomatoes coarsely. Place in a large preserving kettle. Add the onions, peppers, celery, vinegar, hot pepper, salt, pepper, spices and celery seeds. Stir to mix well.

Bring to a boil over medium-high heat. Reduce heat to medium-low and simmer, uncovered and stirring often, until the sauce is dark red and thickened, about 2 ½ hours. Add the sugar and simmer, uncovered and stirring often, for 30 minutes.

Pour the hot chili sauce into hot 2-cup (500 mL) preserving jars, leaving a ½-inch (1 cm) headspace. Seal with prepared discs and rings. Boil in a boiling-water canner for 20 minutes. Remove the jars and let cool on a rack. Store in a cool, dark, dry place.

Makes about ten 2-cup (500 mL) jars

TOMATO AND MARINATED BOCCONCINI SALAD

¼ cup olive oil

1 clove garlic, minced

2 tsp finely chopped fresh oregano or ½ tsp dried oregano leaves

¼ tsp hot pepper flakes

8 oz (250 g) bocconcini, drained

1 tbsp finely chopped parsley

1 tbsp tiny basil leaves

2 tsp well-drained capers, coarsely chopped

Salt to taste

6 ripe medium tomatoes

6 cups lightly packed mesclun (spring mix)

6 sprigs fresh basil

My son Allen and his wife Cherrie are very fond of Caprese salad, the Italian salad of fresh tomatoes and bocconcini cheese. Since their summer wedding was at our house, I wanted to include all their favourites on the menu and served the salad as a sit-down starter. To make it special, we served everyone a beautifully ripe tomato on a bed of mesclun, with the cheese slices standing up in the tomato. Cherrie and my daughter Anne asked one of my favourite vendors at the Cambridge, Ontario, farmers' market if they could choose 85 perfect tomatoes from his bushel baskets!

In a small saucepan, heat the oil, garlic, oregano and hot pepper flakes over low heat until the garlic sizzles and just begins to colour, 1 to 2 minutes. Remove the saucepan from the heat and let cool to room temperature.

Cut each bocconcini ball into 4 slices and place in a bowl. Pour in the oil mixture. Add the parsley, basil leaves and capers. Stir gently to coat well and let stand at room temperature for several hours, stirring occasionally.

Just before serving, cut out the stem ends from the tomatoes and make 3 or 4 deep cuts in each, cutting almost but not quite through.

Season the bocconcini to taste with salt. Place a cheese slice in each cut in the tomatoes, reserving the oil mixture in the bowl.

Line each of 6 salad plates with some mesclun. Place the cheese-filled tomato on each and drizzle with some of the reserved oil mixture. Arrange a basil sprig on top of each.

Makes 6 servings

CHERRY TOMATO AND MARINATED BOCCONCINI SALAD

Substitute 2 cups cherry or grape tomatoes for the larger ones and mini bocconcini for the regular-sized balls. Marinate the bocconcini in the flavoured oil as above. To serve, spread the mesclun out in a large shallow bowl or on a platter. Remove the cheese from the flavoured oil with a slotted spoon and arrange in the centre. Add 1 tbsp (15 mL) balsamic vinegar to the flavoured oil. Add the tomatoes and toss well. Arrange the tomatoes around the cheese. Drizzle any remaining oil mixture over the tomatoes.

3 ripe medium tomatoes, peeled, stem ends removed and coarsely chopped (see page 143)

1 each, sweet green and red pepper, seeded and coarsely chopped

1 English cucumber, peeled and coarsely chopped

1 small onion, coarsely chopped

1 small hot pepper, seeded and diced, or ½ tsp hot pepper sauce

3 cloves garlic, chopped

2 tbsp each, red wine vinegar and olive oil

1 tbsp Worcestershire sauce

3 cups vegetable cocktail

Salt and freshly ground black pepper to taste

Hot pepper sauce to taste

Croutons (see sidebar)

Diced cucumber, sweet green pepper, tomato and onion for garnish

Gazpacho originated in Andalucía in southern Spain but is now popular in Canada as a refreshing cold soup for a hot summer day. Originally made by farm workers using whatever was in the fields, this "liquid salad" always showcases field-ripened tomatoes, cucumbers and peppers.

The traditional recipe often includes bread but I prefer making croutons to serve as a crunchy garnish. Most gazpachos are processed only until chunky, but in Spain I have enjoyed the soup puréed and strained into a tall glass as a before-dinner drink.

In a food processor or blender, and working in batches, process the tomatoes, sweet peppers, cucumber, onion, hot pepper, garlic, vinegar, oil and Worcestershire sauce until the vegetables are finely chopped.

Transfer the mixture to a large bowl. Stir in the vegetable cocktail, and salt and pepper to taste. Cover and refrigerate for several hours or up to 5 days.

Just before serving, taste and add more vinegar, salt or hot pepper sauce, if necessary. Serve the soup in chilled bowls, passing small bowls of croutons, diced cucumber, sweet pepper, tomato and onion so everyone can garnish the soup as they wish.

Makes about 6 servings

CROUTONS

In a large skillet, melt 2 tbsp butter over low heat. Add 1 clove of crushed garlic, then bread cubes (make from 6 slices of white bread with crusts removed), stirring to coat with the butter. Cook, stirring occasionally, until golden and crunchy, about 30 minutes. Makes about 1 ½ cups.

SEE ALSO:

TURNIPS AND RUTABAGAS

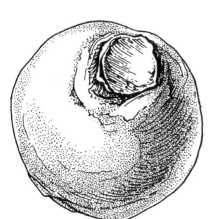

There has always been confusion surrounding turnips and rutabagas, with many thinking they're just different names for the same vegetable.

Turnips (sometimes called summer turnips) are small, white members of the mustard family. They have a delicate flavour that is very different from the stronger-tasting rutabaga.

Rutabagas are large, yellowish-orange roots. The ones we see in supermarkets have been waxed to prevent dehydration. The name comes from the Swedish *rotabagge* meaning "round root." Introduced into Scotland in 1879, the rutabaga shortly made its way to Canada where the pioneers relied on it as food for themselves and their livestock.

Our bigger, sweeter, modern rutabaga was developed in Quebec and, although first referred to as yellow turnip or Swede turnip, in 1967 Canada Fresh Fruit and Vegetable Regulation made rutabaga the vegetable's official name.

Turnips contain vitamin C, calcium and other minerals. Rutabagas are slightly higher in nutrients, having a good amount of vitamins A and C and significant amounts of iron, thiamin, riboflavin and niacin. Both are low in calories.

CHOOSING

Whether buying turnips or rutabagas, look for smooth, firm, well-formed roots that are heavy for their size. Smaller turnips (2 inches/5 cm diameter) are less likely to be spongy. Many gardeners believe rutabaga is sweeter if left in the ground until after a light frost.

About 2 pounds (1 kg) of turnips or rutabaga yield 4 servings.

STORING

Because of their higher water content, turnips cannot be stored as long as rutabagas. Store turnips in the refrigerator for up to 1 week. Rutabagas will keep well in the crisper or a cool basement for up to 2 months.

Cooked, puréed turnip or rutabaga can be frozen. You can also freeze peeled, diced, unblanched rutabaga.

PREPARING

Tiny, new turnips do not need peeling, but older ones should be peeled thinly.

To prepare rutabaga, slice off the top, then place cut side down on a cutting board and cut into several slices. Turn over to place the other flat surface down and complete the slicing. Peel off the thick skin, including the bitter band that runs underneath. I always try to find local, unwaxed rutabagas at farmers' markets in the fall but in the winter I rely on the waxed roots.

To remove the wax, place the rutabaga on a large piece of paper towel and microwave on high for about 5 minutes to melt the wax, which will run down to be absorbed by the paper. Leave to cool for several minutes, then cut as described above.

COOKING

Turnips and rutabagas can be cooked in similar ways, although the milder, soft turnip will require a shorter time.

Boil cubes of each in a small amount of water until tender, about 8 minutes for turnip, 20 to 30 minutes for rutabaga. Steaming takes a little longer. Whether boiled or steamed, mashed rutabaga is delicious mixed with potatoes, parsnips or carrots.

Braising is a good method for turnips, and baking works well for both.

Both vegetables are an interesting, crunchy addition to a crudité platter and the tops of tender young turnips can be cooked like spinach.

BRAISED TURNIPS

1 lb (500 g) small turnips (about 4 turnips)
¼ cup butter
¼ cup chicken broth
Freshly ground black pepper to taste

This is a quick and tasty way to cook small, young turnips. Try it with red radishes, too.

Peel the turnips and cut into 3-x ½-inch (8 x 1 cm) julienne strips.

In a small, heavy saucepan, melt the butter over medium heat. Add the broth and bring to a boil.

Add the turnips. Reduce the heat to medium-low and cook, covered, until just tender, about 7 minutes (do not overcook). Sprinkle with pepper to taste.

Makes 4 servings

JULIENNE OF TURNIP AND LEEK

⅓ cup unsalted butter
8 small turnips, peeled and cut into 3- x ¼-inch (8 cm x 6 mm) pieces (2 lb/1 kg total)
4 leeks (white and pale green parts only), cut into 3- x ¼-inch (8 cm x 6 mm) pieces (1 ½ lb/ 750 g total)
1 tsp granulated sugar
Salt and freshly ground black pepper to taste
1 tbsp finely chopped parsley

If you trim and slice the leeks and turnips ahead of time and wrap them tightly in plastic wrap, this tasty side dish can be on the table in just 10 minutes.

In a large skillet, melt the butter over medium-high heat. Add the turnips and stir-fry for 1 minute. Add the leeks and stir-fry for 2 minutes.

Reduce the heat to low and simmer, covered, until the vegetables are tender but still slightly crisp, about 5 minutes (do not overcook).

Stir in the sugar, and salt and pepper to taste. Transfer to a heated dish and sprinkle with parsley.

Makes 8 servings

CARAMELIZED RUTABAGA

1 large rutabaga (about 3 lb/1 ½ kg)

2 tbsp butter

2 tbsp granulated sugar

¾ cup chicken broth

5 cloves garlic, thinly sliced

⅛ tsp each, freshly grated nutmeg and dried thyme leaves

Salt and freshly ground black pepper to taste

¼ cup whipping cream (35% MF)

2 tbsp chopped chives or parsley

Rutabaga makes a homey and comforting side dish simply mashed with butter, salt and pepper, but if you are looking for something a bit different for entertaining, try this make-ahead side dish.

Peel the rutabaga thickly and cut it into 1-inch (2 ½ cm) cubes. Cook in boiling, salted water until just tender, about 12 minutes. Drain well.

In a large skillet, melt the butter over medium heat. Add the rutabaga and sugar and cook, stirring often, for 10 minutes. Add the broth and garlic and reduce the heat to low. Cook, covered, until the rutabaga is tender and most of the liquid has evaporated, about 20 minutes. If there's any liquid left, uncover the skillet and boil until most of the liquid has evaporated, about 1 minute.

Stir in the nutmeg, thyme and salt and pepper to taste. (The rutabaga can be prepared to this point, covered and refrigerated for up to 6 hours. Reheat gently before proceeding.)

Stir the cream into the rutabaga and heat through gently, stirring often. Season to taste with salt and pepper, if necessary. Serve sprinkled with chives.

Makes 8 servings

BAKED GLAZED RUTABAGA

1 medium rutabaga (about 2 lb/1 kg)

¼ cup melted butter

¼ cup liquid honey

¼ tsp ground mace or ground ginger

Salt and freshly ground black pepper to taste

Mace is the orange web that encases a whole nutmeg as it grows. Ground mace, available in the spice section of most supermarkets, has a distinctive, delicate nutmeg flavour.

Preheat the oven to 350°F (180°C). Peel the rutabaga thickly and cut into ½ inch (1 cm) slices. Brush some of the butter into a shallow roasting pan large enough to hold the slices in a single layer. Place the rutabaga slices in the pan and brush with more of the butter.

Bake, uncovered, for 15 minutes. Turn the slices over, brush with the remaining butter and drizzle with honey. Sprinkle with the mace, and salt and pepper to taste.

Bake, uncovered and turning and basting once, until the rutabaga is tender when pierced with the point of a sharp knife, about 15 minutes.

Makes about 6 servings

RUTABAGA AND CARROT PUFF

1 medium rutabaga (about 2 lb/1 kg)

4 medium carrots

1 ½ cups chicken broth

½ onion, chopped

¼ cup butter, divided

1 tbsp brown sugar

⅛ tsp freshly grated nutmeg

2 eggs, lightly beaten

2 tbsp all-purpose flour

1 tsp baking powder

Salt and freshly ground black pepper to taste

¼ cup finely chopped pecans or hazelnuts

During Canada's winter months, we have available a good variety of locally grown root vegetables which contain more nutrients than fresh vegetables imported from countries far away. Rutabaga has long been a Canadian favourite as a side dish with roast turkey or chicken. Here, carrots add their own special sweetness to a lovely make-ahead dish. You can, of course, omit the carrots and use an extra-large rutabaga if you'd prefer a straight Rutabaga Puff.

Peel the rutabaga thickly and trim and peel carrots. Cut both into ½-inch (1 cm) chunks.

In a large saucepan, combine the rutabaga, carrots, broth, onion, 3 tbsp of the butter, the sugar and nutmeg. Bring to a boil over high heat. Reduce heat to medium-low and cook, partially covered and stirring occasionally, until the vegetables are very tender, about 45 minutes. With a slotted spoon, transfer the vegetables to a food processor or blender.

Set the saucepan over high heat and boil the remaining liquid, stirring constantly, until reduced to about 1 tablespoon, 2 to 3 minutes. Add the reduced liquid to the food processor and process until a very smooth purée forms. Transfer the purée to a large bowl and let cool to room temperature.

Stir the eggs, flour, baking powder and salt and pepper to taste into the cooled purée. Transfer to a buttered, 6-cup (1 ½ L) baking or soufflé dish.

In a small saucepan, melt the remaining butter. Add the nuts and stir well to combine. Sprinkle the nut mixture evenly around the edge of dish to make a border. (The casserole can be covered and refrigerated for up to 1 day. Bring to room temperature for 30 minutes before reheating.)

When ready to bake, preheat the oven to 350°F (180°C). Bake, uncovered, until puffed, firm and golden brown, about 30 minutes.

Makes 8 servings

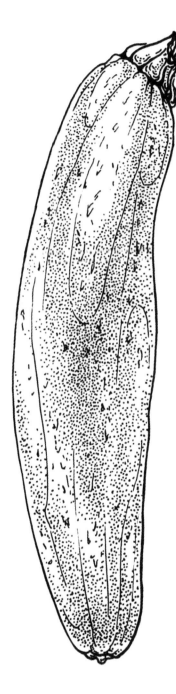

ZUCCHINI AND OTHER SUMMER SQUASH

Numerous types of summer squash are grown in other countries—pattypan or scallop, cocozelle, opo, chayote—but the best-known in Canada are zucchini, and yellow crookneck and straightneck squash, although I can also find pattypan squash at our Cambridge, Ontario, farmers' market.

Unlike the hardier winter squash, summer squash will not tolerate frost, and their skin and seeds are edible. Spaghetti squash falls in between summer and winter squash with slightly hard skin, seeds that must be removed and interesting flesh resembling spaghetti.

If you have your own zucchini plants, it is often a great challenge to find ways of using this prolific vegetable that seems to multiply overnight. Remember when you plan your garden each spring that one or two plants are plenty.

Zucchini has become very popular because it is easy to grow and very versatile. Somewhat bland on its own, it quickly assumes interesting flavours from other ingredients. Because of its moisture content, it is also a good addition to cakes or breads.

There is a great deal of water in zucchini, but the vegetable also contains vitamin A, with the yellow varieties of summer squash containing more of the vitamin. All are low in calories.

CHOOSING

Choose summer squash that is firm and heavy for its size, with tender, glossy skin. Ideally, zucchini should be less than 4 inches (10 cm) long. Other summer squash is good at 6 to 8 inches (15 to 20 cm) long, just after the blossom drops off the end.

One pound (500 g) of summer squash yields 2 to 3 servings.

STORING

Store summer squash in a perforated plastic bag in the crisper for up to 4 days. Because of their high water content, zucchini and other summer squash do not freeze well, but slices can be blanched for 2 minutes, then frozen for use for soups.

PREPARING

Tender squash like zucchini and other summer squash are normally cooked without peeling and seeding. Wash and cut off the stem and blossom ends.

Because summer squash contains so much water, it is best to try to remove some of it before cooking. Place grated or cut squash in a sieve and toss lightly with salt. Allow to sit and drain. If you are sautéing grated

A B C D E F G H I J K L M N O P Q R S T U V W X Y Z

squash, you can squeeze out even more water before cooking by placing the squash in a clean tea towel and twisting it firmly.

COOKING

Summer squash is good raw in salads or as a crudité with dips.

Zucchini and other summer squash can be deep-fried (with or without batter), stir-fried with garlic and oil, or sautéed in butter with herbs. Steam or boil tiny, whole squash for 10 minutes or pieces for 5 minutes.

Larger squash can be hollowed out to make containers for other foods. For a colourful side dish, blanch whole zucchini briefly, hollow out the centres and fill with Carrot and Parsnip Purée (page 46). Heat in a 350°F (180°C) oven before serving.

Summer squash blossoms are considered a delicacy. Pick only male blossoms (they're longer and skinnier than the female flowers), dip in batter, then deep-fry until golden, 1 to 2 minutes.

ZUCCHINI BREAD

4 cups grated, unpeeled zucchini

4 eggs

1 ¾ cups firmly packed brown sugar

1 cup canola oil

1 ¾ cups all-purpose flour

1 ¾ cups whole wheat flour

2 tsp baking powder

1 tsp baking soda

1 tsp freshly grated nutmeg

1 tsp ground ginger

1 tsp salt

½ tsp ground cinnamon

¼ tsp ground allspice

1 cup chopped walnuts or pecans

1 cup raisins

The moisture content of zucchini ensures a quick bread like this is moist and delicious. Grate the zucchini on the medium holes of a box grater or in a food processor fitted with the grating disc. Store the loaves in an airtight container at room temperature for up to 5 days. Or wrap the whole loaves, or individual slices, in plastic wrap, pack in an airtight container and freeze for up to 1 month.

Preheat the oven to 350° (180°C). Grease two 9- x 5-inch (2 L) loaf pans or line the pans with parchment paper.

Place the grated zucchini in a sieve and let drain for 30 minutes. If the zucchini is very moist, squeeze it lightly with your hands to remove any excess moisture.

In a large bowl, beat the eggs until thick. Add the sugar and oil and beat well.

In a separate large bowl, sift together the all-purpose and whole wheat flours, baking powder, baking soda, nutmeg, ginger, salt, cinnamon and allspice.

Make a well in the centre of the dry ingredients and pour in the egg mixture. Stir just until combined. Quickly stir in the zucchini, nuts and raisins.

Divide the batter between the prepared pans. Bake in the centre of the oven until a skewer inserted in the centre of one of the loaves comes out clean, about 1 hour and 10 minutes.

Let the loaves cool in the pans on a wire rack for 10 minutes. Run a long, thin knife around the sides to loosen the bread from the pans. Remove the loaves and let cool completely on the rack. Wrap tightly and store for 1 day before serving.

Makes 2 loaves

ZUCCHINI-ALMOND CAKE

3 cups finely grated, peeled zucchini

3 cups all-purpose flour

2 tsp baking powder

1 tsp baking soda

1 tsp salt

4 eggs

3 cups granulated sugar

1 ¼ cups canola oil

1 tsp almond extract

1 cup ground almonds

ALMOND GLAZE

1 ½ cups icing sugar

2 tbsp milk

¼ tsp almond extract

¼ cup sliced toasted almonds (see page 16)

This moist cake is so well-loved, a friend of mine made several for his son's wedding.

Preheat the oven to 350°F (180°C). Grease well and flour a 10-inch (3 L) tube pan.

Place the grated zucchini in a sieve and let drain for 30 minutes. If the zucchini is very moist, squeeze it lightly with your hands to remove any excess moisture.

In a large bowl, sift together the flour, baking powder, soda and salt.

In a separate large bowl and using an electric mixer, beat the eggs until thick and light. Gradually add the sugar, ¼ cup at a time, beating well after each addition. Stir in the oil and almond extract.

Blend in the dry ingredients, mixing until smooth. Stir in the ground almonds and zucchini.

Pour the batter into the prepared pan. Bake in the centre of the oven until a skewer inserted in the centre of the cake comes out clean, about 1 hour and 15 minutes.

Let the cake cool in the pan on a wire rack for 15 minutes. Remove the cake from the pan and let cool completely on the rack.

For the almond glaze, stir together the icing sugar, milk and almond extract in a small bowl, until smooth. Spread the glaze evenly over the top of the cooled cake, letting it run down the sides. Sprinkle the top with sliced almonds.

Makes 12 servings

ZUCCHINI WITH BASIL PESTO

2 lb (1 kg) small zucchini, unpeeled

Salt to taste

¼ cup unsalted butter

½ cup basil pesto (page 173)

Freshly grated Parmesan cheese (optional)

Strips of fresh summer squash tossed in flavourful homemade pesto make a tasty low-calorie and gluten-free substitute for pasta.

Cut the zucchini into fine julienne strips. Place in a sieve or colander and sprinkle lightly with salt. Let drain for 30 minutes. Drain well.

In a large skillet, melt the butter over medium-high heat. Add the zucchini and sauté until heated through.

Stir in the pesto and toss until well combined. Serve hot, sprinkled with Parmesan cheese (if using).

Makes 6 servings

BROILED GARLIC ZUCCHINI

2 lb (1 kg) zucchini, unpeeled and cut into
  ¼ inch (6 mm) slices
⅓ cup white wine vinegar
2 large cloves garlic, minced
⅔ cup olive oil
Salt and freshly ground black pepper to taste
¼ cup melted butter
Freshly grated Parmesan cheese to taste

Marinating the zucchini slices before broiling infuses them with a lovely hint of garlic.

Place the zucchini slices in a shallow dish just large enough hold them more or less in a single layer.

In a small bowl, stir together the vinegar and garlic. Whisk in the oil and salt and pepper to taste. Pour the vinegar mixture over the zucchini and marinate in the refrigerator for several hours or overnight, stirring occasionally.

Preheat the broiler to high. Drain the zucchini and arrange in a single layer on a greased large broiling pan. Brush the zucchini with melted butter and sprinkle with Parmesan to taste. Broil 4 inches (10 cm) from the element until bubbling, 3 to 4 minutes. Serve hot.

Makes 6 to 8 servings

SPICY ZUCCHINI RELISH

10 cups ground, unpeeled zucchini
  (about 10 medium)
3 cups ground onions (about 3 onions)
4 sweet green peppers, seeded and ground
⅓ cup coarse pickling salt
10 small sweet red peppers, seeded and ground
3 cups lightly packed brown sugar
3 cups white vinegar
1 tbsp cornstarch
2 tsp celery seeds
2 tsp mixed pickling spice
1 tsp ground turmeric
1 tsp dry mustard
1 tsp freshly grated nutmeg
1 tsp coarsely ground black pepper

When your zucchini patch is prolific, this delicious relish recipe is a good way to use it up. A food processor makes fast work of grinding the vegetables. For more detailed instructions on how to make relish, see Preserving on page 9.

In a large stainless steel preserving kettle or large glass bowl, stir together the zucchini, onions, green peppers and salt. Cover and let stand at room temperature overnight.

The next day, rinse the vegetables thoroughly by tipping the mixture, in batches, into a sieve under cold running water. Drain well.

Return the vegetable mixture to the preserving kettle and stir in the remaining ingredients. Bring to a boil over high heat, stirring well. Reduce the heat to medium-high and cook, uncovered and stirring often, until thick, about 30 minutes.

Pour the hot relish into hot 2-cup (500 mL) preserving jars, leaving a ½-inch (1 cm) headspace. Seal with prepared discs and rings. Boil in a boiling-water canner for 15 minutes. Remove the jars and let cool on a rack. Store in a cool, dark, dry place.

Makes about five 2-cup (500 mL) jars

SEE ALSO:

VEGETARIAN MAIN DISHES

Vegetarian food is far from boring. In fact, meatless meals are often more interesting than a meat-and-potatoes dinner. Although I love juicy roasted or grilled meat served with a couple of simple sides, it's often a vegetarian main course on a restaurant menu that piques my interest.

Without meat on the plate, you need a combination of certain ingredients to give the meal sufficient protein. The main courses in this chapter are all nutritionally balanced and tasty enough to tempt the whole family. So, whether you opt for a regular Meatless Monday or need to please a vegetarian guest at a dinner party, you'll find something here. Better still, almost all of the recipes can be prepared in advance, which is a great help when you are entertaining.

CURRIED HARVEST VEGETABLES WITH LENTILS

2 tbsp canola oil

2 onions, chopped

2 cloves garlic, minced

1 tbsp each, ground cumin and ground coriander

2 tsp turmeric

¼ tsp hot pepper flakes

⅛ tsp each, cinnamon and ground cloves

Freshly ground black pepper to taste

1 cup dried red lentils, picked over, rinsed and drained

2 ½ cups vegetable broth

2 tbsp fresh lemon juice

2 carrots, cut into 1-inch (2 ½ cm) slices

1 small winter squash, peeled, seeded and cut into 1-inch (2 ½ cm) pieces

1 small cauliflower, trimmed and divided into small florets

1 sweet red pepper, seeded and cut into strips

8 oz (250 g) green beans, trimmed and halved

½ cup salted or unsalted roasted peanuts

Salt to taste

When fall harvest arrives with its bounty of colourful squash and peppers, this is one of my favourite vegetarian main dishes. Serve it over basmati rice and accompany with a chutney. Choose a squash that's relatively easy to peel such as butternut; pepper squash, with all its ridges, is more difficult.

In a large saucepan, heat the oil over medium heat. Add the onions and garlic and cook, stirring often, until softened, about 3 minutes. Stir in the cumin, coriander, turmeric, hot pepper flakes, cinnamon, cloves and pepper to taste. Cook, stirring, for 30 seconds.

Stir in the lentils to coat well with the spices. Stir in the broth and lemon juice and bring to a boil over high heat. Reduce the heat to medium-low and simmer, covered, for 5 minutes.

Add the carrots, squash and cauliflower to the lentil mixture and bring to a boil over medium-high heat. Reduce the heat to medium-low and simmer, covered, for 5 minutes.

Add the red pepper and beans and simmer, covered, for 5 minutes. Add the peanuts and season with salt to taste. Cook, uncovered, until the vegetables are tender and the lentils have formed a thick sauce, about 5 minutes. Season to taste with salt and pepper. (The curry can be made up to 1 day ahead if you undercook the vegetables slightly. It will thicken if made ahead; thin with more broth or water, if desired, and reheat gently, stirring often.)

Makes 4 to 6 servings

VEGETABLE LASAGNA

2 tbsp vegetable oil

2 onions, chopped

8 oz (250 g) mushrooms, sliced

1 sweet green pepper, seeded and chopped

2 cloves garlic, minced

1 can (28 oz/796 mL) whole tomatoes with their juice

1 can (14 oz/398 mL) tomato sauce

2 carrots, grated

¼ cup finely chopped parsley

1 tsp each, dried basil and oregano leaves

⅛ tsp hot pepper flakes

Granulated sugar, salt and freshly ground black pepper to taste

1 pkg (10 oz/284 g) fresh spinach

5 to 9 lasagna noodles, depending on size

1 lb (500 g) low-fat ricotta cheese, drained if necessary

2 eggs

⅛ tsp freshly grated nutmeg

1 lb (500 g) mozzarella cheese, shredded

1 cup freshly grated Parmesan cheese

I've had many people tell me this moist and hearty vegetarian lasagna has been their go-to recipe since it first appeared in *Homemaker's Magazine* several years ago. Served with garlic bread and a crisp green salad, it's perfect for a party.

In a medium saucepan, heat the oil over medium heat. Add the onions, mushrooms, green pepper and garlic and cook, stirring often, for 5 minutes.

Add the tomatoes, cutting them up as finely as possible with the edge of a metal spoon. Stir in the tomato sauce, carrots, parsley, basil, oregano, hot pepper flakes and sugar, salt and pepper to taste. Bring to a boil over high heat. Reduce the heat to medium-low and simmer, covered and stirring occasionally, for 30 minutes.

Meanwhile, in a medium, heavy saucepan, cook the spinach, covered, in just the water clinging to its leaves after washing, until just wilted, 2 to 5 minutes. Drain well in a sieve and, when cool enough to handle, squeeze any moisture out with your hands. Chop the spinach finely and set aside.

In a large pot of boiling salted water, cook the noodles according to the package directions. Drain and rinse with cold water. Drain again and spread out on clean tea towels on a flat surface.

In a food processor, process the spinach, ricotta cheese, eggs and nutmeg until fairly smooth.

Spread one-quarter of the tomato sauce in the bottom of a greased 13- x 9-inch (3 L) baking dish. Arrange one-third of the noodles in a single layer on top. Spread with half of the ricotta mixture, then one-quarter of the tomato sauce, one-third of the mozzarella and one-third of the Parmesan. Repeat layering the noodles, ricotta, tomato sauce, mozzarella and Parmesan once.

Arrange the remaining noodles on top. Spread with remaining tomato sauce and sprinkle with remaining mozzarella and Parmesan. The dish will be quite full, but will accommodate everything. (The recipe can be made ahead, covered and refrigerated for up to 24 hours. Add 10 to 15 minutes to the cooking time if refrigerated.)

When ready to bake, preheat the oven to 350°F (180°C). Bake the lasagna, uncovered, for 30 minutes. Cover the dish with foil and bake until hot and bubbly, 10 to 15 minutes. Let stand for 10 minutes before cutting in squares to serve.

Makes 10 to 12 servings

TWO-CHEESE BAKED PENNE WITH ROASTED VEGETABLES

2 sweet red or yellow peppers, seeded and sliced

8 oz (250 g) mushrooms, quartered

2 small zucchini, unpeeled and sliced

2 small red onions, diced

4 cloves garlic, minced

¼ cup olive oil

½ cup finely chopped parsley, divided

2 tbsp finely chopped fresh basil or 2 tsp dried basil leaves

2 tsp finely chopped fresh rosemary or ½ tsp crumbled dried rosemary leaves

Salt and freshly ground black pepper to taste

5 cups penne pasta with ridges (1 lb/500 g)

3 cups meatless pasta sauce

1 lb (500 g) provolone cheese, shredded

1 cup freshly grated Asiago or Parmesan cheese, divided

High on everyone's list of favourites, this pretty make-ahead casserole is just the kind I like to serve to company. A crisp green salad goes well with the smooth texture of the melted cheese. Use a homemade sauce, such as Cooked Tomato Sauce (page 146) or a good commercial one.

Preheat the oven to 450°F (230°C). In a large, shallow roasting pan, toss the peppers, mushrooms, zucchini, onions and garlic with the oil. Spread out in the pan and roast, uncovered and stirring once or twice, until softened, about 25 minutes.

Stir in ⅓ cup of the parsley, the basil, rosemary and salt and pepper to taste.

Meanwhile, cook the pasta in a large pot of boiling, salted water just until al dente, about 8 minutes. Scoop out and reserve ½ cup of the pasta cooking water. Add 2 cups cold water to the pot, then drain the pasta well. Return the pasta to the pot and let cool.

Add the ½ cup reserved pasta cooking water, the roasted vegetables, pasta sauce, provolone and half the Asiago to the pasta and stir gently.

Transfer the pasta mixture to a greased, shallow, 12-cup (3 L) baking dish. Sprinkle with remaining Asiago and parsley. (Pasta can be prepared to this point, covered and refrigerated for up to 1 day, or frozen for up to 2 months. Thaw the frozen pasta in the refrigerator, then bring to room temperature before reheating.)

When ready to bake, preheat the oven to 375°F (190°C). Bake the pasta, covered, for 30 minutes. Uncover and bake until bubbly, 10 to 15 minutes.

Makes 8 servings

1 ½ lb (750 g) eggplant, peeled and cut into
 ½-inch (1 cm) cubes
1 ½ lb (750 g) zucchini, unpeeled and cut into
 ½-inch (1 cm) cubes
Salt to taste
½ cup olive oil
2 ½ cups coarsely chopped onions
2 lb (1 kg) ripe tomatoes, peeled, seeded and
 stem ends removed
1 sweet green pepper, seeded and cut into strips
1 sweet red pepper, seeded and cut into strips
1 hot pepper, seeded and finely chopped
1 large clove garlic, minced
1 bouquet garni (see sidebar)
Freshly ground black pepper to taste
Additional olive oil (optional)

RATATOUILLE

This versatile vegetable stew makes good use of late-summer vegetables. Serve with crusty bread, as a filling for omelettes or crêpes, or tossed with pasta. It's also good topped with cheese and served as Ratatouille Gratin (see sidebar).

Place the eggplant and zucchini in 2 separate colanders or sieves and toss each vegetable gently with a sprinkling of salt. Let drain for 30 minutes.

In a large, deep skillet or pot, heat the oil over low heat. Add the onions and cook, stirring occasionally, until softened but not brown, about 10 minutes.

Add the tomatoes and cook, stirring occasionally, until the tomatoes break up, about 10 minutes.

Add the eggplant, sweet and hot peppers, garlic and bouquet garni. Cook, covered, for 45 minutes. Add the zucchini. Cook, covered, for 45 minutes.

Drain the vegetable mixture through a colander set over a medium saucepan. Discard the bouquet garni. Set the vegetable mixture aside in a warm serving dish, cover and keep warm or let stand at room temperature.

Bring the cooking liquid to a boil over high heat and boil, stirring often, until syrupy. Add the reduced cooking liquid to the cooked vegetables and season to taste with salt and pepper, if necessary. (The ratatouille can be cooled, covered and refrigerated for up to 2 days or frozen for up to 1 month.)

When ready to serve, reheat the ratatouille and serve hot, or bring to room temperature. If serving at room temperature, stir in a little olive oil before serving.

Makes 8 to 10 servings

BOUQUET GARNI
Between 2 short pieces of celery and using kitchen twine, tie 2 or 3 sprigs of parsley, 2 or 3 sprigs fresh thyme (or a pinch dried thyme leaves) and 1 bay leaf.

RATATOUILLE GRATIN
Place the ratatouille in an ungreased 8- to 12-cup (2 to 3 L) baking dish and top with 1 ½ cups shredded cheddar. Bake in a 425°F (220°C) oven until bubbly, 20 to 25 minutes.

2 tbsp olive oil

3 leeks (white and light green parts only), thinly sliced

2 sweet red peppers, seeded and diced

4 cloves garlic, minced

2 tsp dried marjoram or oregano leaves

1 tsp dried thyme leaves

Salt and freshly ground black pepper to taste

2 pkgs (10 oz/284 g each) fresh spinach, large stems removed and leaves shredded

8 oz (250 g) soft goat cheese or cream cheese

2 eggs

16 sheets phyllo pastry

½ cup butter, melted

⅓ cup dry bread crumbs

Team this colourful strudel with a crisp green salad and it will satisfy everyone round your table.

In a large skillet, heat the oil over medium heat. Add the leeks, red peppers, garlic, marjoram, thyme and salt and pepper to taste. Cook, stirring often, until softened, about 5 minutes.

Increase the heat to medium-high and add the spinach, in batches, letting each batch wilt before adding more. Cook, stirring often, until all the spinach is wilted and any liquid has evaporated. Remove the skillet from the heat and let cool to room temperature.

In a large bowl, beat the cheese and eggs until smooth. Stir in the leek mixture. Set aside.

Keeping the remaining phyllo covered with a damp tea towel to prevent it drying out, place 1 sheet, with a long side closest to you, on another damp tea towel. Brush lightly with some of the butter and sprinkle lightly with some of the bread crumbs.

Top with another sheet of phyllo, brushing with butter and sprinkling with bread crumbs as before. Repeat the layering with 6 more sheets.

Arrange half of the spinach mixture in a strip 2 inches (5 cm) from the side nearest you and leaving a 2-inch (5 cm) border at each short side. Fold long side nearest you over the filling and, using the towel as an aid, roll up the pastry, folding in the sides as you roll.

Place the strudel, seam side down, on a greased baking sheet and brush with butter. Repeat with remaining phyllo and filling to make 2 strudels. (Strudels can be covered and refrigerated for up to 2 days.)

When ready to bake, preheat the oven to 400°F (200°C). Cut 5 slits in the top of each strudel. Bake in the bottom third of the oven until golden brown, 25 to 30 minutes. Cut each strudel into 6 slices.

Makes 12 servings

ROASTED CHERRY TOMATO CLAFOUTIS

2 cups cherry tomatoes (about 1 lb/500 g)

2 tbsp olive oil

1 tbsp finely chopped fresh thyme or 1 tsp dried thyme leaves

2 cloves garlic, crushed

2 tsp granulated sugar

Salt and freshly ground black pepper to taste

1 cup half-and-half cream (10% MF) or table cream (18% MF)

3 eggs

2 tbsp all-purpose flour

8 oz (250 g) mozzarella cheese, shredded (about 2 cups)

Traditional clafoutis (a kind of cakelike custard) is a French dessert made with black cherries or other fruit. I've added cheese and cherry tomatoes for a savoury version to serve for a company breakfast, perhaps with some back bacon and interesting bread.

Preheat the oven to 400°F (200°C). Remove the stems from the tomatoes. Arrange them in a single layer in a shallow, 6-cup (1 ½ L) baking dish. Drizzle with the oil and sprinkle with the thyme, garlic, sugar and salt and pepper to taste. Roast until the skins shrivel slightly, 10 to 15 minutes. Reduce the oven temperature to 350°F (180°C).

In a blender, combine the cream, eggs and flour and blend until smooth. Pour the cream mixture over the tomatoes. Sprinkle with the cheese. Bake until puffed and golden, about 25 minutes. Serve at once.

Makes 4 servings

BLACK BEAN CHILI

1 medium eggplant, unpeeled and cut into ½-inch (1 cm) cubes

Salt to taste

2 tbsp canola oil

1 onion, chopped

1 carrot, diced

4 oz (125 g) mushrooms, quartered (about 1 ½ cups)

1 tbsp chili powder

2 hot peppers, seeded and minced, or ½ tsp cayenne

1 each, sweet red and green pepper, seeded and cubed

3 cloves garlic, minced

1 tsp each, dried oregano and basil leaves

1 tsp ground cumin

1 can (28 oz/796 mL) whole tomatoes with their juice

1 can (19 oz/540 mL) black beans, drained and rinsed

1 can (12 oz/341 mL) whole kernel corn, drained

2 stalks celery, sliced

2 small zucchini, unpeeled and cubed

Dice the vegetables coarsely for this colourful meatless meal. It's great served over steamed rice but, for a change, why not spoon it over roasted sweet potato cubes or split baked regular potatoes? Whatever accompaniment you choose, top it with a dollop of low-fat sour cream and a sprinkling of cheddar.

Place the eggplant in a colander and sprinkle lightly with salt. Let stand for 30 minutes to drain off any bitter juices. Rinse the eggplant and drain well.

In a large saucepan, heat the oil over medium heat. Add the eggplant, onion, carrot, mushrooms, chili powder and hot peppers and cook, stirring often, for 7 minutes.

Stir in the sweet peppers, garlic, oregano, basil and cumin and cook, stirring often, for 3 minutes.

Stir in the tomatoes, beans, corn and celery. Bring to a simmer, breaking up the tomatoes with the back of a spoon. Reduce the heat to low and cook, covered, for 20 minutes. (The chili can be prepared to this point, covered and refrigerated for up to 1 day. Reheat gently before proceeding.)

Add the zucchini to the chili. Cook, uncovered, until the chili has thickened and the zucchini is tender but still crisp, about 6 minutes. Season to taste with salt, if necessary.

Makes 4 servings

1 small eggplant (about 1 lb/500 g)

2 zucchini (12 oz/375 g total)

¼ cup olive oil, divided

Salt to taste

1 focaccia (7 to 8 inches/18 to 20 cm across)

⅔ cup soft goat cheese or cream cheese (about 4 oz/125 g)

½ tsp finely chopped fresh rosemary or ⅛ tsp crumbled dried rosemary leaves

Freshly ground black pepper to taste

⅔ cup roasted red pepper (see page 111) or drained, bottled roasted red pepper

I tested this recipe for *Canadian Family* magazine on some visitors who came for lunch. When my friend, Bernie Yen, heard we were having a vegetable sandwich, he was not excited but ended up eating two helpings and is still talking about how good it was.

Focaccia is an Italian-style flatbread, sometimes garnished with herbs. Look for it in the bread or deli section of your supermarket. Roasted peppers are available in jars in the condiment section of the supermarket if you don't want to roast your own.

Preheat the broiler to high. Trim the stem ends from the eggplant and zucchini and cut them lengthwise into ¼-inch (6 mm) slices.

Reserving 1 tbsp oil, brush the vegetable slices on both sides with the remaining oil, then sprinkle with salt to taste. Arrange the vegetable slices in a single layer on a large broiler pan or in a shallow roasting pan. Broil, 4 inches (10 cm) from the element, until tender and golden brown, 8 to 12 minutes, turning once. Remove the vegetables from the broiler pan and set aside. (You may need to do this in 2 batches.) Leave the broiler on.

Cut the focaccia in half horizontally. Lightly brush the cut sides with the remaining oil. Broil the focaccia, cut sides up, until lightly toasted, 2 to 4 minutes. Keep warm.

In a small bowl, stir together the cheese, rosemary and pepper to taste until smooth. Spread the cheese mixture on the toasted sides of focaccia.

Arrange the eggplant, zucchini and red pepper on the bottom half of the focaccia, then top with the other half of the focaccia. With a large serrated knife, cut the focaccia into quarters and serve at once.

Makes 4 servings

OLD-FASHIONED BAKED MACARONI AND CHEESE WITH TOMATOES

8 oz (250 g) elbow macaroni (2 cups)

1 lb (500 g) old cheddar cheese, divided

1 can (28 oz/796 mL) whole tomatoes

1 tsp granulated sugar

1 tsp Worcestershire sauce

½ tsp dried summer savory or thyme leaves

½ tsp Tabasco sauce

Salt and freshly ground black pepper to taste

1 cup milk

2 eggs, beaten

My son Allen and his wife Cherrie often treat me to my own recipe for macaroni and cheese when I go for dinner, but Allen has tweaked it by doubling the cheese and adding some Tabasco sauce. I must admit, I like his new version. If you wish, divide the pasta mixture between two 6-cup (1 ½ L) baking dishes and reduce the baking time to 35 minutes. Freeze one dish to have on hand when the craving strikes for macaroni and cheese like your mother—or son—used to make.

Preheat the oven to 350°F (180°C). In a large pot of boiling, salted water, cook the macaroni until just tender, about 8 minutes (do not overcook). Drain well and transfer to a well-buttered 12-cup (3 L) baking dish.

Meanwhile, shred half of the cheese and set aside. Thinly slice the remaining cheese and set aside.

Drain ¾ cup of the juice from the tomatoes and reserve for another use. Pour the tomatoes and their remaining juice into a bowl. Chop the tomatoes by snipping them with a pair of kitchen scissors.

Add the shredded cheese, sugar, Worcestershire sauce, savory, Tabasco sauce and salt and pepper to taste to the tomatoes. Stir well. Pour the tomato mixture over the macaroni and stir well. Top with the sliced cheese.

In a small bowl, whisk together the milk and eggs. Pour the milk mixture over the cheese-covered macaroni but do not stir. Bake, uncovered, until the top is golden brown, 40 to 50 minutes.

Makes 6 to 8 servings

HEARTY CHILI SOUP

4 tsp canola oil

2 onions, chopped

4 cloves garlic, minced

1 can (28 oz/796 mL) whole tomatoes with their juice

2 stalks celery, diced

2 carrots, diced

1 sweet green pepper, seeded and diced

2 tbsp chili powder (or to taste)

1 tsp each, dried oregano and basil leaves

⅛ tsp hot pepper flakes (or to taste)

Salt and freshly ground black pepper to taste

2 cans (each 19 oz/540 mL) red kidney beans, undrained

Shredded cheddar cheese for garnish

Quick to make, probably with ingredients already in your pantry, this simple main-course soup is perfect served with crusty bread or rolls.

In a large saucepan, heat the oil over medium heat. Add the onions and garlic and cook, stirring often, for 3 minutes.

Add the tomatoes, mashing them with a fork. Stir in one tomato can of water, the celery, carrots, green pepper, chili powder, oregano, basil, hot pepper flakes and salt and pepper to taste.

Stir in the beans, with their liquid, and one bean can of water. Bring to a boil over high heat. Reduce the heat to medium-low and simmer, covered, for the flavours to blend, about 30 minutes. (The soup can be cooled, covered and refrigerated for up to 5 days or frozen for up to 2 months. Heat gently before serving.) Serve in wide soup bowls and sprinkle each portion with cheese.

Makes 8 servings

TOMATO AND CHEESE TART

One 9-inch (23 cm) unbaked pie shell

2 cups cherry tomatoes

1 tbsp Dijon mustard

8 oz (250 g) Gruyère cheese, shredded (2 cups), divided

1 tsp dried basil leaves

¼ tsp dried thyme leaves

Freshly ground black pepper to taste

1 tbsp olive oil

Over the years my husband and I have taken many vacations in southwestern France, and this simple but elegant tart is typical of the food we've enjoyed there. Serve it as an appetizer, or add a green salad and make it a lovely main course for lunch. Garnish with a fresh sprig of one of the herbs, if available.

Preheat the oven to 400°F (200°C). Prick the bottom of the pie shell all over with a fork. Press a piece of foil or parchment paper into the pie shell and fill with uncooked dry white beans or rice. Bake in the bottom third of the oven until the edges of the pastry are pale golden, 15 minutes. Reduce the oven temperature to 375°F (190°C).

Remove the beans and foil and prick the pie shell all over with a fork. Return to the bottom third of the oven and bake until the pastry is pale golden, about 15 minutes. Let cool. Leave the oven on.

Cut the tomatoes in half and arrange cut sides down on paper towels. Set aside while you prepare the remaining ingredients.

Spread the pie shell with the mustard and sprinkle with half of the cheese. Arrange the tomatoes cut sides up on top of the cheese. Sprinkle with the basil, thyme and pepper to taste. Sprinkle the remaining cheese evenly over the tomatoes and drizzle with the oil.

Bake in the bottom third of the oven until the cheese melts, about 30 minutes. Let cool slightly in the pan on a wire rack. Serve warm.

Makes 4 to 6 servings

HARVEST FRITTATA

4 eggs

2 egg whites

Salt and freshly ground black pepper to taste

1 tbsp each, butter and canola oil

1 each, onion and small zucchini, sliced

Half sweet red pepper, seeded and diced

1 clove garlic, minced

1 ½ cups cooked corn kernels or 1 can
(12 oz/341 mL) whole kernel corn, well
drained

½ tsp dried basil leaves

1 ½ cups shredded Swiss cheese

This quick, meatless main course is lightened with a couple of extra egg whites. Serve with chili sauce (see page 144) and toast triangles for a quick lunch, brunch or light supper.

Preheat the oven to 400°F (200°C). In a medium bowl, whisk together the eggs, egg whites and salt and pepper to taste. Set aside.

In a large, heavy, ovenproof skillet, melt the butter with the oil over medium heat. Add the onion and zucchini and cook, stirring often, until lightly browned, 6 to 7 minutes.

Add the red pepper and garlic and cook, stirring often, until softened, about 4 minutes. Stir in the corn and basil. Remove the skillet from the heat.

Spread the vegetable mixture evenly over the bottom of the skillet. Pour the egg mixture over the vegetables. Return the skillet to medium heat and cook for 1 minute.

Sprinkle evenly with the cheese. Transfer the skillet to the oven and bake until golden brown and set, 15 to 20 minutes. Cut into wedges to serve.

Makes 3 to 4 servings

SAVOURY HERB CHEESECAKE

1 ½ cups fresh bread crumbs

⅔ cup finely chopped walnuts

3 tbsp butter, softened

1 ¼ lb (625 g) brick cream cheese, at room
temperature (two-and-a-half 250 g pkgs)

¼ cup freshly grated Parmesan cheese

4 eggs

2 tbsp each, finely chopped fresh tarragon, basil
and oregano

2 cloves garlic, minced

¼ tsp freshly ground black pepper

I love the creamy texture of this easy savoury cheesecake, and the addition of fresh herbs makes the flavour so good. It's excellent for a company lunch cut into thin wedges and served warm on top of dressed mixed salad greens, like Lettuce Herb Salad (page 83) dressed with Basic Vinaigrette (page 170).

Preheat the oven to 350°F (180°C). In a food processor, combine the bread crumbs, walnuts and butter until well combined. Press the bread crumb mixture over the bottom of an 8-inch (2 L) springform pan. Bake in the centre of the oven until golden, about 15 minutes. Leave the oven on.

In a medium bowl and using an electric mixer, beat together the cream cheese and Parmesan until smooth. Beat in the eggs, one at a time, beating well after each addition.

Stir in the tarragon, basil, oregano, garlic and pepper. Pour the cream-cheese mixture into the prepared pan. Bake in the centre of the oven until golden and puffed, about 1 hour.

Run a sharp knife around the edge of cheesecake and let cool in the pan for 15 minutes. (The cheesecake will fall slightly as it cools.) Carefully remove the sides of the pan and slide the cheesecake onto a serving platter. Serve warm or at room temperature.

Makes 6 servings

SQUASH AND BEAN STEW WITH CHIPOTLE CREAM

2 tbsp canola or olive oil

2 onions, coarsely chopped

2 tsp ground cumin

½ tsp cinnamon

Salt to taste

1 sweet green pepper, seeded, sliced and divided

2 jalapeño peppers, seeded and chopped

2 tbsp chili powder

4 cloves garlic, minced

2 lb (1 kg) buttercup or Hubbard squash, peeled, seeded and cut into 1-inch (2 ½ cm) cubes (about 5 cups)

1 can (19 oz/540 mL) diced tomatoes with their juice

2 cans (each 19 oz/540 mL) red kidney beans, drained and rinsed

Chipotle Cream (recipe follows)

Finely chopped fresh coriander (cilantro) or parsley for garnish

CHIPOTLE CREAM

1 cup sour cream

1 canned chipotle pepper, minced (or more to taste)

This warm, flavourful vegetarian stew makes a satisfying supper served with rice, warm tortillas and a crisp green salad.

In a large saucepan, heat the oil over medium heat. Add the onions, cumin, cinnamon and salt to taste. Cook, stirring often, for 5 minutes.

Stir in half of the green pepper, the jalapeños, chili powder and garlic. Reduce the heat to low and cook, covered and stirring occasionally, for 5 minutes.

Stir in the squash and toss to coat with the onion mixture. Stir in the tomatoes. Bring to a boil over medium-high heat. Reduce the heat to medium-low and cook, covered, until the squash is tender but not mushy, about 20 minutes.

Gently stir in the beans and remaining green pepper. Cook, covered, for 5 minutes. Season to taste with more salt, if necessary.

Serve hot, topping each portion with a dollop of chipotle cream and a sprinkling of chopped coriander.

Makes 4 to 6 servings

CHIPOTLE CREAM

Chipotles are smoked, dried jalapeño peppers usually sold packed in cans with adobo sauce. Once opened, store in a tightly closed container in the refrigerator for up to 2 weeks. Or, for longer storage, pack the peppers and sauce in a freezer bag, gently pressing out the air. Manipulate the bag to separate the peppers so it will be easy to break off a section of pepper and sauce without thawing the whole package. The chipotles can be frozen for up to 3 months.

In a small bowl, whisk together the sour cream and chipotle pepper until well combined.

Makes about 1 cup

1 cup tiny new potatoes, unpeeled and scrubbed

1 cup baby carrots

1 cup each, green and yellow beans, trimmed and halved

1 cup snow peas, trimmed and halved diagonally

1 cup shelled peas

2 green onions, chopped

½ cup whipping cream (35% MF)

1 tbsp butter

Salt and freshly ground black pepper to taste

2 tbsp finely chopped parsley

I've included this traditional east-coast recipe in memory of Marie Nightingale, the wonderful food writer who made the rest of Canada aware of Nova Scotia's good food in her classic cookbook *Out of Old Nova Scotia Kitchens*. The vegetables listed were Marie's suggestions for what to include in this early summer vegetable stew, but use whatever you have on hand. Just remember to add the firmer vegetables to the pot first, ending with those that cook very quickly, so none overcook. And for best flavour, use the freshest vegetables you can find.

Place the potatoes in a large pot with about 1 inch (2 ½ cm) of boiling water. Cover the pot and boil gently over medium heat for 2 to 3 minutes. Add the carrots and cook, covered, for 1 to 2 minutes. Add the beans and cook, uncovered, for 2 minutes.

Add the snow peas, shelled peas and green onions. Reduce the heat to medium-low and simmer gently, uncovered, until all the vegetables are just tender, about 3 minutes. Drain only if a lot of water remains.

Add the cream and return the pot to medium-low heat. Cook until the cream has thickened slightly, 2 to 4 minutes. Stir in the butter, and salt and pepper to taste, stirring until the butter melts. Serve sprinkled with parsley.

Makes 2 main-course and 4 side-dish servings

SEE ALSO:

DRESSINGS AND SAUCES

Any simple salad or vegetable dish can be dressed up with a flavourful dressing or sauce. Many appear in the recipes throughout this book, but here are some of my favourites, old and new. Feel free to use your imagination and any available fresh herbs and other ingredients you like to turn these basic sauces and vinaigrettes into something unique.

BLUE CHEESE SALAD DRESSING

1 cup crumbled blue cheese (see recipe introduction; about 5 oz/150 g)
2 tsp dried chives
1 tsp dry mustard
Salt and freshly ground black pepper to taste
1 cup olive oil
½ cup white wine vinegar

Because it does not have the usual cream base and uses dried chives in place of fresh, this dressing will keep for 2 to 3 weeks in the refrigerator. If you use a stronger-tasting blue cheese, such as Roquefort, you may wish to use slightly less than 1 cup.

In a medium bowl, mash the cheese with a fork. Add the chives, mustard and salt and pepper to taste. Blend in until well combined.
   Whisk in the oil and vinegar until the dressing is fairly smooth.

Makes about 2 ¼ cups

MRS. ANDERSON'S BOILED SALAD DRESSING

1 cup granulated sugar
3 tbsp all-purpose flour
1 tbsp dry mustard
Salt to taste
2 eggs, beaten
1 cup water
1 cup white or malt vinegar
1 cup milk
Half-and-half cream (10% MF); optional

My friend Marg Anderson's mother used this lovely dressing on the tender leaf lettuce she picked from her garden in Sutton, Ontario. Mrs. Anderson always used malt vinegar, which gives the dressing a punchy flavour, but I find white vinegar makes the dressing a nicer colour.

In the top of a double boiler or in a stainless steel bowl, whisk together the sugar, flour, mustard and salt to taste. Stir in the eggs until smooth. Whisk in the water, vinegar and milk until well blended.
   Place over simmering water and cook for about 10 minutes, stirring constantly at first, then stirring often. The cooked dressing will be fairly thick and will thicken more as it cools. Remove from the heat and let cool, stirring occasionally.
   Pour the cooled dressing into a clean jar, cover and refrigerate for up to 2 weeks. Stir well and thin with a little cream (if using) before adding to salad greens.

Makes about 4 cups

BASIC VINAIGRETTE

2 tbsp white wine or red wine vinegar
½ tsp Dijon mustard (or more to taste)
Salt and freshly ground black pepper to taste
6 tbsp oil (olive, canola, walnut or a
 combination)

This is my everyday dressing for green salads. If using olive oil, find a good-quality extra virgin oil. Vary the proportions and ingredients to suit your own taste.

In a small bowl, whisk together the vinegar, mustard and salt and pepper to taste. Gradually whisk in the oil until the vinaigrette is creamy.

   If making ahead, cover and store in the refrigerator for several days, but let stand at room temperature for about 20 minutes, then whisk vigorously before using.

Makes about ½ cup

GARLIC VINAIGRETTE
Add 1 or 2 cloves crushed garlic, according to taste.

HERB VINAIGRETTE
Add 1 ½ tsp finely chopped fresh herbs or ½ tsp dried herb leaves.

CREAMY VINAIGRETTE
Add ¼ cup whipping cream (35% MF) or sour cream.

LEMON VINAIGRETTE
Substitute fresh lemon juice for the vinegar.

LIGHT ASIAN DRESSING

2 tsp granulated sugar
2 tbsp hot water
2 tbsp rice wine vinegar
1 tbsp soy sauce
½ tsp sesame oil

Low in fat but high in flavour, this simple dressing is great on shredded radishes, sliced cucumbers or any salad greens.

In a small bowl, dissolve the sugar in the hot water. Whisk in the vinegar, soy sauce and sesame oil.

Makes ⅓ cup

CLASSIC MAYONNAISE

2 egg yolks*
1 tbsp fresh lemon juice or white wine vinegar
½ tsp Dijon or dry mustard
Salt to taste
1 cup canola or extra virgin olive oil, or a
   combination
Freshly ground white or black pepper to taste
Additional fresh lemon juice or vinegar to taste

A popular cold sauce for more than three centuries, homemade mayonnaise is far superior to commercial brands and is easy to make if you remember to have the all ingredients and utensils at room temperature and add the oil very slowly. If the mayonnaise does curdle or doesn't thicken properly (perhaps if you're making it during very hot weather or a thunderstorm), beat another egg yolk in a clean bowl and add a few drops of oil to it. Very slowly beat in the curdled or unthickened mayonnaise, adding it drop by drop at the beginning, then gradually adding up to a tablespoonful at a time until all is incorporated.

In a medium bowl, beat the egg yolks with a wire whisk or an electric hand mixer for about 1 minute. Beat in the lemon juice, mustard and salt to taste.

Slowly beat in ½ cup of the oil, adding it drop by drop until the mixture thickens. Gradually beat in the remaining oil, adding it by tablespoonfuls and making sure each addition is incorporated before adding the next.

Season with pepper and more lemon juice to taste. Refrigerate in a tightly covered jar for up to 5 days and stir well before using.

Makes about 1 cup

* When using raw eggs in a recipe, choose Canada Grade-A eggs within their best-before date; these eggs have been properly handled and graded by a registered farmer.

SAUCE VERTE (GREEN MAYONNAISE)
Stir in finely chopped parsley or a combination of finely chopped fresh tarragon and chervil after the oil is added.

MAYONNAISE DIP
Add enough fresh lemon juice or plain yogurt to thin the mayonnaise to a dipping consistency. Flavour with your favourite finely chopped herbs, Dijon mustard, drained capers, drained green peppercorns, puréed avocado and/or finely chopped onion or shallots. Serve in the centre of a tray of crudités.

AIOLI (GARLIC MAYONNAISE)
Combine ½ cup mayonnaise with 4 minced cloves of garlic.

QUICK MAYONNAISE

1 large egg*
1 tbsp white wine vinegar or fresh lemon juice
1 tsp Dijon or dry mustard
⅛ tsp each, cayenne and granulated sugar
Salt to taste
1 cup canola oil

This speedier mayonnaise, made in a blender or food processor, keeps slightly longer than the hand-made version. As with Classic Mayonnaise (page 171), be sure all your ingredients and utensils are at room temperature and add the oil very gradually.

In a blender or a food processor fitted with a steel blade, place the egg, vinegar, mustard, cayenne, sugar and salt. Blend for 4 seconds.

With the motor running on slowest speed, add the oil, adding it drop by the drop until the mixture thickens, then in a thin, slow stream until all the oil is incorporated. Refrigerate in a tightly covered jar for up to 2 weeks. Stir well before using.

Makes 1 ½ cups

* When using raw eggs in a recipe, choose Canada Grade-A eggs within their best-before date; these eggs have been properly handled and graded by a registered farmer.

CREAM SAUCE

2 tbsp butter
2 tbsp all-purpose flour
1 cup hot milk
Finely chopped fresh herbs or other seasonings, as desired
Salt and freshly ground black or white pepper to taste

You can adjust this sauce in all kinds of ways, depending on how you want to use it: for a thinner sauce, use more milk; for a thicker sauce, use more butter and flour; for a richer sauce use a mixture of milk and cream. If preparing a cream sauce to serve with a boiled vegetable, reserve some of the vegetable's cooking liquid and use in place of some of the milk for extra flavour.

In a medium, heavy saucepan, melt the butter over low heat. Add the flour and cook, stirring constantly, for 2 minutes. Be careful not to let the mixture brown.

Remove the saucepan from the heat and gradually whisk in the hot milk, then the seasonings of your choice.

Place the saucepan over medium heat and cook, stirring constantly, until the sauce is thick and smooth, 1 to 2 minutes. Season to taste with salt and pepper.

Makes about 1 cup

CHEESE SAUCE
Off the heat, add ¼ cup to 1 cup shredded cheddar or Swiss cheese (according to taste) to the hot sauce and stir until melted.

LOW-FAT HOLLANDAISE

¾ cup plain yogurt
3 egg yolks
2 tsp fresh lemon juice
½ tsp Dijon mustard
¼ tsp granulated sugar
Dash of hot pepper sauce
Salt and freshly ground black pepper to taste

No one will guess this rich-tasting hollandaise contains low-fat yogurt instead of butter. Enjoy it on steamed asparagus or fiddleheads, or make a spring version of eggs Benedict using roasted asparagus instead of ham.

In a heatproof bowl, whisk together the yogurt, egg yolks, lemon juice, mustard, sugar, hot pepper sauce and salt and pepper to taste.

Set the bowl over a saucepan of simmering water and cook, stirring constantly, until the sauce is thick enough to coat the back of a spoon, 6 to 8 minutes. (The sauce can be set aside at room temperature for up to 1 hour, then reheated gently over simmering water.)

Makes 1 cup

BASIL PESTO

2 cups packed fresh basil leaves
½ cup olive oil
¼ cup pine nuts or chopped walnuts
3 large cloves garlic
Salt and freshly ground black pepper to taste
½ cup freshly grated Parmesan cheese
2 tbsp room temperature unsalted butter

When fresh basil is in season, buy a large bunch at your local farmers' market to make this delicious Italian sauce. It's usually served tossed with fresh pasta but also adds interesting flavour to pizzas and sandwiches. Since pesto freezes well (pack it in small airtight containers), you can make a winter's supply when basil is at its best. If freezing, omit the Parmesan cheese and butter and beat them in after the sauce thaws.

In a food processor or blender, combine all the ingredients, except the Parmesan and butter. Process until a fairly smooth purée forms, scraping down the sides of the food processor once or twice.

Transfer to a medium bowl and stir in the Parmesan and butter.

Makes about 1 cup

SEE ALSO:

Chipotle Cream	167	Onion-Honey Dressing	86
Classic Cabbage Roll Sauce	42	Parsley Cream	45
Cooked Tomato Sauce	148	Pesto Mayonnaise	95
Fresh Tomato Sauce	148	Quick Tomato Sauce	19
Hazelnut Vinaigrette	16	Rémoulade Dressing	80
Kale Caesar Salad Dressing	141	Sour-Cream Sauce	20
Leeks Vinaigrette	83	Tarragon Vinaigrette	91
Lemon-Mustard Sauce	15	Watercress Sauce	92
Mustard Sauce	40	Winter Bean Salad Dressing	21
Old-Fashioned Chili Sauce	147		

ACKNOWLEDGEMENTS

I gratefully acknowledge the assistance of government agencies that provided information for the original publication of the book: Agriculture Canada; the staff of the Ontario Agricultural Museum, Milton, Ontario (now Country Heritage Park); the Agricultural Marketing Boards across Canada, especially the Prince Edward Island Market Development Centre; the Ontario Vegetable Growers' Marketing Board; the Marketing and Economics Division of the Saskatchewan Department of Agriculture; and the Manitoba Vegetable Producers' Marketing Board.

I am grateful for all those friends and relatives who willingly shared recipes and time for the original publication, and my thanks to Gary and Diane Slimmon for carefully going through the book to make suggestions for the revised version. Thank you to those who shared new recipes for this edition: Julia Aitken, Carla Azevedo, Elizabeth Baird, Nancy Brent, Corrie Burke, Marlen Chase, Meghan Collins, Anne Noronha, Hannah Pahuta, Monda Rosenberg, Judy Shultz, Diane Slimmon and Linda Stephen.

Many thanks to James Lorimer and the staff at Formac Lorimer Books, as well as my meticulous editor and friend, Julia Aitken, for all their hard work in bringing the 1983 version into this century.

As always, I appreciate the unfailing support of my husband Kent.

INDEX